KT-514-582

ACC. No: 05118270

LEFT FOR DEAD?

LEFT FOR DEAD?

THE STRANGE DEATH AND REBIRTH OF THE LABOUR PARTY

LEWIS GOODALL

WILLIAM
COLLINS

For Grandad, for teaching me

William Collins
An imprint of HarperCollins*Publishers*
1 London Bridge Street
London SE1 9GF
WilliamCollinsBooks.com

First published in Great Britain in 2018 by William Collins

1

A catalogue record for this book is
available from the British Library

ISBN 978-0-00-822669-5

Graphs redrawn by Martin Brown
Image on page 204 by In Pictures Ltd/Corbis via Getty Images

Printed and bound in Great Britain by
CPI Group (UK) Ltd, Croydon

MIX
Paper from
responsible sources
FSC® C007454

This book is produced from independently certified FSC paper
to ensure responsible forest management

For more information visit: www.harpercollins.co.uk/green

CONTENTS

Acknowledgements vii

Prologue: Longbridge 1

1 What Went Before: New Labour and the Left 11
2 The Curious Case of Jeremy Corbyn 50
3 What is Corbynism? 81
4 The 'A-Word' 102
5 Corbyn the Culture Warrior 115
6 A Class Apart 137
7 The Takeover 144
8 Fear and Loathing in the Labour Party 192
9 The Night Everything Changed: The 2017 General Election 224
10 What Comes After: The Next Election and the Future of the Left 269

Postscript: Grandad 333
Notes 342

ACKNOWLEDGEMENTS

I work in a profession in which my working days are essentially a series of sugar hits. In TV news, our deadlines are short, our working days long but our time horizons truncated. While most people's jobs and projects can spread out for weeks, if not months at a time, in ours the complications, the highs, the lows, the screw-ups are compressed into a single day. For us, a week is a long-term gig. As a consequence my brain has been rewired by a thousand two-minute lives, three hundred three-minute packages, ten score of online instant analyses.

Writing a book then, all 130,000 words of it, has been a major challenge, the ultimate slow burn. And then, every time I was able to concentrate for long enough, everything would change. In the time I've been writing, Jeremy Corbyn has gone from zero to hero (and some would say back again). Every time I thought I understood what was happening, political life would find a way of making me reach for the delete button, once again. In three years, the Labour Party has moved from extinction to the precipice of government, and therefore this book, its premise and its contours have fluctuated almost as much as Corbyn's reputation. What began as an obituary became a living history of rebirth. At the same time, and to my surprise, it became infused with my own history. For this I am indebted, principally to my family, especially my mum and dad, for giving more political insights and wit and wisdom than I could glean from a lifetime in Westminster. I also have to say an enormous thank you to Tom Killingbeck, my editor, for encouraging me to strike out beyond my working life, beyond Westminster and the corridors of power, and for encouraging me to explore my own story – and how both were mutually reinforcing. I owe him special gratitude for his patience – especially given he inherited the book from his colleague Joe Zigmond, to whom I am very grateful for believing in the idea in the first place. The same is true of my agent Claudia Young – she took half an idea, in the *Newsnight* green room, and helped develop it into the book you're holding. Iain Hunt, also of William Collins, handled the final stages of the edit brilliantly. I'd also like to thank the dozens of people, politicians, journalists, aides, activists and the rest, who spared the time to be interviewed. I hope they feel everyone, of every opinion within the Labour Party and without, has had a fair shake.

Special thanks must go to my employers, Sky News, especially the former head of politics Esme Wren, for giving me the space and time to write the book – and so many opportunities more generally, many of which have fed into the contents of these pages. In that vein I'm also grateful to the whole of the senior Sky News management team, especially Esme's successor Dan Williams, Jonathan Levy, head of newsgathering, and John Ryley, the head of Sky News, for their interest and willingness to throw me new challenges. My colleagues, too, in the Millbank bureau are too many to mention, but are a never-ending source of inspiration, humour and fun. They make me, in so innumerable ways, a better journalist. After eighteen months at Sky News, I can say without hesitation that I am extremely proud to work for an organisation which reports politics without fear or favour and which, in my entirely impartial opinion, has the best political team in Westminster. In particular, my colleague and best friend in TV, Zach Brown, has worked with me since the beginning at *Newsnight* and now Sky. My best work – especially on matters Labour – has been with him. Long may it continue.

I'm grateful too to my friends, many of whom have contributed ideas to the book – apologies in advance if I've stolen them. In particular I'd like to thank Marc Kidson and James Stafford, two brilliant minds, who over the years since our Oxford days have helped shape my thinking on so many things. If you read something here that makes you think, chances are one of them had a hand in it.

As you wade through these pages, there is one man who looms large. My dear grandad, Alan. It is no exaggeration to say that without him there would be no pages. A more thorough tribute is reserved for him at the end – but it would still be remiss not to mention him here. His imprint, his essence, is in every bit of what you're about to read. I only wish he could read them for himself. With his no longer being here, I will have to leave that to his darling wife, my beloved nan. My dearest, this book is for him.

And to my darling girl – my imp, my Cherie, the cleverest person I've met, the one who has had to hear all my stupid thoughts again and again and then read them in print and still be kind about them – I can't give all those evenings and holidays back but I promise, no matter what happens to the Labour Party, this is my last word on the subject.

Probably.

Lewis Goodall
London
July 2018

Prologue

LONGBRIDGE

Son, where we're from, you could put a donkey in a Labour rosette and it'd win.

My dad, many, many times

I'm not sure there's been a time when my family wasn't involved in making things. Some of my earliest memories involve my grandad coming home and presenting the three- or four-year-old version of me with some samples of buttons, medals or coins that he'd helped make at the Birmingham mint. Grandad, as its works manager, got my dad a job there too. He was a lanky 22-year-old, just moved to Birmingham to be with the 17-year-old mum who had just given birth to me. They'd met at a Scarborough holiday camp a year or so before – my dad's first ever holiday. He was from Middlesbrough, the son of a dockworker, and before then he'd barely left the town as a kid. He later said it put him off holidays for life. He didn't have a qualification to his name, except a GCE in needlework. This didn't help at the mint, where the only job my grandad had available was on a machine that needed a delicate approach and small fingers, which probably explained why all the other workers in the department were women. He didn't, Grandad told me later, excel himself but he tried his best.* We all lived cheek by jowl in Erdington in north Birmingham: me, my two aunts, Mum and Dad, and my grandparents. I was the apple of my family's eye; it probably explains why I'm unafraid of the limelight. It was a mindlessly happy existence for a little boy. But after my grandad could fiddle the figures for Dad no more, my nan phoned up the Rover plant, on the other side of the city in Longbridge, where she'd heard they needed some new workers. She asked if they had any openings for her son-in-law (just about – he'd married my mum weeks before; I was page boy at the ripe old age of four). So we left Erdington and crossed the city to the south Birmingham suburb of Northfield, just next to the vast Rover plant. I walked past it to secondary school for five years.

For more than a decade my dad worked there nearly every working day. Each morning I'd leave for school just as he was getting in after a night shift; then, not long after I'd got home at around 4.30 p.m. Mum would instruct me (probably for the third or fourth time) to go and tell him to wake; he had to get up and eat before he started again. We were ships in the night. I didn't mind. It was a given. Mum and Dad worked, and Dad worked more hours because he had to look after me and my younger sister. He worked incredibly hard (and still does), without complaint. These were the comforting rhythms of my childhood.

These days, I imagine it must be hard for kids in the playground to describe what their fathers and mothers do for a living. How, as a child, do you go about describing what Mummy, the management consultant, does? Or Daddy, who works as a computer software programmer? Or project managers? Or account directors? Or procurement experts?

But for many of us in Turves Green Primary School's playground, we knew what our dads did. They worked at the Rover. They made cars. And most of them drove in the cars they had made. And I knew which bit my dad worked on: the doors. He was a welder. Today, in

* He survived through a combination of Grandad's munificence and a bit of light form-fiddling.

the increasingly unlikely event that you see a Rover on the roads, my dad probably welded it on its hinges.

I wasn't uncommon. When I think back to my friends and classmates, so many of us had fathers and mothers who were employed on the Rover site and even more in the wider supply chain of the plant. Rover was ubiquitous, part of the bloodstream. They even sponsored our school technology labs and our curriculum, their branding and emblem proudly on display on many a classroom wall. Our families were connected through Rover socially via the 'Austin' Social Club, just down the road from the main site. I remember every Christmas Eve Dad taking me there for the afternoon, as he enjoyed a well-earned break and pint, played some snooker, or watched a football match. As we got older, some of my friends got their first jobs collecting glasses there a couple of nights a week. The company arranged trips to Weston-super-Mare and other seaside towns. Rover's presence punctuated almost every aspect of life. It was, on reflection, an impossibly traditional working-class childhood, almost stranded out of its own time.

The plant's quotidian certainties reassured not only our present but our futures too. I remember very clearly one lunchtime talking to another boy in my class. Like me, his father worked at the Rover. Somehow, as kids do, we started to talk about what we would do when we 'grew up'. Even today I remember the confidence with which he talked about his own nine-year-old plans. He told me he would work at the Rover and that it would be easy; after all, his dad could easily get him a job. This was more than just the lack of imagination and naivety of a child not yet a decade old. It reflected the esteem a job there enjoyed. Longbridge was the Rover and the Rover was Longbridge.

Some 18 years or so later, I'm not sure what happened to him. I am certain, however, that he had to make a few changes to his career plans. For in the space of our schooldays the deep certainty attached to a life at the Rover gave way to the apprehension and unease of the twenty-first century. Globalisation came to Longbridge and shattered the quiet insularity of our lives. By the 1990s and early 2000s, as me and my friends grew up, changed schools and went into the sixth form, it had become ever clearer that our community was living on borrowed time.

By the time of my childhood, Rover had been manufacturing cars on the site for a hundred years. Ever since a young industrialist, Herbert Austin, discovered a disused printing works there in 1905, it had been a hive of industry. A century later, in 2005 it had largely closed. At its peak, 100,000 people were employed on that site alone; even by the dawn of the millennium, five years before closure, my father was one of 25,000, with an estimated 100,000 in the wider supply chain.

So, as its troubles mounted in the late 1990s and early 2000s, we all of us were aware of just how potentially devastating the factory's closure would be. As the national media poured in to witness the slow decay of this last British brand of motor car, we kids went to school every day in something akin to grief. I remember seeing the worry in my mum's eyes, I remember her asking my dad, every night before he'd even had chance to take off his coat, what news there was from the union, from management – something, anything that might give us some hope and if not hope then at least some certainty. This was reflected and amplified for me in the playground, all of us exchanging fragments of half-truths that had been ricocheting around our fevered imaginations. The plant's travails, every twist and turn of the story, gripped us and the wider community like an all-too-real soap opera. I can recall, as an eleven-year-old, praying, on more than one occasion, that the factory would be saved and Dad would keep his job.

It wasn't and he didn't. As BMW pulled out in 2000 and the factory was 'rescued' by a consortium of local businessmen, Dad decided to take redundancy. By his own reckoning, it was 'one of the only good decisions I've ever made'. Although not exactly flattering for my mother and for me, it had the benefit of being true. By leaving when he did, he received a full redundancy package to reflect his decade-long service. Those 6,500 who chose to stick with the plant until 2005, when it finally closed its doors, received no more than half a month's pay packet. At the same time, the plant's newish and final owners made a pretty penny. While profits plunged and the news became grimmer, it transpired that the British Towers group, which in 2000 had bought the plant from BMW for £10, had been siphoning considerably more than a tenner of investment into their own pockets. In 2002, they pumped £12.95m into a trust fund for their retirement. At the end of its five-year tenure the Phoenix consortium had been remunerated with £42m while the company went into administration with debts worth over £1.4bn. The day after closure, while being interviewed by the BBC, John Towers announced the set-up of the Longbridge Trust Fund for ex-workers – where he pledged the assets of the company, which he hoped would raise up to £50m for the workers' severely damaged pensions. As of 2018, those workers were yet to see a penny. Later, it became clear that 6,000 workers would receive next to nothing from the pensions they had paid into for years. The money had vanished. The news broke that Nanjing, a Chinese consortium about which nothing was known in Birmingham, was buying the intellectual property, branding and remaining assets of what was the Rover MG Group. A tiny handful of workers remained in Longbridge, with the rest of production moving to China.

At the same time, BMW had taken the only assets that made the brand profitable, including the iconic Mini that had been produced on the site for decades. When I look back, I can see it as a textbook indictment of the worst elements of globalisation and corporate greed, and it left our community bewildered and bereaved.

This canvas is the one on which my childhood and early life were painted, in colours that millions of others would recognise too, in Britain and across the West. Those same forces, and the anger and resentment left in their wake, also form the base coat for the politics of our own age.

My family were not especially political. Both my parents' families were quintessential congenital Labour types, the sort of people whose politics is motivated by an atavistic but powerful instinct: 'We vote Labour because they are for us and the other lot are for them.' One of my earliest political memories, perhaps my earliest political imprint, was my grandad telling me that Margaret Thatcher 'made the rich richer and the poor poorer' and Mum nodding sagely as he did so. As simplistic as it may sound, these are the fundamental political reflexes on which most people rely, the lenses through which they view and make sense of the world around them. Grandad read the papers and watched the news but they largely reaffirmed his own views; the rest of my family didn't do much of that but they knew how they felt. None of them were much troubled by party politics; if they remembered to vote, they would vote Labour – and that was that.

And that's why, at the time of Rover's travails, I simply couldn't understand why the then Labour government wasn't helping my dad. My eleven-year-old brain, small but curious, was flummoxed by the events leading to the factory's closure. I knew that the Tories were for them and Labour was for us. Yet Labour didn't seem terribly interested in helping us, any more than the loathsome Tories were.

I remember walking around the by then rather tumbledown Grosvenor Shopping Precinct up the road from our house, looking at my mum as she nipped around the shops and thinking, Why doesn't the government just buy the factory, employ the workers, they'll pay tax and there won't be a problem?* But there would be no question of much assistance. There was endless talk, and a lot of hype – one Labour cabinet minister after another (from the very top down) traipsed to our little corner of Brum – but there was certainly no question of nationalisation or a rescue package. In fairness, the government did offer a £100m bridging loan to lure a separate Chinese company to invest in the business, but when they got cold feet, there was nowhere else to go. I remember my dad, late one night, over a bottle of Newcastle Brown Ale in our kitchen, musing, almost to himself, how funny it was that the fate of all his old mates was being decided in a boardroom somewhere, in another language, by people we'd never met, by a company we'd never heard of, in a country none of us were ever likely to visit. After a moment's contemplation,

* I didn't know it, but looking back, I'd stumbled upon Keynesian economics without realising.

he took another swig, shrugged his shoulders and said, ruefully: 'That's the modern world, I suppose.'

What my young brain also found difficult to understand was that our government, the body in which so much awesome power was said to reside, appeared so impotent. How pathetic, it seemed, to have British ministers, the chancellor of the exchequer himself, shuttling back and forth to China, begging a company that was itself owned by the Chinese state, to reconsider. Worse, even those efforts were for naught.

But my dad and his mates got on with it, and this fortitude wasn't uncommon. Rover's death had been a slow one; most had been braced for it. There was never any serious expectation that the government would step in directly. Ever since the 1980s, plenty of working people had seen their employers bite the dust and been told, rightly or wrongly, that the government ought not and could not step in, that it would distort the market, that the world had globalised, that the buck no longer stopped with the government. There was, then, no real backlash. The hard-working local Labour MP was re-elected in the subsequent general election, despite the factory's closure. The BNP, and later UKIP, gained in strength but never seriously threatened. Most voters carried on voting Labour, in the knowledge, perhaps, that though Labour would do little, they would at least try and do a little more than the obvious alternative.

But eleven years later, in 2016, Longbridge, like hundreds of other places that had been forgotten, that seemed so powerless, discovered a political vent, discovered that alternative in its rejection of the European Union. Longbridge, and all of the other Longbridges, had had enough, they fought back.

And little wonder. Many promises were made in Rover's wake. On the eve of its demise, Tony Murphy, then of the Amicus union, said: 'Yet again I'm having to write an obituary for another stalwart of the British engineering and manufacturing industry. Longbridge and the whole of the West Midlands are becoming ghost towns. We are going to fight for every job possible at Longbridge … We don't want to see another supermarket built.'

On a grey, December afternoon, the sort of midwinter day sunlight barely troubles, I returned to Longbridge and met up with my oldest friend, Liam. We'd met at our local primary school some twenty-three years earlier. My dad had worked at Rover, so had his neighbours. The place had changed much in twelve years, and yet not enough. Half of the old site had been transformed. At its centre was the biggest Sainsbury's I'd ever seen. Later that afternoon, I found out Liam's neighbour now worked there.

The Sainsbury's wasn't alone. It had been joined by a Hungry Horse pub, a Boots, a small shopping precinct, a Poundland, a large youth centre called (in what I can only assume to be the product of a town planner's dark humour) 'The Factory' and a small business technology park. The promised industrial jobs never came. In truth, I doubt anyone expected them to. And the site of the main factory, the one I walked past every day on my way to school? Well, that had been replaced only by detritus, mainly plastic bags and rubbish, willowing in the wind. There was nothing there. Twelve years on, no one could think of anything to do with it.

This is not a book about Rover, nor is it one solely about my own experiences. This is a book about the decline, near-death and potential rebirth of social democracy and the left in Britain. It's a story of how the left lost touch with the economic and cultural lives of its voters. How those voters became disillusioned with a party that seemed unable to imagine how to improve its own voters' lives or tell a convincing story about their so doing. How, as a result, the centre left has withered but how also, a new Labour Party, a new left has emerged to take its place; but which, ironically, is no closer to the voters who became alienated in the first place. It's a story of transformation, of Labour leaving its historic working-class moorings behind and sailing into a new world, depending on new people, new classes and new places. It's a story that begins with Labour, centred in Britain, but which holds lessons for its left-wing sister parties and students of politics around the wider world. It's a story that asks how Labour came so close to death only to be rescued, in the end, by forces not of its own making.

I feel I'm in a decent place to evaluate all this: I've been following what has happened ever since the 2015 general election. I've interviewed Jeremy Corbyn and nearly every single senior Labour figure. I've spent more hours than I care to remember travelling the length and breadth of the country speaking to Labour clubs, voters and members in all four corners of the kingdom.

Yet it's more than that; I was born into a working-class Labour family but doing the thing that they wanted most of all – getting educated, moving away, going to Oxford, leaving the familiar and making anew. In doing so, in lots of ways, I feel removed from my family and our old way of life, in which I was happy. But on the other, I don't entirely feel at home with the new world that has taken its stead, nor with the new Labour Party that has been created which looks, feels and sounds so much like the new rarefied world I've entered. Perhaps then, as a journalist, I'm in the right place, not as I used to think as a politically obsessed kid as a participant in the arena, but as a passionate observer.

In the interest of full disclosure, I should say at the outset that I joined the Labour Party when I was 15 years old, as soon as I was able. There's no point in not being up front about that. I was a very political young man – I still am. For me, as a 15-year-old, I felt my sense of class very deeply. Labour was for kids like me and families like mine. It was the simplest and most basic lesson of politics. I wanted to change my life and that of those around me and joining Labour, my eyes dazzled by the New Labour politics of the age, seemed natural. I sat in dusty leisure centres and school halls on Thursday evenings, debating motions and resolutions, and gave up my teenage Sundays to leaflet in the drizzle. It felt right. Today – with the bonds between Labour and the sort of kid I was frayed – I don't know whether the 15-year-old me, now, would do the same. This is why I tell you this. Certainly, as a reader you deserve that honesty. You might argue that such history (and such openness) is incompatible with my job as a political correspondent. I would emphatically reject that. I have long left any party affiliation behind me. Every political journalist has a past and often a political one – indeed, given our borderline obsession with all things politics, it would be peculiar if we didn't. Other journalists' past (or present) political predilections are well known. But straightforwardness is not the only reason. Most importantly, I talk of my past here because it is directly relevant to the story I propose to tell. I was born into the automatic Labourism of my class and birth. As I have changed, moved on and grown up, so in a peculiar way has Labour. These pages tell the story of the evolution of the party I knew. I hope to tell the story of that evolution as fairly and dispassionately as I can. But it is nonetheless also a personal one.

The only living remains of the Rover factory today is the Austin Social Club, where I spent so many of those childhood Christmas Eves and my dad a fair bit of his wage. It's a lingering remnant of what was: a workers' club for a workplace long gone.

Around the new precinct, through the rapidly descending December fog, I noticed what appeared to be two road signs outside the shops. On closer inspection, I could see they weren't road signs but instead each carried a phrase. They stopped me dead: on the left 'WE SLEPT TO THE SOUND OF HAMMERS' and on the right 'IT WASN'T ABOUT CARS, IT WAS ABOUT PEOPLE'. Many of my friends find the notion of working in industry almost quaint. To us, it wasn't just a way of life, it was a reason to be. It was under those hammers, and those like them up and down the country, that the Labour movement was forged. And now they've ceased to sound, the old movement has withered. But out of its shed skin something else has emerged, something new. It feels, with the 2017 general election result, that the new is half-formed. The old is not quite dead. But its new party is not yet quite born. Perhaps, like me, Labour is betwixt and between two worlds.

Chapter 1

WHAT WENT BEFORE: NEW LABOUR AND THE LEFT

I assessed that there were three types of Labour: old-fashioned Labour, which could never win; modernised Labour, which could win and keep winning, which was my ambition from the outset; and plain Labour, which could win once, but essentially as a reaction to an unpopular Conservative government.

Tony Blair, *A Journey*

If she wants a PR war, then she can have a PR war … I'll Mandelson her. Nobody wanted New Labour, Jeremy. But we all know how it works.

Mark Corrigan, *Peep Show*, 2008

What we want to know is what kind of society this government is trying to create.

Barbara Castle, 1998

I'm a New Labour kid. That's not to say anything about my politics especially; rather it's a matter of my pedigree. The earliest political memory I have is John Major giving way to Tony Blair. I was seven years old, nearly eight, and had some dim conception of this grey man in big glasses being in charge. Mum had previously explained to me that, contrary to my assumptions, the Queen was not in fact the leader of the country. This struck me as being very peculiar: the Queen, after all, had a crown. No, Mum insisted, it wasn't anything to do with the crown, power was actually exercised by this drab man in a suit rather than the old lady in the jewels. Put right, I forgot about it and focused on something else, like Lego.

But I remember the morning of the 1997 election, watching it on TV. This younger man driving up in front of a black door. Mum explained to me there had been a vote and a change. I was captivated by the idea. That the leader could change just because people willed it.* I asked Mum – worriedly – if she might change if there were a vote and be replaced. No, she laughed, that wouldn't happen. I was relieved.

But I kept on watching. And watching and watching and watching. I can't tell you why I'm interested in politics. I just am. In the same way that some people can't explain why they're interested in football, or cooking or butterflies, I am just fascinated by politics. I am addicted. There hasn't been a day since I was about ten or eleven years old when I haven't thought about it to some degree or other. The drama of it, the importance and scope of it, the power and vitality of it. I can't understand why anyone wouldn't be.

My political 'education', if you can call it that, started quite early, thanks to one man – my grandad. I used to spend every Easter, summer and half-term with my grandparents on the North Wales coast. Grandad, having been made redundant when the Birmingham mint closed, opened a small souvenir shop in the coastal town of Towyn, near Rhyl. Every day I'd work behind the counter, and there, or in his van, on our way to top up his stock, I would pepper him with questions: 'What does the prime minister do?' 'What were the names of the old prime ministers?' 'What were they famous for?' 'Do you remember them?' 'Which one did you like best?' 'Did you like Harold Wilson?' 'Why didn't you like Margaret Thatcher?' 'How often is an

* I think children to begin with are natural authoritarians, responding to one leader is all they know.

election?' 'Grandad, I've read about the miners' strike – what was that?' 'How big is this Chief Whip I've read about?' I must have done his head in but he never once expressed the slightest irritation or impatience, he just chuckled, took another puff on a cigarette and talked to me not like a child but an equal. I gorged on his knowledge and wisdom and words. It was the foundation of everything I was to learn later.

But, in a way, the knowledge he gave me and that I imbibed from book after book was secondary. I think that from quite a young age I was aware of how important politics was, not because I read about it in some theoretical or abstract way but because I could see, even as a child, the import and impact of political change around me. Not just with my dad's work, in Longbridge as I've described, but on each and every aspect of my little life.

When I was small we lived in a pretty dilapidated council house. The worst part was that it had no heating upstairs. I remember as a little four- or five-year-old begging Mum to let me sleep with her when my dad was on his night shifts because it was just so cold upstairs. Mum didn't mind,* but in the end she bought me an electric blanket and we left it on all night. God only knows how we didn't set the house ablaze. Especially when you consider she occasionally gave me a hot-water bottle to go with it. Even with both, I rarely wanted to get up in the mornings – just now and again, in winter, you could see your breath inside.

I didn't know any different: it was home, I was happy. I had two kind, loving parents, a mum and dad who although so young did everything they could to give me the best beginning that they could. But, looking back, the fact that a little boy and then a baby sister were allowed to live in a state-owned house without proper heating in the early to mid-1990s was appalling.

At some point, near the dawn of the new millennium, those houses on Willets Road in Northfield were declared unfit for habitation. They were rightly pulled down and we moved to a better house on a

* Not least because she was cold too!

rougher estate but which nonetheless my mum and dad eventually bought under the right to buy scheme. One day, not long after we moved there, on my way home from school, I was beaten up by some older kids. They kept accusing me of 'cussing' their mum. I replied meekly, tearily, that I'd never even met their mum. It didn't stop the next round of punches; I learned then that there's nothing quite like the sound of the impact of fist on jawbone. Mind you, I was so fat at the time they probably rightly intuited that if they'd gone for anything else their hands might have disappeared under endless rolls of flesh. I was so ashamed that I didn't admit it for days. When the indigo bruises began to appear, I told Mum I'd walked into a door at school. When she asked why they appeared to be on every side of my face I replied that it was, in fact, a revolving door. Unsurprisingly she wasn't fooled. For a while I didn't walk home from school any more. Mum worried we'd moved into the worst neighbourhood in south Birmingham; my dad, by comparison, who had been brought up in proper poverty as the youngest of a big Irish family in Middlesbrough, seemed to think it was, if anything, moderately swish. The trouble peaked one night when the garages around the back of our house were set on fire. I watched it from my bedroom, wondering to myself why anyone would want to do it. The truth is, though they might not have had much more than me materially, they lacked my real blessing: two loving parents, who both wanted me to achieve. In the end, the council put in a new neighbourhood team to sort out the estate. Over time, things got better. After a few years, the problems more or less disappeared.

I attended a lovely school, Turves Green Primary, just down the road. A year or two before I left, me and a few of my friends who were quite bright got an extra teacher, Mrs Clinton, who worked just with us on advanced English and maths lessons. It really helped bring us along and stretched us in ways we might not otherwise have been. Embarrassingly, I remember being thrilled she shared her surname with the then president and asked if there was any chance she might be related and could arrange a tour of the White House. I was more than a bit disappointed by the reply. Around the same time, we started doing something called 'Literacy and Numeracy hour'. I remember my teacher Mrs Hicking, doubtless aware of this little weird boy already showing an odd, precocious interest in politics, telling me it was a new idea from the new government. I was puzzled but intrigued that teachers, the summit of all power, were being instructed from elsewhere. It was the first of many changes over the next few years.

Then the school was refurbished. I was disappointed to be leaving just as everything was unveiled. I didn't get into King Edward's Grammar School a few miles away and so accompanied my (male) friends and travelled a few hundred yards up the road to the local comprehensive, Turves Green Boys' Technology College. It was a school that had its problems and that did its best with lots of kids who didn't have that much in life. Many of the boys there didn't think learning would help them and didn't see much point in the subjects or knowledge the teachers, with varying degrees of enthusiasm, tried to impart. In my early days, you didn't get the sense some of the teachers were doing much to help matters. I remember one maths lesson, the teacher, who usually taught PE, gave up trying to keep control of an especially riotous afternoon session. He called for the deputy head, the austere, taciturn Mr Williams. He remonstrated with us: 'You're some of our brightest lads, if you actually apply yourselves, you can get Ds and Cs … maybe more, if you're lucky.' Educational rallying call, it was not. The lack of ambition, on both sides of the teacher's desk, was occasionally profound.

Over time, things improved and as they did a fair number of opportunities came my way. A 'Gifted and Talented' fund was established and (thanks to some very dedicated teachers) paid for me to learn GCSE Drama and GCSE Spanish after school. It also paid for a hotel in London for me to do a week's work experience in Parliament, chaperoned by (you guessed it) Grandad. You can imagine my 14-year-old giddiness ('Was that David Blunkett?! MY GOD, THAT'S DAVID BLUNKETT, GRANDAD!'). It was also the first time I'd properly visited London. I walked poor Grandad's legs off. He spent the afternoons recovering before we set out on our travels again: Piccadilly Circus, the Embankment, Whitehall, Oxford Street,

Leicester Square – places I'd hitherto known only on a Monopoly board. As I walked around Parliament and in London's bright lights, I swore to myself that one day I'd come back to work in both. Sometimes, as I'm walking past Big Ben on my way to work, or dashing to meet an MP or going to do a live in Downing Street, I think back and can almost see my podgy 14-year-old ghost walking with his grandad, and I pinch myself.

Towards the end of my time at school, a senior teacher handed me a brochure with the words 'Aim Higher' emblazoned across its front. Inside, its pages outlined a new programme, a series of summer schools that had just been established across British universities to encourage kids from state schools without much history of sending students to Russell Group universities to apply. Everything was paid for, accommodation, train fare, food – the works. 'You should think about the one at Oxford,' he told me. I acted on his advice, applied to the programme and was accepted. I had the time of my life. Up to then I used to dream of what it would be like to escape my happy but small world and in that week, surrounded by the books and the buildings and the spires, I began, for the first time, to see the shape of a new, bigger existence that might take its place. From then on all I wanted to do was go and I was determined to do everything I could to make it happen. I spent weekends scouring the internet (dial-up, when not interrupted by calls from Nan, aunts and Mum's friends) for every scrap of information I could to help me get there, be it about interviews, extracurricular activities, practice entrance examination techniques and the rest. I worked like a dog for my GCSEs, now knowing how important they were to the application process. All of it flowed from that week. Two years later, in what was then the proudest moment of my life, I was able to tell my crying, jubilant mum that I'd won a place at St John's College, Oxford, to read History and Politics. I will never forget opening that letter, in full Charlie Bucket mode, reading the words aloud again and again lest they vanish from the page. Mum literally jumped for joy; once she came back down to earth, I noticed she had a look in her eyes. At the time I thought it was pride. But looking back I think it was more: it was vindication.

Vindication in the face of all the people who had written her off as a hopeless teenage mum all those years before. I think much of the rest of my life has flowed from the contents of that letter, opened on that December afternoon. And yet I'm quite confident that the words inside would neither have been read nor written had it not been for that precious week in midsummer, two years before.

Just as I was packing my bags for Oxford, work was about to start on a new £3m sports hall at Turves Green Boys. Birmingham was changing around me too. Slowly but surely, with the new Bull Ring and revamped city centre, Brum had a spring in its step. The city was shining with fresh glass and things felt hopeful. My mum's sisters, who had lived with us all together in Erdington, were by then starting to have kids of their own (waiting to the grand old age of their early and mid-twenties, which is pretty late in my family*). They seemed better off than we had been. Not so much because their income was greater – if anything it was probably a touch less – but it was topped up by the new sprawling system of tax credits created by Gordon Brown. I couldn't help but be aware of this because occasionally, in the car on the way home after we had been visiting, Mum's eyes would flash and invariably she'd spit out something like: 'They don't know they're born, we didn't get tax credits or anything like that with you.' Nothing quite like sisterly love, sometimes.

Much if not all of what I've just relayed followed inexorably from my watching the New Labour government to office, on that 1997 day. They put the money in to refit old dilapidated council housing on its last legs. They established the Gifted and Talented fund. They invested in regional cities. They refurbished schools. They established the Aim Higher Summer School Programme.† In short, I have no doubt that I wouldn't be where I am today were it not for the New Labour government. They say the personal is political. It doesn't get more personal than that. You can say it was all on tick, all on borrowed

---

* I've got to the age of 28 without any so I'm pretty sure they think I'm infertile.

† To my sadness and frustration, one of Michael Gove's first acts as education secretary was to abolish the scheme.

time. You can say that Blair didn't achieve enough, that he was a neoliberal, a Tory, a Thatcherite wolf in Labour clothing. You're perfectly entitled to think this and you're perfectly entitled to make the accusation (I'm sure some of you will). None of this is true – I'm a journalist and like all journalists I can only relay to you lived experience as I see it and experience it. I can only tell you that those things were transformative to me and to those around me. I think it's also the reason why – you wouldn't know it from reading the editorials in the *Guardian* or listening to many of the bien pensant voices in London – in many working-class communities there are plenty of people (my parents and their friends included) who don't have a bad word to say about Tony Blair. They remember their lives before his time in office and they felt their material lives tangibly improve. My own life is among that number. Many people I know want someone to arrest Tony Blair. I confess to you that when I met him for the first time as a journalist, part of me – a not insignificant part – wanted to thank him for what his government had done.

I got older, I saw many of the government's imperfections, began to appreciate Blair's and Brown's personality defects, the endless tedium of their interminable psychodrama. I, like many others, felt disillusioned by the horrors of Iraq. By the end of my period at university, watching the results programme on my iMac with friends, drinking cheap wine in plastic cups right in the middle of my finals week, it felt like New Labour's time was exhausted, tarnished in a thousand ways, in the sands of the Middle East, in the expenses office of the House of Commons, in the pages of the Hutton Report, in the meeting rooms of Downing Street where the Election That Never Was was called off. But it's clear, now we can look at the period with a more neutral, dispassionate lens, that in most ways Britain got better in those years, especially for the people Labour was established to defend and promote, the working classes.

It is then a matter of some curiousness that Blair's name is mud and that period of Labour government, the longest in the party's history, is considered an embarrassing aberration by so many within and without the Labour Party. The fate of its reputation tells us much, not only about the inadequacies of both New Labour and its replacement but of the entire breed of 'moderate' centre-leftism that has all but disappeared around the world.

I don't propose to give a blow-by-blow account of the New Labour years. It's already been done. Instead, we need a different approach in our attempts to understand that era. The most common accusation against New Labour is that it had become a pale imitation of the Tory Party, that it had mutated into a form of Thatcherism with, at best, a human edge. This accusation was made in its earliest days. Even by 1996, before Blair became prime minister, the mid-1990s seminal state of the nation TV drama *Our Friends in the North* lambasted the project as a sell-out. The son of one of the main characters, Mary (who had started out on the left of the party as a local councillor only to become leader of Newcastle City Council in the 1980s and a Blairite MP), accosts his mother at a political meeting: 'Mother, man, if you and your New Labour party sound any more like the Tories they'll sue you for plagiarism.' This belief was to embed itself, then multiply, before it finally became received wisdom in the party, and is the main reason, alongside his foreign policy decisions, why Blair has been disowned as a pariah.

There are many legitimate criticisms to be made of Blair. His decisions in the wake of 9/11, to religiously stick with a neoconservative American administration in particular, deserve much of the ire for which they are now known. Blair's development into a political masochist, irritating his base, attacking students, the public sector, led to a drift from his social democratic beginnings. However, it is a gross, ahistorical and absurd contention that the New Labour years were 'Tory-lite'. For all of its faults, the Labour government was not a Conservative (or conservative) one and did things that a Tory administration would never have countenanced. It fails to understand either what New Labour was or the historical and political moment in which the Labour Party found itself in the early to mid-1990s. Nonetheless, even though it was in fact a recognisably Labour government, it did, in its rhetoric, if not in its actions, sow the seeds of the leftist Corbynist revival that it was its *raison d'être* to banish and destroy. This is my attempt, 25 years on, to offer a rounded perspective on New Labour and its place in history.

NEW, NEWER AND NEWEST LABOUR

New Labour was an election-winning machine: it presided over by far and away the most successful electoral period in the party's century-long history, achieving 13 years in office and three terms in government. It is nearly always forgotten now that before the 1997–2010 ministries the longest period the party had been continuously in office was five and a half years. Prior to 1997, the last time the party had won a decent majority was in 1966, under Harold Wilson. Yes, 1966. In other words, by the late 1990s it wasn't just England fans enduring thirty years of hurt; decent Labour majorities felt nearly as rare as England winning the World Cup. The Conservatives were in office for sixty-six out of one hundred years of the twentieth century, about the same length of time as the Communists in the Soviet Union – and the Soviets hadn't had the minor inconvenience of periodically having to secure the population's consent. The Tories were election-winning dynamos and had moulded a nation in their own image. Labour's performance, by contrast, had been anaemic.

New Labour, then, was a movement born out of desperation. The party, especially after the shock defeat of 1992, was questioning its very survival as a credible governing force. The original British (and better!) television series of *House of Cards* summed up well the mood of the early 1990s. The Machiavellian protagonist, Francis Urquhart, succeeds Thatcher as prime minister and goes on to win three more general election victories, each victory being narrow but absolute. At one point, Urquhart, seeking a new political adviser, asks a candidate to assess his government's performance:

SARAH: Extremely effective. By not seeking the approval of all of the people all of the time you've put yourself in a very strong position. You've got 46 per cent of the people and that means you can afford to ignore all of the rest. And you do. Labour has no chance because it has no power base. Most of the underclass isn't registered to vote. You've virtually destroyed the two-party system.

URQUHART: Good.

The exchange, initially broadcast in 1993, not long after the Conservatives' fourth victory, is an insight into the now lost mindset of the mid-1990s political observer, especially when you remember that it was written by a Conservative peer. The Conservatives having enough people in the right places could dominate the House of Commons through the 'first past the post' system in perpetuity, especially given that Labour's appeal was so limited. This theory was pre-eminent at the time: that Labour's social base had proved too narrow and brittle, that as a party born in the fires of the smelter and the soot of the mines, of the manual and unionised working class, in an economy increasingly based on services, it was doomed to failure. The Tories, it was argued, had trapped Labour in a demographic cage. New Labour was an attempt to escape from its confines.

Such an attempt was hardly novel though. Today some talk in a way which seems to suppose that before New Labour came along the Labour Party was one monolithic bloc, 'Old Labour', comprised exclusively of miners, flat caps and whippets from the Jarrow marches onwards before the yuppies with the suits and briefcases and flat whites came along and snatched it from those to whom it truly belonged. In other words, that New Labour was unduly obsessed with and beholden to the middle classes. There's truth to that charge but our problem comes with the assumption that New Labour was somehow unique in its bourgeois courtship; rather the Labour Party had been wrestling with expanding its appeal for a very long time, before Blair and Brown were even born.

As far back as the early 1950s, as the Attlee government slipped from power and an age of rationing and queuing gave way to one of affluence, Labour had been fretting about the salience of its ideological and social appeal. Much to socialists' horror, many of whom had seen the 1945 government as the beginning of a destined age of socialist government, it was the Conservatives who would govern for the next thirteen years. It began to look as if the Attlee government, for all its achievements, would be socialism's high-water mark, an apotheosis, an end, rather than a beginning. A new age of individualism and consumerism beckoned for which Labour seemed temperamentally and congenitally ill-suited. As one Conservative journalist observed, the English working class were characterised less by an interest in Marx and Engels, than in Marks and Spencer.

Thus the 1950s were a period of deep soul-searching for the party, and concern abounded that its reach was far too shallow. One study commissioned concluded that 'Labour is thought of predominantly as a class party and the class that it represents is objectively and subjectively on the wane.' Moreover, even members of that class were not necessarily friendly to Labour. As Hugh Gaitskell, by then party leader, said to the party's 1959 conference in Blackpool: 'We assumed too readily an instinctive loyalty to Labour which was all the time being gradually eroded.' Harold Wilson's 'white heat' speech, which came a few years after and today is remembered best as a call for state planning and investment in technology and science, was neither nearly so lofty nor futuristic as it appeared. It – and Wilson's entire electoral strategy at the time – was an attempt to bring in new middle-class and technically educated voters. Wilson ran a campaign arguing that Labour was the *classless* party, the party of aspiration, for those who aspired to dispose of the primitive and outmoded distinctions of the place and status in which people were born. While the Tories of the grassmoor held back people of talent for reasons of snobbery, so a technocratic Labour government would liberate people of ability irrespective of class, so that socialism was for you if you wore a white coat or a flat cap. This built on Gaitskell's observation at the party conference in 1959, where he said the worker (and voter) of the future would be 'a skilled man in a white overall watching dials in a bright new modern factory'. Wilson was, he said privately, 'making myself acceptable to the suburbs'. The language was different – Gaitskell and Wilson spoke of 'intermediate voters' rather than Blair's 'Mondeo Man' or 'Middle England' – but the ambition was the same: to expand the Labour Party's appeal in new quarters.

Wilson's strategy worked for a while. In 1964 Labour scraped in and won big 18 months later, in 1966. By the 1980s, though, Labour's white heat had long since cooled and the issue of the party's social appeal once again seemed profound. MPs and leftists darkly whispered of the party's 'London effect'. As the party retreated to its old industrial heartlands of the Scottish central belt, the pit villages of the north-west and east Midlands, and the shipyards of the north-east, Labour struggled most of all in the capital. It seems hard for us to imagine now, but London – deindustrialised, service-dominated, liberal, full of non-unionised younger workers – represented all that Labour Party strategists and thinkers feared most. It was at the centre of the Thatcher revolution and potentially a harbinger of things to come elsewhere. By the late 1980s the party was 17 per cent behind the Tories in London, compared to only 9–10 per cent in the country overall.

Blair, interviewed standing for the 1982 Beaconsfield by-election, was alive to all this early on. He told the BBC's *Newsnight*, with Michael Foot at his side:

'The image of the Labour Party has got to be an image which is more dynamic, more modern, more suited to the 1980s. I don't think it's as much about right and left as people make out. We live in a different world now, 50 per cent owner-occupiers, many people working in services. Large numbers of people working in services rather than manufacturing and that means a change in attitudes and a change of attitudes we've got to wake up to.' At its core, Philip Gould, Blair's close confidant and personal pollster, wrote, would be 'the new middle class; the aspirational working class in manual occupations and the increasingly insecure white-collar workers with middle-to-low level incomes.' It would also include the urban poor, the inner cities, the suburbs, as David Marquand observed, every voter from 'Diane Abbott's Hackney as well as Gisela Stuart's Birmingham Edgbaston'. Looked at in this way, New Labour wasn't just a branding exercise or, ironically enough, that new: rather it was the latest version of a series of iterations of a new type of Labour Party, attempting to attract a new coalition of voters to a party whose electoral performance since the war had been lamentable.

OUR SURVEY SAYS ...

Today there are some who argue that the New Labour victories came at too great a cost; that effectively Blair, in his courting of 'Middle England' and so-called 'Mondeo Man' and 'Worcester Woman', hemmed himself in, reduced Labour's room for manoeuvre, and reined in radicalism all in the name of respectability, and that this was unnecessary. The academic Neal Lawson, for example, has argued that Blair's 1997 majority was too large: 'The tent was too big and you spent the next ten years trying to keep the wrong people in it: the very rich, for example.'[1]

That a political party is electorally successful but then spends the years afterwards self-flagellating because it had the wrong sort of votes cast by the wrong voters seems to me an argument that only the Labour Party could have. But even taken on its own terms, there are two key reasons why it is a wretched analysis. For a start it's ahistorical. It looks that way now because Blair did achieve what he did. It seems the party was destined to win and win big. That is not how it seemed at the time: Labour politicians did not have the reassuring benefit of hindsight that we possess. Read any diary entry, any memoir or account of that period, and the scars of four successive defeats run deep in the psyches of the Labour politicians of the age. Even though the party had been ahead in the polls for years, even though the country was thoroughly sick of the Tory government, it didn't seem a certainty that Labour would finally get over the line. Chris Mullin, in his safe Labour seat of Sunderland Central, still didn't think it was going to happen until the last moments, as his diary entry from 24 April 1997 (exactly a week before polling day) records:

> We're going to lose. Blair knows it, too. I can see it in his eyes every time he appears on the TV news. The magic is fading. He looks exhausted. Major, by contrast, is as fresh as a daisy. The massive rubbishing to which our man has been subjected is paying off. The Tories have succeeded in turning him from an asset to a liability.[2]

Moreover (ironically given the accusation that all Blair wanted to do was achieve office at any cost), getting into government was not New Labour's only aim. Blair's objective was not to secure power once. Lawson is probably right that most (though by no means all) mainstream Labour leaders in 1997 would have won – the country was sick of the Tories after 18 years and the democratic elastic had been stretched to its maximum. But that was not the sum of Blair's or Brown's ambition. They wanted to govern for a sustained period in office. At the time that was mistaken for pragmatism over principle, but up to then one of the key critiques of the Labour Party was that it had never been able to enact a truly transformative programme because it had never governed for long enough – that too is forgotten now. Rather it had had periods of minority government followed by the stop-start governments of the 1940s and 1950s and especially the 1960s and 1970s. Blair didn't believe that simply expelling the Tories from office every now and again was enough: he wanted to, in effect, displace them as the natural party of government. Listen to any speech, read any pamphlet written by Blair or Brown at the time, and the idea of securing that objective drips off the page; that, in their view, required fundamental political accommodations. In the 1940s, after the Labour government enacted some truly socialist policies, socialists were dismayed not just at losing office in the 1950s but because the scales fell from their eyes. Part of the ideological makeup of prewar socialism was that once the working class had had a taste of the truly transformative powers of the ideology, it would usher in a golden age in which Labour would rarely be dislodged. History had not turned out that way and Blair's generation held no such illusions; they assumed they must act accordingly.

But there's another reason why it's easy to ridicule the Blair big tent, why it seems almost quaint as a political notion: because, for good or ill, it was precisely that – a big tent. Blair genuinely believed his was a new approach, a new conception of politics, and that much of the population could be brought into the tent's shelter. His politics was not one based on antagonism but on unity. The contrast with what came before him, of Margaret Thatcher's constant quest for enemies to slay, of her rhetoric of 'our people' and 'one of us', was a million miles away from Blair's soft and conciliatory tones, of 'one people', transcending left, right and all the old dogmas. Francis Urquhart would not have approved. In as much as anything, this was rooted in Blair's personality, in a tremendous self-belief in his own persuasive abilities and capacity to bring people together. As Professor David Marquand argued years later: 'the central premise of his statecraft was that society was naturally harmonious: that apparent differences of interest or belief could always be compromised or transcended'.[3]

That contrast is not only striking for what came before Blair but for what has come since. New Labour's big tent partly seems so kitsch because its open and pluralist approach seems so foreign to the politics of our own age. Today's politics, of remain and leave, of heroes and villains, of identity politics, of authenticity and virtue and vice, is a politics that fundamentally rests on enmity just as much as did that which characterised the 1980s. It relies on showing who you are for and who you are against and in so doing revealing your truly authentic self. In this regard, the bonhomie of the settled politics of Blair's 1990s seems as distant as Baldwin's 1930s or Macmillan's 1950s – indeed our own politics has manifested itself to some extent as a counter-reaction to it. Consequently, Blairism can appear unprincipled or rootless. The 'authenticity' of big characters like Donald Trump, Nigel Farage, Jeremy Corbyn and the rest must surely arise as a counter-reaction to the 1990s era of spin, PR politics and the idea of politicians trying to please all of the people all of the time. Better, it is said, to have politicians who really say what they think, even at the risk of being divisive, rather than those who try to be all things to all people. Today, as Britain is ravaged by new political and cultural schisms, I've lost count of the number of times I've heard friends or colleagues or columnists yearn aloud for a unifier, a politics less coarse, less bellicose, someone or something that can bring people together. Yet it was exactly that sort of openness, and its accompanying rootlessness, which so many came to revile and which now makes Blair's approach seem so antiquated and his political personality dismissed as a libertine.

Of course, Blair and Brown said the big tent couldn't be constructed on a foundation of presentational changes alone; they believed deep policy shifts would be necessary as well. In the same way that the hunt for new voters and appeal is sometimes today considered a unique and grubby affliction of the New Labour years, so likewise the abandonment of certain policies and adoption of others is considered to be a distinct piece of New Labour treachery. Rather, it makes more sense to think of New Labour as the party's latest attempt to respond to the changing material world around it, in a way that Labour hadn't done in a comprehensive fashion for a very long time, probably since the revisionist Anthony Crosland attempted to update the Attlee settlement for the 1960s in his seminal work, *The Future of Socialism*. Blair's and Brown's thinking, nursed through the 1980s and '90s, resulted in the so-called 'Third Way', in which the dynamism of the free market was combined with traditional social democratic goals of social justice and fairness.* As Blair was himself to say in 1999: 'It was important for me to try and explain to people what the nature of my political project was about, this idea you could get beyond left and right but have a pro-business, pro-enterprise but also pro-fairness party.' Decades after it had fallen out of favour, Blair was to reanimate that sentiment to me, saying that the Third Way and New Labour are

* Note, not necessarily equality, of which more later.

just rhetorical vehicles 'to describe an attitude, a way of looking at politics, the label is insignificant. What's significant is the idea that social democracy has to keep renewing its policy applications and principles.'

This didn't come out of a vacuum and it was a theme Blair spoke about often, throughout his leadership and after. When I asked him why he thought New Labour was successful he returned to the idea: 'I think the reason is that we broke this stranglehold that elements of the progressive left had over associating policies which were appropriate at one time with principles for all time. It's not complicated but it is essential; if you don't break that stranglehold you have the world changing but you are in the same place over policy.' In other words, he challenged the view that Labour policy had to be constant, that it would always look the same, and that to deviate from it was heresy, that there was only one road to socialism.

Blair won that argument for only a short time, and perhaps he never could win it in the end, because for most of his party the only road to socialism still runs to and from 1945 and hasn't changed much since.

1945 AND ALL THAT

Clement Attlee's 1945–51 government remains the party's most important administration, one of the three most significant governments of the twentieth century. Its achievements are ones of which the party can be justly proud. Its ability to stir hearts in members of the party is unparalleled, despite the fact that no one even elected to that Parliament remains alive, much less anyone who held ministerial office. In the summer of 2015, I made a film about the seventieth anniversary of that government's coming to power. As part of that I interviewed Margaret Beckett. She described an occasion when, in 1994, not long after John Smith's death, she attended the fiftieth anniversary of D-Day in Normandy, as leader of the opposition:

'We had a ceremony at the cemetery at Bayeux. The Queen was there, President Clinton, the Prime Minister and so on and so on. After the ceremony, the people broke and there was an opportunity for people to mix informally. And I was mobbed ... by veterans and their families. I remember looking around and there were lots of people around the Prime Minister of course but I was mobbed. And it's not just me who thinks that I was, because the Defence Secretary [Malcolm Rifkind] was there and said to everyone a few days later, did Margaret tell you, that she was mobbed by the D-Day veterans? And I thought ... that was for Attlee's government.' As she told the story, she became quite overcome with tears.

It's hard to compete with that, and every government before and since hasn't. It is the only Labour government of the half-dozen or so there have been that has emerged with its reputation intact. Perhaps because of this and because of the strength of its achievement, it has acted as a sort of eternal litmus test against which each and every government since is judged within the Labour movement. It has become Labour lore.*

But just as subsequent Labour governments and prime ministers struggle to compete with its emotional pull, so they struggled to compete with Attlee's greatest gift: the moment in which he lived, a moment primed for socialism. The total-war strategy articulated by Churchill entailed doing all the things that the Conservatives under Chamberlain and Baldwin had told the country were not possible: nationalising swathes of industry, huge government intervention in every sphere of existence, taking profound stakes in not only the economy but the day-to-day affairs of life. It controlled what you ate, what you did, whether or not your children lived with you, how much you paid for consumer goods, where you worked, whether or not you fought in the war, whether you lived or died. Public expenditure as a

* Yet it is forgotten now just how disappointing many socialists found the government at the time, how shoddy they thought it had become, how irritated they were with the compromises they had to make. The Conservatives have no equivalent – it would be like judging Theresa May against the actions of Macmillan or Baldwin.

proportion of overall national spending and income skyrocketed.* As a result, the ideological superstructure of the country changed. It was a unique moment and one that couldn't last.

The new consensus Attlee and his ministers bequeathed held for the next thirty years or so, with both Labour and Conservative governments managing Attlee's inheritance. But by the late 1970s Labour (and Conservative) governments had found it increasingly difficult to manage that settlement, which was by then decaying. As Britain struggled economically and the rest of the world fell into economic malaise, the traditional Keynesian methods of reflating the economy through public spending were in trouble across the globe. Jim Callaghan, who endured a pretty unsuccessful stint as chancellor and was now prime minister, sounded its death knell. He told the Labour Party conference in 1976: 'We used to think that you could spend your way out of a recession and increase employment by cutting taxes and boosting government spending. I tell you in all candour that that option no longer exists, and in so far as it ever did exist, it only worked on each occasion since the war by injecting a bigger dose of inflation into the economy, followed by a higher level of unemployment as the next step.'

The cosy Keynesian postwar balloon was slowly leaking air. As it did so, the social ideas that underpinned it were also dissolving. As we've seen, the party's grip on the working class was never entirely firm but by the 1970s it appeared almost loose. One of the central problems was the idea of greater public spending and, in a portent of things to come, a dissatisfaction with newer streams of more liberal leftist thought focusing on minorities and individual rights. As Denis Healey was to relay to his cabinet colleagues in 1975:

> At the Labour clubs, you'll find there's an awful lot of support for this policy of cutting public expenditure. They will tell you all about Paddy Murphy up the street who's got eighteen children,

---

* By 1943 it accounted for 54 per cent of GDP, against 24 per cent in 1938. It turned out that total war was extraordinarily egalitarian.

> has not worked for years, lives on unemployment benefit, has a colour television and goes to Majorca for his holidays.[4]

In other words, as the years of postwar plenty gave way to a harsher economic climate, so the social solidarity that had paved the road to 1945 diminished. At the same time, globalisation, membership of the European Economic Community and increasing integration of global markets continued to lessen the power of social democratic governments to enact the policies that they might like: the idea that socialism or social democracy in one country was possible seemed less and less likely. Globalisation, the end of dollar convertability and the development of a truly international capital market had disrupted the cosy world of 1940s Britain, where socialist or social democratic governments could pursue their dreams of a new Jerusalem without much regard to the rest of the world. The experience of the 1968 devaluation crisis under Wilson and the 1977 IMF crisis under Callaghan was searing to the Labour movement, but also illustrated how powerful international capital flows and financiers had become and how weak national governments now paled when set against them. Blair showed himself alive to these forces early in his leadership. In a university lecture in 1995 he said:

> Governments can no longer adopt stimulative policies that boost demand without risk of being punished by markets and higher interest rates. We must recognise that the UK is situated in the middle of the global market for capital, a market which is less subject to regulation today than for many decades. An expansionary fiscal or monetary policy that is at odds with other economies in Europe will not be sustained for very long ... to that extent the room for manoeuvre of any government in Britain is already extremely circumscribed.[5]

Blair and Brown were obsessed with this idea; from their earliest days in office it's clear now that they were genuinely quite scared of the market reaction against their government. Harriet Harman, in her memoir, recounts a story that is revealing of her bosses' mindset. As the new Labour government's social security secretary, she had been tasked with finding several billion pounds' worth of cuts, so the government could stick to its election pledge of matching Conservative spending plans (something the man who drew them up, Ken Clarke as chancellor, later said he wouldn't even have done had the Tories been re-elected). This entailed cutting child benefit for new claimants by £6 a week, a move deeply unpopular within the wider Labour Party. She recalls that she went to see Brown to spell out the problems and find a remedy:

> But he said it was a manifesto commitment and that it would have to be carried out. If we didn't, it would send a signal that we weren't going to be financially prudent in the way we'd promised, it would cause instability in the money markets, there would be a loss of confidence, the government would fall, and I would be responsible for bringing down the first Labour government for eighteen years ... Our government still felt fragile to me, I couldn't do anything to threaten it.[6]

In retrospect, this seems quite incredible. The Labour administration was only a year old, elected with a stonking majority, the economy was booming, the markets were sanguine, the world economy was enjoying stability and growth, but a Labour chancellor and cabinet minister were worried that a £6 a week cut in benefits for lone parents might be the issue on which the government's fortunes turned and which risked sending money markets into a spin. Perhaps Brown was over-egging the pudding to get his way, but what is striking reading the accounts of the time is just how commonplace fears like this were.

So in every direction by the 1990s, whether it was economic, social or ideological, the world seemed to have given way beneath social democracy's feet. The postwar social democratic settlement seemed to be increasingly unobtainable because the pillars on which it had been constructed were vanishing. Callaghan could see what was happening better than anyone. When polls indicated he might be doing a bit better in the run-up to the 1979 election than he might have hoped, his aide, Bernard Donoghue, ventured to suggest he might win after all. 'Bernard,' the old warhorse replied, 'I'm afraid to say I think there's been a sea change and it is for Mrs Thatcher.'

It is sometimes spoken of as if Blair and Brown 'abandoned' socialism all on their own. That's putting the cart before the horse. By the time New Labour came along the process of abandoning the trappings of the old Attlee settlement (which many people then took, and today continue to take, as the quintessential socialism) was already well underway. Because New Labour was not only an attempt to broaden the party's sociological appeal: it was also an attempt to respond to a world where traditional methods of social democracy and socialism had been deemed bankrupt, in a metaphorical and a real sense; and many of the people who declared them so were – guess what – the social democratic politicians of the day.

And while the old leftist ways withered the right wasn't sitting idly by, it was seizing the moment. The next decade and a half after the 1979 election transformed the political and social landscape in Britain, a more economically liberal, individualistic and enterprising culture was born and much of the time Labour was nowhere to be seen. Thatcher clocked up three general election victories and her successor, John Major, secured an unprecedented fourth in 1992.

In the meantime, a betrayal myth developed across some parts of the Labour Party that not only had Blair and Brown sold out but that Wilson and Callaghan had done so before them, that they had given in to international capital, and that if they had taken a properly left-wing approach to managing the economy, things might have been different and Thatcherism might have been resisted. We will never know for certain, but there are two important indicators that might suggest such revisionism is without much basis. The first is that the idea of betrayal might be more credible if similar phenomena were not taking place all across the West. Britain might have led the way, but the entire world was heading in a more 'neoliberal' direction. Whether it was Reaganomics in the United States or Rogernomics in

New Zealand,* the picture was much the same everywhere. Even governments that were ostensibly left wing, like François Mitterrand's in France, implemented more economically liberal policies once in office. The same phenomena that were running the left ragged in Britain were much the same elsewhere; the malaise and stagflation of the 1970s gripped the world; the corresponding decline in social democracy took hold partly as a result of changing technology and work patterns, and partly simply as a result of the final dissipation of some of the solidarity that had so characterised the immediate post-war world. There had, in other words, been an ideological changing of the guard around the world in favour of markets and their creative potential. Just as in the 1940s, the sweep of leftist governments across Europe led the historian A. J. P. Taylor to lament that belief in private enterprise seemed as hopeless as Jacobitism after 1688, so in the 1980s and 1990s did an untrammelled statism appear equally futile.

The left had to respond to these changes and more which were to come: the Soviet Union was collapsing, the Berlin Wall was coming down, and the ideological and geopolitical underpinning of much of twentieth-century leftist thinking was coming down with it. This was the era of the supposed 'end of history', as the academic Francis Fukuyama (sort of) said. Liberal market-based democracies had triumphed – it would have been bizarre if no reckoning had come and doubly bizarre if the response had been to double down with policies of nationalisation, higher taxation and stricter economic controls. Indeed, what is striking is that the left responded in a similar way across the West. Wherever you look, whether it's Clinton's Democrats or Schroeder's SDP, there was a conspicuous move to the centre and an acceptance of market methods. New Labour might have embraced it with more brio than the others, but the pattern was the same. The left fundamentally changed because the world around it had done so too, including the attitudes and beliefs of the voters. Thus, even if the dreaded Blair and Brown hadn't led Labour, even if

* So-called for Finance Minister Roger Douglas. He was a Labour minister by the way.

New Labour had never been created, there is no doubt as to what the direction of the party in the late 1990s would have been because we have a control: the rest of the world. New Labour and Blairism were just a British version of an attempt across the West to respond to the profound crisis of social democracy that had taken place in the late 1970s and beyond.

Blair's personal take on Labour's lack of success in the 1980s and 1990s period was a simple one. He told a 1996 BBC documentary analysing the party's 18 years in the wilderness: 'The problem of the Labour Party of the seventies and eighties is not complex it's simple. Society changed and the party didn't. So you had a whole new generation of people with different aspirations and ambitions in a different kind of world. And we were still singing the same old song that we were singing in the forties and fifties.'[7]

Brown agreed. He told the same documentary: 'I don't think anybody believed that you would have a Conservative government that would be able to maintain itself over four elections and be in power for now 16 years. I think what Mrs Thatcher understood in 1979 was the need for change. I think what Labour failed to understand then was that change had to come about and that Labour should have been sponsoring that change and I think we've had to come to terms with that over a period of 16 years.'[8]

But what would that change look like when all the old tools of tax and spend had been taken out of the toolkit? Well, the truth is, as we shall see, that New Labour did dust off some of the tools in the end – but in the early days, before Brown's tax hikes of the early 2000s, things were different. Harriet Harman, then shadow chief secretary to the Treasury and Brown's deputy, described the approach:

> Gordon developed the mantra that, to have growth, we needed to build the supply side of the economy. He was determined that our economic policy, which had been our electoral Achilles' heel over so many years, would shift from taxing and spending the proceeds of growth to focus instead on increasing the rate of economic growth. He wanted to move beyond the idea that our

> economic policy was only about taxing the rich and spending more on benefits. Government policy should not just be about dividing up the cake but increasing the size of the cake as well. This was the background to his 'endogenous growth' speech in 1994, in which he said that economic growth could come not just through increasing demand but through increasing the capacity of the economy by investment in people, through education and training; in industry, through research and development. And in infrastructure, like roads and public transport … This was a huge change. For so long, the only thing people knew about Labour's approach to the economy was that we would raise taxes and use the money to improve benefits and public services. The public perception was that they would have to pay more taxes and that, subsequently, their money would be thrown down the drain … Now our weekly Treasury team meetings would always begin with Gordon intoning that Labour was not just about taxing and spending but about investment. To get our message across, we had to invoke the supply-side investment strategy as the frame for every point we made.[9]

This idea, of unleashing people's latent talent and investing in training and education in order that they might release latent potential was not exactly red-in-tooth-and-claw stuff – it wasn't bailing out my dad's job in Rover as the Labour governments of the 1940s and 1960s might have done, but it was still recognisably a Labour innovation. Its transformative impact, on the public realm and on people's lives, is often underestimated and damned by some on the left and right today who, frankly, would never have come within a thousand feet of feeling its effects. But it was the underlying philosophy that directed government money into my Aim Higher programme and Gifted and Talented. It was the approach that allowed my mum, a woman who had had me at 17 years of age and had had to quit her education early, to retrain as a midwife and start a new life as her kids were growing. It was the philosophy that led to the reinvigoration of the public realm and civic infrastructure that I could see all around me growing up. I'm not convinced that would have happened had New Labour not come to power and the best thinking Conservatives, including David Cameron and his team, learned its lessons. It was a quiet radicalism to befit a benign age.

The irony is, as the government grew in confidence, it quietly became much more bullish about redistribution and the tax and spend policies from which it resiled in its early days. But you wouldn't have known it; that hushed radicalism led to its own decline.

DIDN'T THEY DO WELL?

Aside from its foreign policy,* there are several powerful critiques of the New Labour years. The first is an egalitarian critique. Although the New Labour government can objectively be considered among the most redistributionist and empowering of its predecessors, it was perhaps the first not to place equality as part of its central and organising political mission. This was genuinely new for Labour. The fundamental Labour critique, which underwrote its view of political economy, was that society would not only be better to live in if it were more equal but that it would be more just. It was a profound political insight and one that endured. As early as the late 1990s, senior figures worried the party was drifting away from it and, *ergo*, the basis of its political and philosophical power. Roy Hattersley, a man partly inspired to become a socialist because of his reading R. H. Tawney's seminal work *Equality* as a schoolboy, said in 1995:

> We had a big idea, a more equal therefore a better country. Sometimes we called it fairness. Sometimes we called it social justice. But our idea was a more equal and free society. Now that

* This is a vast area and an important one. There is no doubt that Blair's foreign policy helped incubate the leftist revival that was to occur in the 2010s. However, I do not go into the details of the foreign policy decisions in any great detail in this book. It seems to me to have been very well documented elsewhere.

> was the idea we should have propagated with determination and consistency and we should sell to the people, the idea we've failed to sell to the people. But it's still the only idea that socialism could possibly stand for.[10]

It was not entirely clear that Blair and others did share that idea. Equality didn't improve much in the New Labour years, although there's plenty of evidence to suggest that it would have got worse than it did had New Labour's policies not been in place. Regardless, it wasn't something the leadership seemed very concerned about. Tony Blair famously said that he wasn't 'especially interested in controlling what David Beckham earns, quite frankly'. Peter Mandelson likewise observed that New Labour was 'intensely relaxed about people getting filthy rich ... as long as they pay their taxes'. Under the Conservatives the Labour rallying cry had always been, just as my grandad used to say to me, that 'the rich got richer and the poor got poorer'. Under Labour, the poor got richer but the rich got richer too (and faster). For a while it was satisfactory enough, but inspiring rallying call it was not.

The important thing, it was argued, was to create the right conditions that allowed individuals to thrive, that equality of opportunity, not outcome was what mattered. As I've said, this isn't to be underestimated. My life was transformed. I was and am exactly the sort of person Blair's socialism would benefit. But once I succeeded and had skyrocketed up, the gap in income between me and my old classmates back in Longbridge was something about which New Labour seemed to have little to say, especially in the post-industrial Midlands and north, the small towns and the left behind, what we would one day come to call 'Brexitland'. That was a clear weakness in New Labour's political strategy and one that gave its opponents on the left and the right the space to destroy its reputation in years to come – and more importantly, weakened the social and political fabric of the country.

Nonetheless, the last part of the Mandelson quote is still important and often forgotten: that getting filthy rich was acceptable 'as long as they pay their taxes'. Because, as it turned out, Brown was slowly redistributing vast sums of money, especially after 2002, when he increased National Insurance to pay for greater NHS spending. The tax credit network redistributed money from rich to poor. Take a look at this chart, from the Institute for Fiscal Studies. It shows how much the population gained or lost as a percentage of their income.

The distributional impact of Labour from 1997 to 2000

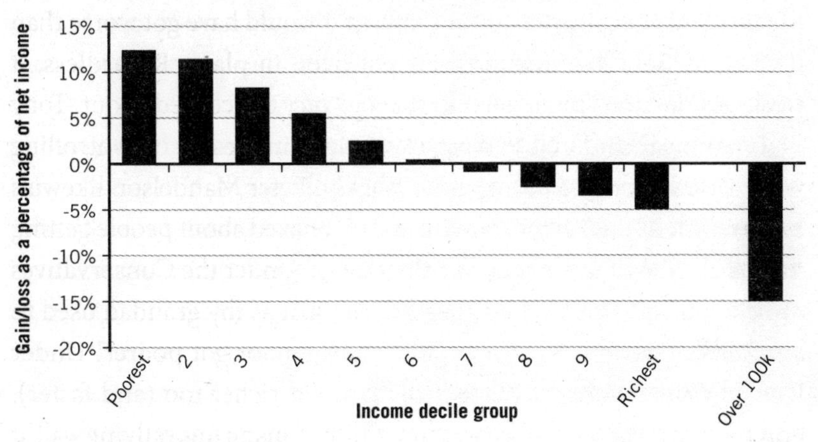

Source: Institute for Fiscal Studies

The impact is clear. In terms of what the government was doing, there was one sort of person you really didn't want to be. And it was rich. Quietly, without much fanfare, in a way that it barely dared to say aloud, the New Labour government was redistributing money hand over fist.

But the people who didn't make a song or dance about it most were the Labour government itself. It was so desperate to appear respectable, not to hark back to Labour governments of long ago, that the most social democratic things they did were never presented as such. They were offered to the country and to their own voters, from conception to implementation, through the way they were explained and communicated, in terms of the market and of individual empowerment. Consequently, what they didn't do is sew the threads together in a moral critique of capitalism, or of politics more generally. It revelled in its banality, in its dull managerialism. New Labour was often radical but it usually pretended that it wasn't. Today's leftists are the opposite. New Labour did social democracy on the quiet, in deed if not in spirit. Corbynism does it through a loudspeaker.

But the sense of mission matters much more than Blair thought it did – as Peter Shore, the former Labour cabinet minister, once said:

'You've always got to have in mind with a Labour Party that if it isn't a radical party, if it isn't a party of change, if it isn't a party that's committed to making Britain a fairer more equal society then that idealism, that enthusiasm, that energy that goes with that, will be denied it. And if the Labour Party plays too safe for too long then it really will be denying its own heritage.'

Too often, New Labour, desperate to be accepted and to be seen to be in the middle ground, was insufficiently proselytising about just how radical its own achievements were. Looking back it's clear it was, broadly speaking, a social democratic government. But it didn't always look or feel that way at the time. As a result, it allowed its internal opponents to cast it as dull technocrats and themselves as the true inheritors of the party's radical flame. At times, inexcusably, Blair and others acted as if they weren't political at all. Indeed, he would say in 1999 that 'I was never really in politics. I never grew up as a politician. I don't feel myself a politician even now. I don't think of myself as being a politician in that sense of someone whose whole driving force in life is politics.' And in so doing he managed to lay the foundations of his own unmaking within the Labour Party.

James Graham's 2017 play *Labour of Love* wrestles with recent Labour history and, in so many words, this precise tension. The plot revolves around a Midlands MP, David Lyons, and thirty years of tribulation and trial within the party. In one scene, the MP's caseworker, Jean Whittaker, offers a killer assessment of the New Labour period: 'All looks good on the outside but it only takes one little tremor to bring the whole thing down.' Lyons jumps to the government's defence, listing all of the new schools and hospitals that have popped up in the area and the new-look town centre, but Whittaker is unimpressed: 'Yeah, spending, good, fine, but not the actual difficult work of digging deep down into the underlying factors woven into the rotten fabric of this unfair fucking country.'

In other words, New Labour did not in any way challenge the fundamental economic assumptions of the British economy. It believed – as most people did – that at base the British economy was working well and that it was a new sustainable settlement. The basic economic model did not need to be challenged or changed; the sole question was about what you did with the bounty of the untrammelled free market – and New Labour's answer was, among other things, spend it on kids like me. The problem was, as Whittaker says in the play, that as soon as the good times ended, it was all too easy to turn the taps off. This happened again and again across the West where social democrats had governed. As the academic Shiri Berman told me:

'These new centre-left politicians celebrated the market's upsides but ignored its downsides. They differed from classical liberals and conservatives by supporting a social safety net to buffer markets' worst effects, but they didn't offer a fundamental critique of capitalism or any sense that market forces should be redirected to protect social needs. When the financial crisis hit in 2008, this attitude repelled those who viewed globalisation as the cause of their suffering and wanted not merely renewed growth, but also less inequality and instability.'

It was all too easy for such measures to be reversed by the Tories, as soon as the good times ended. By contrast, as a signifier of the power of their achievement, Labour did not attempt to reverse the changes to Britain's political economy that the Tories augured in the 1980s. By way of illustration, Labour's enduring reforms – which were substantial – were usually structural ones: the Scottish Parliament, the Welsh Assembly, the London mayoralty, the minimum wage, civil partnerships to name but a few. But New Labour was too dewy-eyed about the virtues of the market. As a result, the question Giles Radice posed on that heady day in 1997 is still apposite: 'What will Tony's success consist of: election victories or something more permanent? The jury is out.' The answer, we now know, was somewhere in between. Some permanent structural changes, a reinvigoration of the public realm but not a new settlement in favour of social democracy.

In fairness, it is easy now to say with hindsight what they should have done. Moreover, it seemed before 2008 at least as if New Labour had created a new settlement. When they assumed the leadership of their party, David Cameron and George Osborne did not initially dare to question Labour's spending. On the contrary, they called on the government to increase spending on public services. It would not even explicitly commit to tax cuts, the *raison d'être* of Toryism; only cautiously, gingerly, daring to say that they would 'seek to share the proceeds of growth' at some undefined point, probably far in the future.

This, as we now know, did not endure. The New Labour settlement was not as successful at changing the minds of its opponents as the Thatcherite one had been. But perhaps one of the reasons for that is Blair himself, who was dedicated not only to the market but to the idea that he wasn't even political at all. This critique is perhaps the most damaging.

HOOK, LINE AND SINKER

At times New Labour seemed to go out of its way to undermine the very notion of political change itself. So convinced did Blair become about the virtues of the market and of the overweening power of globalisation (and the cultural changes with which it was associated) that New Labour appeared to forget that many of its voters voted Labour to protect themselves from those same forces. Over time, Blair's rhetoric adopted increasingly determinist and fateful overtones. His interpretation of the globalised world came to imply that political action was barely possible. That was because globalisation was an unstoppable, inexorable force that could be neither halted nor much changed. In conference speech after conference speech a parade of government ministers trotted out the same mantra. Blair's conference speech of 2005 is the most chilling example:

> Change is marching on again. The pace of change can either overwhelm us, or make our lives better and our country stronger. What we can't do is pretend it is not happening. I hear people say we have to stop and debate globalisation. You might as well debate whether autumn should follow summer.
>
> The character of this changing world is indifferent to tradition. Unforgiving of frailty. No respecter of past reputations. It has no custom and practice. It is replete with opportunities, but they only go to those swift to adapt, slow to complain, open, willing and able to change.

These are not words you'd expect from a social democratic prime minister. Social democracy, if it is to mean anything, must surely be about doing its best to protect its citizens from the harsh winds of international capital and globalisation, to preserve personal sovereignty. This was a very different vision. It was a vision of an almost nihilistic politics. As we've seen, leftist governments all over the West were wrestling with the challenges of globalisation and the constraints that its associated processes implied, but Blair seemed to come to embrace that new order with zeal. That zeal led New Labour to accept and encourage high levels of migration (especially the immediate extension of free movement to the new EU accession countries of eastern Europe in 2004), without much thought to the reaction of its culturally conservative voters, the consequences of which would prove profound. Blair was not merely wearing the 'golden straitjacket' of the global economy, perhaps as any social democratic prime minister would have had to do or will yet again, but appearing to enjoy the fit that little bit too much. Tony Benn used to say that the most powerful letters in the English language were 'TINA', or 'There is no alternative.' It was one thing taking that from a Conservative prime minister, but hearing the remorseless market logic from a Labour one – and worse still a Labour premier who seemed to salivate at the thought – felt like a bitter pill.

Today, Blair is unrepentant. He maintains that he was right to be straightforward about the inevitability of globalisation, telling me:

'I wasn't zealous about globalisation the way you described it; I was saying it was a fact. I haven't decided as a matter of policy that the world is changing in this way, it is changed in this way and it's changing for reasons to do with technology, with trade and migration; things that no single government or country either can stop or will stop ... I was aware of the potential for a populist backlash from early on. So the thing I find odd about today is that people accuse me of allowing populism to develop; yes, sure, they were developing when I was in power it's true but I was dealing with them. Social democracy is shifting because the workplace has also been shifting – therefore many of the things that are happening today are the product of new coalitions in politics and new fragmentation of politics that has been going on for a long period of time. What we did very consciously was create a coalition that could see us through that process – why was it both before becoming leader and after, I obsessed about law and order? Some people thought it was some sort of fetish. But it was because I could see that for working people who we traditionally represented a mere economic message was not enough, we also had to be dealing with their problem with security and the changing nature of their communities because of migration. These were questions that we were actively working on and we should have been actively carrying on working on, but what happened after 2007 was a feeling that we went too far on that stuff, that we should actually pull back – whereas that was never the answer; the answer was to carry on; all of those issues were going to intensify.'

It is true that Blair rightly identified the social conservatism of many of his voters (something often ignored by the current Labour leadership) and acted accordingly. But often that sat uncomfortably with New Labour's deep economic liberalism and laissez-faire approach to globalisation – for example, the 2004 decision to allow untrammelled migration from eastern European accession states to the EU was thought permissible because it pleased Blair's economic liberalism – but no matter what safeguards he put in place in the form of ID cards or extra police, he seemed little able to assure his voters. Rather, as so often, he found himself in the worst of all worlds, annoying every constituency of opinion. His traditional working-class voters were irritated by his openness to migration while his culturally liberal middle-class voters were lured to the Lib Dems and others on the basis of the draconian social policies Blair instituted to compensate. This helps explains the hollowing of the Labour vote, to only 35 per cent by 2005 – bleeding in every direction, to the authoritarian right and the liberal left. Both offending strands of Blair's thought became more pronounced and problematic as time proceeded. Even for critical friends of New Labour this is difficult territory. All the more difficult because it isn't where Blair began, as Jon Cruddas explained to me:

'The danger is we get further away from it and we look at it more and more in the one-dimensional sense through the rearview mirror: New Labour was this or that. I remember going into Downing Street the day after we won in '97 and at that stage there wasn't one Downing Street, there were many Downing Streets – more liberal Downing Streets, more communitarian, more European, more Eurosceptic, people who wanted a more systematic labour market structure, or refinancing the public services or tax policy – but what I'm trying to get at is that it was a lot more plural political project than people give it credit for especially across the left now. The question is how it's shrunk over time – which is very dangerous in terms of the collective memory of the left and the Labour Party, but it has lost nuance, and the character of it has diminished over time. In turn, Blair changed over time: compare the speeches of 1995–6 to 2004–5 – they are very different characters. The arc between those speeches explains that change in dynamics. It lost its ethical components primarily and became quite a dystopian liberal sink-or-swim agenda by the end. Where you can trace it back to is his philosophical reference points, his spiritual and ethical history, who he studied with at Oxford, his letters and communications in Opposition. You can trace a more thoughtful ethical and moral dynamic to a social democratic agenda, and over time it became empty, and more economistic and instrumentalised and cold – it lost its soul over time.'

In other words, to begin with New Labour retained a starkly moral component, a strong critique of and distaste for the worship of

Mammon and the individualism of the Thatcher and Major years. Blair, whose political philosophy, like that of the early Labour Party leaders, was far more influenced by the teachings of Mark and Matthew than Marx and Engels, felt comfortable on this terrain and even invoked scripture. He told a Labour conference in the mid-1990s:

'Socialism for me was never about nationalisation, or the power of the state, not just about economics, or even politics. It is a moral purpose to life. It is how I try to live my life. How you try to live yours. The simple truths: I'm worth no more than anyone else; I am my brother's keeper; I will not walk by on the other side. We are not simply people set in isolation from one another, face to face with eternity, but members of the same family, same community, same human race. This is my socialism.'

He said this at his second conference as party leader. On the platform, as a special guest, was Mary Wilson, the widow of the recently deceased Harold, who had once said that 'the Labour movement is a moral crusade or it is nothing'. Wilson was right. The link, physical, intellectual and ethical, from New Labour to old was there for all to see. It was only later, in the mid-2000s, that Blair appeared to choose to sever that link, in that his philosophy had mutated into something quite alien to Labour tradition. In that, Blair sowed the seeds for the trashing of his own reputation, the Blairites' loss of Labour's crown and eventually even Britain's repudiation of the sort of moderate, centrist politics that Blair had so hoped to permanently embed.

LET'S SEE WHAT YOU COULD HAVE WON ...

In pure Labour terms, the party from its inception had the trappings of religion. We live in an age characterised by a caustic suspicion of politicians and their motives, yet we have not to go back too far into history to see a missionary evangelism about politics and a particular fervour associated with socialism and the Labour Party. It is not for nothing called 'the Labour movement'. That movement and ideological crusade was at its zenith in Attlee's 1945–51 administration. Imagine a contemporary politician of any stripe speaking with the moral and political certainty, if not the evangelical overtones, of his deputy prime minister, Herbert Morrison: 'The good Socialist works with religious zeal for the redemption of mankind from the evils of poverty and ignorance. ... He is conscious of the beauty of the ideal ... he works ... for the deliverance of the human spirit from the enslavement of material things.'[11]

It's hard to imagine Peter Mandelson's grandfather as Moses but there we are. And such a sentiment was not unusual. At Labour's birth, and for much of the twentieth century, for many people it was nothing less than an article of faith that a Labour government, and *ergo* the use of state power, would positively influence their lives. A fusion of class attachment and group thinking led to a solid conviction among a significant portion of the population in the importance of voting Labour. The state could and would tame capitalism and help build that new Jerusalem for the working class. Over time, however, that faith, in both Labour as an entity but perhaps more crucially in the state's capacity to ameliorate social conditions, has eroded. Time and again, up and down the country, I've heard voters tell me some variant of the same thing, as one elderly lady in Manchester explained: 'I've voted Labour always. It's just what we did. My mum told me, we were poor so we voted Labour, for our own kind. The rich vote Tory and we don't.' These are not unique insights, they're sentiments the like of which would have been repeated countless times in families up and down the country for decades, including in my own family. Yet, unfortunately for Labour, what she went on to tell me has become an all too common addition: 'I don't vote Labour any more. Doesn't matter who gets in. Nothing ever changes.' Leave London or any of the big cities and this sense of powerlessness among voters is as palpable as it is ubiquitous, especially among Labour voters.

And, extraordinarily, to some extent Labour brought this on itself. Throughout the New Labour years, the refrain was the same: that voters simply had to accept this new world. Do or die. Sink or swim.

This was hardly inspiring talk for a party whose essential aim since its inception had been to reform industrial capitalism and alter its character. Here, 105 years after the party's birth, its most successful electoral leader was offering it a vision of society that was less a shining city on a hill, but rather a burning one.

This repeated insistence that perpetual change was on the way and that national governments could do little to alter its path did more than just demoralise Labour's party faithful. It helped erode the very basis of Labour's *raison d'être*, in the public's collective psyche. If even the Labour prime minister was of the view that nothing could or indeed *should* stand in the way of global economic forces, then what was the point of their supposed gatekeepers? Why not replace them with stewards of the free market who were true believers and ultimately had more credibility, i.e. the Conservative Party? And, true enough, as soon as Labour's economic credibility was damaged beyond repair in the late 2000s, that is precisely what the public did.

Worse, with Labour's retreat from the state, others have filled the vacuum. Across Europe, a similar phenomenon has occurred. Voters who have become sick and tired of social democratic politicians telling them what they can no longer do have decided to fill that space with politicians on the far right. If you take Nigel Farage's UKIP, or Marine Le Pen's Front National or Donald Trump, one thing unites them: their unabashed enthusiasm for state power and the pitch to voters that contrary to what they've been told, another world is possible. While many liberals may find the populists' rhetoric dark and distasteful, one reason it appeals is its political and economic certainty. There is no hands-up expression of woe, no plea to global forces outside our control – all of this cast of characters offer safety and security to the dominant tribe in their respective societies: we will protect you, and your family, and we'll use the state to do it. Whether that translates into deportation, stronger border controls, or promises of greater economic self-sufficiency, the underlying theme is the same: that of state power; that voting for some – any – sort of political change must be better than voting for parties that offer none at all. This is why the prospect of 'taking back control' was so potent in the

Brexit referendum – it was speaking to a powerlessness that politicians, especially of the centre left, had for too long cultivated. In Scotland, in a different case, lost Labour voters turned to nationalism rather than populism but the phenomenon was essentially the same: a group of politicians expressing the belief that alternatives were possible, that the future was not set in stone. What, social democracy's antagonists in every case implicitly and explicitly argued, do you have to lose? As Sheri Berman told me: 'The decline of the centre left is one of the most important pre-conditions for the rise of the populist right. Not in a narrow way that people have currently focused on – that traditional left-leaning voters have shifted over to the right. That's too simplistic. Something more profound is that in the course of the last decade, the centre left (not necessarily the far left) has lost the ability to speak effectively to the two main challenges that are facing European and American society: economic challenges and social or cultural challenges. The left has lost its voice on both these things, and so it has left the space open for parties to move in with answers to these types of things. Without the decline of the centre left both across Europe and in the US, you'd never had a political space for the rise of populism.'

It is in this where late Blair loses his connection with Labour leaders before him. He too often presented the laws of economics as if they were the laws of physics. Politics became boring and hopeless, trapped by its own confines. It removed the magic of possibility on which politics must rest. Jeremy Corbyn's biggest virtue is perhaps that, under him, that has been restored. And if Berman is right (as I think she is) that the populism of our own age can be attributed to the decline of the centre left, and its modern inability to speak to voters, then Corbyn's achievement to arrest that decline is all the more important. It is vital, then, to understand what he has done, just who exactly this rather curious man is and how he came to be there in the first place.

Chapter 2

THE CURIOUS CASE OF JEREMY CORBYN

Anyone on the real left of any significance was there. Jeremy Corbyn couldn't make it.

Tony Benn, diaries, June 1994

You really don't have to worry about Jeremy Corbyn suddenly taking over.

Tony Blair, 1994

Ooooh! Jeremmmmmyyyy Corrrrbynnnn!

Almost everywhere I went, summer 2017

It's very late September 2017, summer is clinging on by its fingertips, and, yet again, I'm waiting for Jeremy Corbyn. It's the eve of the Labour Party conference in Brighton. It's a home fixture for him here. Draw a Venn diagram of the Brighton population and Jeremy Corbyn supporters, and you'd find yourself colouring the section in the middle a very dark shade of Labour crimson indeed. This park – 'the Level', not far from the city's famous Pavilion – informs its visitors upon entry that it is a 'gender inclusive' amenity. If Corbynism has a spiritual home outside his Islington redoubt, it is surely this great coastal city.

As ever, Corbyn is late. The crowd, a hundred deep or so, don't seem to care. They seem high. Some of them probably are. Most of them, apparently, on sheer possibility, the unadulterated joy of being proved right. One man is dancing in a Pikachu costume while wearing a Jeremy Corbyn T-shirt and no one bats an eyelid. Families have brought their kids on a rapidly darkening late September night and more still have brought their dinner, just to hear a near septuagenarian politician from north London, first elected before many there were even born, address the crowd and give the same speech he's essentially been giving for twenty years.

I watch in the press pen, as I've done many times. Before he appears, he often has a posse of speakers introduce him. Not just one, not just two but usually, five, six, even seven. Believe me, when you're on a deadline, you have no choice but to count them, in pure desperation, making feverish calculations about average speaking time. John McDonnell usually goes last. He has a few anecdotes thrown in from their three-decade bromance. He's preceded by a consortium of local activists, mid-level trade union officials, long-standing councillors, the occasional new party member to remind us all just how inspiring young people find the old man. This one is no exception. The crowd sports a peculiar mix of adulation and detachment. After all, there's only one man they've come to see. Pikachu dances on.

But then someone notices the merest flash of a cream suit. The word diffuses through the masses like quicksilver. A gradually excited roar rips through the crowd. Pikachu stops dancing. As well as being the media area, the cordoned-off section in which I'm standing is also reserved for disabled people. One lady, on a crutch, almost explodes with excitement when she sees the cream.

'Jeremy! Jeremy! He's here … oh my, he's here!' she screams in a Scottish accent.

I ask her why she's so excited. She replies that she loves him.

'But why?' I ask again.

She offers a series of incredulities. She's clearly never wondered why anyone would need to wonder. Nonetheless, she indulges me, considers for a moment, rolling the question around her mind and then: 'Well, for a start, that one. The … the pig fucker. You know who I mean, I can't even stand to say his name without wanting to rip someone's head off, he makes me so angry!'

I ask her, why does he make her angry?

She takes another moment, apparently deep in thought. Then comes the answer: 'I don't know, he just does.'

There's a flash of something across her eyes, just for a moment – is it uncertainty? And then, turning her head to see Corbyn emerging on to the stage, her huge smile returns, and she walks, slowly, unsteadily, but determinedly on her crutches, as fast as she can, to get as close as possible to the politician who makes her beam. Who makes her feel good.

We wait a long time for his speech. When he eventually comes on to the stage, he steps up to the microphone, holding his notes close to his long, pointy nose and Dumbledore glasses, almost like a menu. And he treats his diners to a pretty typical meal chez Corbyn. He meanders from one topic to the other with little in the way of thread. The subjects selected are united only by his belief in their place on the arc of his own moral universe, which, like his speech, is very long indeed. The big issue of the day, the geopolitical mantrap of Brexit, gets as much attention as the burning question of free music lessons for all under-elevens. The dozens holding EU flags aloft continue to hold them high. They see no disconnect between Corbyn the Eurosceptic, the only MP alongside Dennis Skinner to vote against every European treaty and piece of legislation in his 30 years in Parliament, and the folk hero that he has now undoubtedly become. Because he is bigger than any one issue, than any one cause.

He speaks as he always does, laconically in a single register. I've heard him so many times I feel I could deliver his speech myself. But, this time, I sense there's something more. He's savouring every syllable. He's enjoying himself. And who could blame him? How close he must have come to resigning in 2016 as MP after MP shattered like spinning plates falling off their sticks, one after the other. How close Theresa May might have come to not calling the 2017 election, leaving him instead to fester and wade through the most intractable of political treacle, every moment now a living vindication of the right path chosen, the chill of what he might neither have known nor experienced enough to make him grateful. There's a parallel universe where another Jeremy Corbyn is sitting on his allotment, staking his raspberry canes for the next year, wondering what might have been. Not just because Theresa May didn't call the 2017 election but because, in a universe where in 2015, as virtually the last man or woman on the Labour left who hadn't stood for the leadership, he'd consulted his wife, Laura, and decided he'd rather have a quieter life. None of this would have happened.

He finishes. He leaves. But not quickly because the crowds descend. The idea that he's 'like a rock star' is clichéd but there are few other ways to describe it. People, like the lady on the crutches, seem genuinely overwhelmed to see him, to touch him, to exchange a few words: the (people's) king's touch – ridding them not of scrofula, but of the little pessimism they have left about life and about the journey that they're all on together. Not long to go now and when victory comes, as it surely must, as night follows day, he'll still be theirs. Their Jeremy. He's real and he's sending them away with even more hope than they had when they arrived. They are part of his army. His tribe. They call him by his first name because he feels like a friend, like he's one of them but greater than them too. He gives them strength. Just before he leaves the stage, he stops, takes his phone out of his pocket and takes a picture of the crowd. He smiles.

The election of Jeremy Corbyn as leader of the Labour Party must be one of the most important turning points in the party's 118-year existence. At the time of writing, in early 2018, the party is dominated at every level by the left. This is the first time this has ever happened. Moreover, if the 2015 leadership election was a moment for the party, the 2017 election, likewise, was a moment for the nation. It was also another episode when a crack appeared in every shibboleth, every sacred truth, every bit of cement and mortar of the fundamental assumptions of every political strategist, columnist and two-bit hack to have ever worked or wandered in Westminster – that is down to

Jeremy Corbyn. A Labour leader ran on the left. What's more, that leader ran on (what was considered to be) a left-wing platform. Then, he gained seats. Cue collective pundit breakdown.

Why now? Why did this septuagenarian who had crafted a happy life as assiduously tending to his allotment as he does the constituency in which it lies take his party, and then the nation, by storm? How had we got to this moment? If 'cometh the hour, cometh the man', then what was it about this hour and this man? What has happened to Labour and to the country to make this his moment, a moment he must surely have thought would never come? Why were all those families out there that late September night in Brighton, a scene replicated in endless town halls, gymnasia and community centres from Stornoway to the Solent? Was it the man? Was it his ideas? It can't have been his root vegetables. And what are those ideas anyway? This is important stuff, because the Corbyn Labour Party is pretty much the only left-of-centre party to be doing well across the Western world. If there is something about this man and his approach, it could be the panacea that ailing social democrats across Europe and North America have been looking for. To answer takes some delving into history and getting under the skin of a political party and membership buffeted by the most turbulent economic and political storm.

I have been following him around Britain for three years. I've heard his speeches many times. I've witnessed the slow lingering decay of one Labour Party and the changeling replacement take shape behind it. I've seen the people he's inspired and the people he's frightened. I've seen a civil war fought and won. This is what I've learned about Jeremy, his army and his movement.

HOW IT STARTED

I'd wager that the majority of those who joined the Labour Party because of Jeremy Corbyn in that fateful leadership contest in 2015 hadn't heard of him before that summer. Hell, I'd say a fair number of

Labour Party members who were already members in 2015 probably hadn't either. I'd wager again that the vast majority of the 12 million voters who cast their ballot for him in 2017 hadn't heard of him before he became Labour leader.

I had. I knew him not as a great tribune of the left, political shaman or mover and shaker on the parliamentary scene. No, I knew him as a man I might have phoned at a quarter to ten on a Friday night if the guest I'd really wanted had fallen through; and he'd always answer the phone. In the couple of years leading to the 2015 general election and subsequent leadership contest, I was working as a producer on the BBC's *Newsnight.* If I had told my programme editor for that night that I'd booked Jeremy Corbyn for a discussion they'd have looked at me as if I were a Michelin-starred chef who'd just served up a happy meal. It was just too easy. He was just too … accessible. Save for Keith Vaz, he was the easiest booking in Westminster. And, beyond that, I can hear them say: 'Who cares? What would he have to say? Who does he speak for? No one.'

So why did Corbyn stand? The left was determined to field a candidate. It had done so in 2010 with Diane Abbott. John McDonnell had stood twice before but later suffered a heart attack so didn't feel it was possible this time around. As the newly elected left-wing group of MPs gathered, there weren't many other options. But such was the severity of the electoral defeat, the group felt it was especially important that their voice was heard in a contest that was looking pretty anodyne. One of their number, Clive Lewis, told me:

'When I came down here, obviously, we saw where the leadership election was heading. It was awful, it was dry, it was just three people trying to get over the line by saying nothing – just kind of seeming like the best leader. And we had, kind of like, a meeting and Jeremy and John and Diane were the campaign group at the time and got together. As is well known now, we had that meeting and Jeremy volunteered. I think Jeremy and John had thought about it before … Was I surprised he stood? No, because I think the expression he used was, it's my turn, we're going to have a lefty, I haven't had a crack at it yet so why not? So it wasn't a surprise in that sense.

'I think he wanted to do his duty with the left and put forward his politics and remind people what the Labour Party was there for, which he has done. I think his ambition was, if you have been in opposition for all those years, the kind of daydreams of epic victories probably subside quite far back in your mind and you have to think how we can make the case, shift what is debated within the leadership election, to pull the centre of gravity of the debate, how to make those arguments for a different audience and that's a platform: whether you win or you don't. I think also, thirdly, it's about how you build your social movement of the left. You do that by having a platform so anyone on the left who stood, whether it's Diane or John, can use that as a mechanism – to organise and build platforms for your ideas and this one worked exceptionally well. I think the great surprise was how well he did. I think that was a surprise for everyone.'

That surprise meant that from 15 June 2015 booking Jeremy Corbyn on *Newsnight* became, each day, that little bit harder. Today, you'd have to wade through many, many *Newsnight*s before Corbyn crops up. But deciding to stand wasn't enough. Corbyn had to succeed where McDonnell had failed nearly a decade before: he had to get on the ballot. That he did was down to 35 people. Thirty-five MPs, heroes, unlikely revolutionaries or 'morons', depending on your point of view: the gatekeepers not only sleeping on duty but thinking the enemy so weak that when they awake they invite him in for a look around the castle.

To win a place on the ballot to run for leader it was necessary under Labour Party rules in 2015 to be nominated by 15 per cent of the party's MPs. After the 2015 drubbing, when the total number of Labour MPs in the Commons was reduced to 232, that meant getting 35 to sign on the dotted line. That did not mean, however, that they were beholden to that candidate in the ensuing contest. I was sitting in the *Newsnight* office the morning Jeremy Corbyn crawled over the line having reached the required 35 nominations. Of the 35 only 18 would go on to vote for Corbyn in the leadership contest and around the same number had nominated him in the first week of nominations being opened. That was pretty much the limit of the reach of the left in Parliament. He would need a further 17 to sign his name on the ballot paper.

It went right down to the wire. One by one, MPs traipsed down to the offices of the Parliamentary Labour Party. The heart of Corbyn's campaign manager was in his mouth: 'An hour to go, we were in the high twenties and nowhere near,' John McDonnell was to recall. 'Then we got thirty-two and we got to thirty-three and we had five MPs that had promised us that if we got to thirty-four they would nominate. It got to ten seconds and then two of them cracked. I admit I was in tears begging them.' Indeed, one by one those 17 signatures came, including from some very unlikely places. The Bermondsey MP, Neil Coyle, has spent much of the last three years eviscerating Jeremy Corbyn and Momentum day after day but his name was under Corbyn's on the nomination paper. David Lammy and Jo Cox were firm Blairites, yet they put Corbyn forward too. They said they did so for several reasons. Some have since suggested that some of the candidates were playing games. Rival camps accused Andy Burnham, the early favourite, of quietly welcoming Corbyn. Having Corbyn in the race meant he would no longer be the most left-wing candidate and he couldn't be presented as such afterwards. He also felt he could get many of Corbyn's second preferences. Burnham's people vehemently deny it. Others had more straightforward intentions. After a shocking, unexpected and stinging result, many MPs spoke of the need 'to widen the debate' with every wing of the party represented. Emily Thornberry told me: 'I didn't support Jeremy as leader – I supported Yvette – but I was concerned about the great level of caution that was being shown and this tendency for triangulation. And if having Jeremy in the race meant that we didn't fall down a right-wing rabbit hole and some of the things that were being challenged by Jeremy, it was a positive contribution to the debate. I didn't expect Jeremy to be elected but in hindsight I can see how it happened.' David Lammy spoke for many who chose to nominate Corbyn at the time: 'This is a contest and there will be a winner. I will be surprised if he becomes the leader because it is clear that we need to broaden our appeal and move beyond our current tribe. I believe in an open process. It is important that someone like Jeremy is part of the process.'

The thing is, it was a debate that, insofar as they'd thought about it at all, centrist MPs arrogantly and blithely assumed they would win easily. That is the obvious reason Jeremy Corbyn made it on to the ballot. The two slightly less obvious ones are (i) that Labour MPs didn't grasp the new leadership rules and their own role in them, of which more later; and (ii) MPs' own arrogance and lack of understanding of their own party as it was in 2015.

On the day he made it through the nominations, I sat in the *Newsnight* office, working on something else. It was just another new absurdity of the leadership race, something going on in the background, of not much significance to anybody, a symptom of a party in a headspin. The only person I remember speaking to who thought it was an important moment and, at that, an unalloyed disaster was the programme's economics correspondent, the doughty, long-time obsessive of all things Labour history, Duncan Weldon.

Puffing on one of his trademark heavy-duty cigarettes, he spluttered: 'It's crazy. Absolutely crazy. It makes the party look insane. Why nominate someone you don't think should be prime minister, only to widen the debate?'

He was one of the very few who recognised Corbyn's potential. Most of the others who reacted negatively did so less because they thought there was any hope that Corbyn might win than because they thought that in the wake of an electoral defeat, when one of the perceived reasons for the loss was that the party leader was too left wing and metropolitan, the very last thing the party should do now was put forward the honourable member for Islington North. As another Labour MP, John Mann, tweeted that day:

> So to demonstrate our desire never to win again, Islington's Jeremy Corbyn is now a Labour leadership candidate.
> 11:07 AM – Jun 15, 2015

> Quite a number of Corbyn supporters saying to me that principled opposition is better than seeking an electoral majority. The elite speak.
>
> 11:32 AM – Jun 15, 2015

In preparation for the show that night I spoke to one MP who had been reluctant: 'Look, I had John McDonnell phoning me every fifteen minutes and physically begging me. What are you supposed to say? And, besides, he's harmless enough.'

'He's harmless enough.' Looking back, that one sentence encapsulated how Corbyn could get on to the ballot paper. To some extent it speaks to Corbyn's reputation within the parliamentary party. He'd been around since 1983, avuncular, eccentric, spartan but with a charm in his own way. As Chris Mullin, a fellow Bennite traveller turned Blairite minister, was to say later, 'Jeremy really is the sort of man who if you run into on a train he'd halve his sandwiches and share them with you.'

Corbyn's fellow MPs therefore found him a far less worrying or frankly terrifying prospect than McDonnell, who many colleagues considered to be a Trotskyite, on the hard left and extremely doctrinaire. He was also considered much more pleasant company than Abbott, who fairly or unfairly was considered aloof by many of her fellow MPs. As one MP who nominated Corbyn told me later: 'I'd never ever have nominated McDonnell. Just look at him. He's a thug. Diana was and is extremely rude. Jeremy was always nice to everyone. To be honest we got conned.'

But that word 'harmless' spoke to a more profound truth, to another word that would aid the Corbynistas again and again in their hostile takeover of the Labour Party: complacency. Corbyn was the first member of the 'hard left' or Bennite wing of the Labour Party to run for leader since Benn himself in 1988. At one time, the Labour centrists would have done everything possible to avoid such an outcome. But this time it didn't matter. Because the hard left was, in the view of much of the rest of the parliamentary party (and everyone else), almost entirely moribund. It had been dwindling in significance since the 1980s. There were only 15 or so reliable members of the 'left' in Parliament (forming the rather motley crew of the 'Campaign for Labour Party Democracy'), and most of those – John McDonnell, Diane Abbott, Dennis Skinner, Corbyn himself – had been hanging around for decades apparently not doing all that much. Some of them, like Skinner and to a far lesser extent Corbyn, had started to enter the Tony Benn stage of their careers, where they were teetering on the edge of national-treasure status: a charming, living homily to a land and time lost long ago.

Benn liked to remind people that he was still dangerous – 'I received a death threat again the other day!' – but frankly Corbyn would have been lucky if anyone had even noticed him, much less sent a death threat. They spent their days attending worthy public meetings and rallies, turning up on foreign-owned television and radio stations like the Iran-backed Press TV, decrying Western imperialism and carping from the sidelines on the political and moral deficiencies of their own Labour government. The narrative in the minds of most MPs and observers of politics was clear: the internecine battles of the 1980s were as likely to make a comeback as Rick Astley. The left had been vanquished as far back as 1981 and had slowly been bleeding influence and power both within the party and without ever since.

However, as with so much of our contemporary analysis, it could have benefited from a longer view. It was always fantasy to believe the left's fox was permanently shot. Today, we can see instead that the 1990s and 2000s were simply a period when the left was unusually and misleadingly weak. Failing to realise that provided an entirely illusory comfort blanket that Labour MPs refused to pull from their eyes and see what was happening within their own party.

By looking at previous Labour leadership battles in a little more detail, the signs would have been there for all to see that, outside the halls and corridors of the Palace of Westminster, the left had been gathering in strength for some time. Even before the game-changing financial crisis there was discontent in the party's ranks. Jon Cruddas, a backbencher who then passed as the left-wing candidate, did unexpectedly well in the 2007 deputy leadership contest. He ran on a ticket of fundamentally shifting the party's approach to the economy away from the market excesses of the Blair years. He came a solid third, behind the winner Harriet Harman and Blairite candidate Alan Johnson – even then it was clear that the Blairite moment had already slipped. Less clear at first glance was the groundswell that was building up for left-of-centre ideas and for a more 'authentic' Labourism. Cruddas came top of the ballot on first preferences. He was only whittled down to third as second and third preferences came into play.

In the same year, John McDonnell tried to run for leader twice but, unpopular as he was with his own parliamentary colleagues, failed to make the ballot paper when he tried to run against Gordon Brown. One Thursday night, late in 2007, Andrew Neil remonstrated with Diane Abbott, then appearing weekly with him cosily alongside Michael Portillo on the *This Week* sofa: 'It's pathetic. Your lot can't even get forty-five backers.'

But that was as much to do with Brown's dominance (no one else could get any backers either) and some think that had McDonnell managed to get on, he'd have outperformed expectations, especially with the trade union section. This is presumably one of the reasons the Gordon Brown machine was so desperate to keep him off the ballot in the first place.

When Abbott herself ran three years later after the drubbing of the 2010 election, she needed 'help' from several colleagues to get on the ballot paper, not least from David Miliband, who hoped it would siphon votes from brother Ed, who was clearly making a play to the party's left.

Most MPs I've spoken to agree that that experience proved the reddest of red herrings, which itself was a primary contributor to the party accidentally getting its own reddest of red leaders, five years later. The narrative at the time was that Abbott's performance was dire, which proved the thesis that the left of the party was irrelevant. She did indeed come fifth of five, with less than 5 per cent of the vote, and was eliminated in the first round.

But dig a little deeper and she did much, much better than that. Abbott came third in the trade union section. She was only just behind Ed Balls in the membership section. What sent her languishing so resolutely was the party's electoral-college system in place at that time, which gave a third of the college votes to Labour MPs and MEPs. She only got seven (presumably including her own). But had she been running on the reformed system that was to return Jeremy Corbyn five years later, she would have done considerably better, coming third with 33 per cent of the vote – ahead of Andy Burnham and Ed Balls. Moreover, Abbott ran less on an explicitly left-wing message than on one about diversity. She said she was getting into the race because 'it's 2010, we can't have a situation where every one of our leadership candidates are white and male'. This was not an offer that proved especially resonant at the time.* Corbyn's economic prospectus was to prove more powerful.

Her performance (and McDonnell's a few years before) was a chimera. As one senior Blairite MP told me: 'The Abbott example was the best thing that ever happened to the left and the worst thing to ever happen to us. It made them look weaker than they were and made us look stronger. We just thought we could put up a lefty for sport and whack them to show just how right our ideas were. We were so wrong it's painful.'

Even if they had been aware that her performance wasn't as weak as it looked, Labour MPs should have been warier about the changes that had taken place in the Labour Party since 2010. There had been lots of left-wing returnees from the Lib Dems (and other parties on the left), driven away by Iraq but now disgusted with the party's collusion with the Conservatives. But even at the eleventh hour the signs were there if MPs had cared to look for them. A poll of party members published by the website LabourList in June 2015 (before Corbyn got the 35 votes he needed) showed him head and shoulders above all the other candidates, including Burnham, the presumptive favourite. The first glimmers of Corbyn's most potent weapon, his social-media following, had also started to shine.

#NominateJeremy had been tweeted some 50,000 times in the days leading up to deadline day, designed to pressure wavering MPs. Even

* Today, I suspect it would prove more potent.

if those things were all you knew, given all of that, Corbyn should never have been the long shot that he was, and MPs should have taken note. Taking the long view, the Labour Party has always been an organic entity with a Darwinian battle at its heart. Both the right, the 'soft left' and the left have, at one time or another, competed for dominance. Their fortunes are often inversely linked. Occasionally one faction looks like it has become extinct and that one will, *Lord of the Rings* style, 'rule them all'. But they never do, in the end.

The slow revival of the left had been a long time coming but it was real. Ed Miliband ran specifically as a break from New Labour, casting his brother, David, as the candidate of the Blairite right. Ed won with the support of the unions, but David won with the members. What the left desperately needed was a way of breaking out of the cage in which the party's electoral system kept them imprisoned. Fortunately, in another example of how extraordinarily powerful forces can twist and weave with low farce and accident, their salvation would come from the unlikeliest of sources: Eric Joyce's fist.

THE POLITICAL CONSEQUENCES OF MR MILIBAND

Eric Joyce was not alone in Westminster in being an MP with an alcohol problem. He was, nonetheless, one of the relatively small number who would follow it up with a punch, or five, and one of the smaller number still who would do it on the palace grounds. But punch he did and it led to his stepping down as the Labour candidate for Falkirk in the pending general election. The consequences would be greater than even his victim's chin could feel at the time – a left hook that proved a boon, for the left wing. There is a direct line from that punch to me standing waiting for Jeremy Corbyn at the Labour Party conference, at the Durham Miners' Gala, in a Stornoway leisure centre, in Perth conference hall and Zaatari refugee camp in northern Jordan. A direct line to all those people standing there on that

Brighton September evening. Were it not for that, none of it might have happened, or at least happened in the way that it did.

Joyce's stepping down initiated a swift selection contest in Falkirk, the details of which need not detain us long. In brief, it looked like a union stitch-up for Unite. Guess what – it was a union stitch-up for Unite. Hold the front page. It's the Labour Party. Stitching things up has been its MO since 1900. But for some reason that neither I nor anyone else I interviewed can quite remember, it caused fire and fury in the press.* 'Pressure mounted' as it so often apparently does and Miliband concluded that something must be done. To deflect attention, he came up with a wheeze. He would abolish the electoral college where the Labour leadership and deputy leadership were decided via the infamous 'a third, a third, a third' formula. To recap, a third of the weighted votes went to the MPs, a third to the trade unions and affiliate organisations, and a third to the membership at large. The system, designed to diffuse power throughout the party while also maintaining the disproportionate influence of MPs and the unions, had thrown up several arcane anomalies, much loved by the *Mail* and the Tory Party. For a start, it was complex: David Miliband had been ahead for several rounds and the choice of the membership at large. This was the first time since the inception of the system (it had been used three times before) that the winning candidate did not win clearly in all three sections.† It thus created a legitimacy crisis. His younger brother had got the position through union votes. Endless cartoons and editorials implying that Ed was the puppet of Unite's general secretary, Len McCluskey, had been damaging. Ed proposed to cut the strings:‡ he would introduce the principle of 'one member, one vote' to the leadership electoral system. He sold it as a diminution of union power. It would end the absurd situation where certain

* The coalition years now seem almost quaint when I remember the sorts of things we got worked up about.

† Kinnock, Blair and Brown had done so. Though it wasn't much of an achievement for Brown as he was the only candidate.

‡ Obviously not for himself – for leaders in the future.

people had multiple votes by virtue of their being members of different parts of the party.

And Ed Miliband wasn't done there. Not content with changing the nature of the election he wanted to change the people who could vote in it. He proposed wholesale changes to the electorate, making it much easier to get involved with the election as a member of the public. All you had to do was become a 'registered supporter' (not even a full member) of the party for about the same cost as a latte (£3). You could then, under the new 'one member, one vote' rules, have as much influence on the outcome of the leadership contest as an MP of 30 years' standing or a trade union leader or party member who joined under Clement Attlee. This was an extraordinary transformation. As recently as 1981 (and for eight decades before) the leadership had been the preserve solely of Labour MPs. As Miliband said on the day of the special conference in 2014: 'All of these things happened, not because leaders made them happen, but because people and movements made them happen. Today if you vote for these reforms you will be voting for Labour to be a movement again.'

Ed Miliband had no idea just how accidentally prophetic his words were. Whatever the rights and wrongs of the new members, their importance in the 2015 contest can't be overstated. Of 105,598 members who joined the party that feverish summer, no fewer than 88,449 voted for Corbyn. There can be little doubt that they joined specifically to vote for Corbyn, as opposed to being won over during the contest. Miliband had created a system ripe for mass entryism. Just one tiny example by way of illustration: on day one of the leadership contest, literally hours after Corbyn had apparently miraculously made it on to the ballot paper, the Green Party tweeted its support and members began openly discussing the prospect of registering to support his candidacy.

> Good to see @jeremycorbyn as part of @UKLabour leadership race – we welcome your strong anti-austerity voice in UK politics Jeremy
>
> 11:05 AM – Jun 15, 2015

Some members of Natalie Bennett's party even encouraged fellow party members to sign up to Labour as registered supporters to increase Mr Corbyn's chances of winning:

> @TheGreenParty @jeremycorbyn @UKLabour 1. We would love Green Party members to become registered supporters and vote for Jeremy
>
> – J(@SetSpeed) June 15, 2015

The accidental punch had led Ed Miliband to create an accidental system that would create an accidental leader. And all of it devised, created and implemented with about as much thought as the average Deliveroo order. Perhaps a bit less.

Why so little scrutiny or forethought? Simple: Ed Miliband was going to be leader. As one MP put it to me: 'None of them, not one of them, even gave it a moment's thought. It was pathetic. He just thought he was going to be prime minister and no one would be even using the rules for a decade. He's got a lot to fucking answer for.'

Angela Eagle was more diplomatic but no less angry at her former leader's actions: 'It's a fundamental misunderstanding of what the French had done with their primary for the presidential candidate – it's not the same as leader of the party. One candidate for one election is not the same as electing the leader of the party and to lead the PLP. I wasn't asked about the changes to voting – my opinion wasn't sought. The removal of the electoral college was a panic over Falkirk which no one remembers now so shouldn't have been done in that way ... You have to get the balance right between reaching out, and allowing people who don't have your best interests at heart to manipulate a result. No one had any sort of inkling that the influx of people would outweigh the membership and be more important than the membership.'

Another senior shadow cabinet minister at the time the changes were made put the blame specifically on the fact that there was not even a freeze date:

'I think the fundamental error was not to have a freeze date because throughout the whole history of the party we have always had a freeze date on selection and elections for obvious reasons, because if you announce it's coming they can recruit a lot of people. But in effect we said to people, come and pay your fee and get yourself a vote and lots of people did that for a particular candidate … it was done for the right reasons. The introduction of the original scheme was about trying to broaden the base of the party, which is a good thing. Now, we are a voluntary organisation, professional but also a voluntary organisation, and I can't tell you why a view wasn't taken to have a freeze date so that lots of people could get themselves a vote knowing who the candidates were. But once Jeremy was on the ballot paper and once there wasn't a freeze date and the numbers of new members were announced then it was very clear who was going to win.'

Today Miliband's allies find all this rum stuff. They (rightly) point out that many of the same people protesting now were neither to be seen nor heard at the time. Indeed, internally the changes went through largely on the nod. At the special conference convened at the ExCel Centre in late 2014, the reforms were passed by a doughty 86 per cent to 14 per cent margin. At the same time, the party had other problems. At the same point in 2014 the Scottish independence referendum was raging. The future of the kingdom was in jeopardy. These were the leadership rules for a contest most hoped was a long way off – it seemed a bit like a couple drawing up custody rules before they'd even walked down the aisle.

Moreover, in a truly catastrophic misjudgement, the Blairites and right of the party supported the changes. In an ironic twist that would make even Alanis Morissette blush, it was the left who were most sceptical.

At the time, it was generally perceived to be an attack on the power of the trade unions. Tony Blair – yes – Tony Blair welcomed the changes: 'I think this is a defining moment. It's bold and it's strong. It's real leadership, this. I think it's important not only in its own terms, because he's carrying through a process of reform in the Labour Party that is long overdue and, frankly, probably I should have done it when

I was leader.' This was partially drawn from a subtle distinction. Blair and his tribe had always been extremely suspicious of the organised element of the Labour Party, constituency Labour parties, their chairmen and chairwomen and the 'activists'. The word activist made them shudder. It conjured images of long, late-night sittings of constituency meetings, debating subsection 3 of composite 1 of the CLP motion condemning the situation in the Wallis and Futuna Islands. They thought that CLP meetings attracted a certain type of person, the unrepresentative crank. By contrast, they had had enormous faith in the 'member'. Perhaps the husband and wife who had paid their dues for years, might turn out for the Christmas raffle, hadn't had much truck with the preoccupations and vicissitudes of the far left, and, indeed, would vote against them: in other words, the internal Labour Party version of the 'real people' about whom Blair was so fond of talking during his time in government. The Blairites and the right assumed that the 'members' would always guard them against the incursions of the left (as they largely were in the 1980s), rather than be the footsoldiers of their enemy. It was an astonishing miscalculation.

The Blairites and Milibandites can, however, find common cause in blaming the PLP. Today they both argue that the membership question would not have arisen had MPs understood their role as gatekeepers to the system and not nominated someone with whom they could not live as their leader in Parliament. This has truth. MPs simply did not understand the new rules properly. They had not quite clocked that they no longer had a third of the votes under the electoral college on their side.

Curiously they overvalued their importance and yet undervalued it at the same time. They weren't just wine tasters, setting out a series of options. If MPs could not live with one of the candidates winning and leading them in Parliament, then they ought not to put them forward. MPs who dislike Jeremy Corbyn but nominated him have, therefore, only themselves to blame.

If we're looking to answer the questions: 'Why Corbyn? Why now? Why has this never happened before?' then part of the answer has to be the system that elected him. Miliband had put all of the party's chips with the members in a party where, for all the talk, members had almost never had much influence. I said before that the leadership of the party had for most of the party's existence been the preserve of the party's MPs. It's more profound than that. Remember, for most of its history the Labour Party had been a federation of constituent organisations. For a long period in the party's early days it wasn't even possible to be an individual Labour Party member; you could only become one by joining one of its member bodies. One of the many phantoms that should be laid to rest about the way that the party has 'returned to its roots' under Corbyn is that it is once again a mass-membership organisation. Yes, membership numbers were greater in the party's heyday (much greater than they are today), but it was not something that much preoccupied Ramsay MacDonald or Clement Attlee or Harold Wilson. Search through their speeches for references to the mass party membership and its importance and you will do so in vain. Most of those million or so members of the Labour Party of old were members not of the party itself, but through a union or affiliated organisation. They therefore expected little say in the party's affairs. They took part in campaigning but not in party management or directly in policy. The party was top down, almost unashamedly hierarchical. That was the basis of many of the battles of the 1980s, with the left arguing that the party structures were moribund, atrophying and hierarchical, and in need of change. The merits and demerits of all this are beside the point. Rather, at a stroke, Miliband transformed the party. He changed the balance of power, accidentally but fundamentally. It would have been unrecognisable to any Labour leader from the twentieth century. Jeremy Corbyn was the first leader of his kind in the party's history. So was the system that elected him. Those facts are not unconnected.

But it's not the whole story. Nowhere close. Because Corbyn didn't just win among the new members. He won among the old too. That means there was something more profound going on in Labour politics than just entryism. We cannot account for the rise of Corbyn in the party's rule book alone. The political tectonic plates were shifting, in no small part thanks to another legacy of Mr Miliband, the general election result of 2015.

After the herculean task of getting on to the ballot paper, the bookies made him a 20/1 outsider. Unbelievably, Liz Kendall on that day was at 5/2 only just behind Andy Burnham. The bookies and MPs had failed to understand just how painful 2015 was and what had happened to the Labour Party.

One supporter, elated that finally a left-wing candidate had made it on to the ballot paper, tweeted her new hero this:

> Jacky Burdett
> @trivychatter
> @jeremycorbyn well done – now the really difficult stuff – bonne chance X
> 11:08 AM – Jun 15, 2015

Those changes within the party, not of the new members but of the old, would mean that, unlike his nomination itself, Corbyn wouldn't need it.

THE LONG MARCH OF MILIFANDOM HALTED: 2015

It's easy to forget now but the 2015 general election result, when David Cameron won a majority of 12, was a tremendous shock; indeed, it was a rout.

As he addressed his election count at Doncaster's metropolitan council offices, Ed Miliband told his supporters: 'This has clearly been a disappointing night for the Labour Party.' He could say that again. After five years, five slow, grinding, hard years, the party had lost 26 seats and gained a paltry 1 per cent of the vote share. It had lost seats across England to the Conservatives and lost 40 of its golden treasure chest of Scottish seats to the SNP, possibly for good. Labour MPs used to delight in tormenting Conservatives that there were more pandas in Scotland than Tory MPs. You don't hear the joke so often these days.

Almost no one had predicted the majority Conservative result. The weekend before the poll I was working on a *Newsnight* programme from Birmingham. David Gauke, now a cabinet minister, then financial secretary to the Treasury, was on batting for the Tories. Conversation with Evan Davis quickly turned to the inevitable coalition negotiations that would come after the election:

GAUKE: We're aiming for a majority Conservative government ...

DAVIS: Look, let me stop you right there, we all know you're not going to get a majority, that it's impossible so let's discuss the real issue ...

How we rolled our eyes. How we pitied Gauke for having to parrot the absurd and trite government line. How stupid he must have felt, we thought. Turns out, joke was on us. Except of course that Gauke probably did feel stupid and was squirming in his seat. He, like the rest of the political and media class from Cameron and Miliband down, were stunned by the result and had little reason to predict it. And with good reason: virtually every poll put Labour and Tories neck and neck. The final polls on the eve of voting day gave Labour a one-point lead. Only one survey, from Survation, reflected the correct result – and it was suppressed by the organisation. On the day before the election, our own *Newsnight* Index (never repeated), which collated and processed all the polling data to give a daily prediction of seat numbers, forecast a 99 per cent probability of a hung Parliament.

The working assumption was that Labour would probably cobble together a sclerotic minority government propped up by SNP support. Lest I ever think or try and tell myself otherwise, I will always know my own assumptions as to the outcome. I spent election day in Oxford, filming with historians in what would be a two-day shoot.

The second day would be spent in Dublin and the flights were all booked. The subject? The 1910 Liberal government, the last left-of-centre government propped up by nationalist support in the House of Commons.* Once filming was done, I sat outside the King's Arms pub on Holywell Street in the early May sunshine, supping a pint or two with my producer (and general TV partner in crime), Zach Brown. As anyone who knows me will tell you, I get insanely excited at the thought of elections. Sadly, I had literally been counting down the years until this one, not least because it was the first I was covering professionally as a journalist. As we chewed the fat as to the sort of political landscape we might be covering when the sun next rose, I joked that, of course, this whole film could be for nothing if the Tories got a majority. We both stared at each other and then literally laughed out loud – 'No way!' we guffawed. We went back to our pints. The next day, we cancelled our flights.

The extent of the surprise meant that the 2015 election was like a sudden bereavement for the Labour Party, and the grief that flowed from it was one of the main factors that led to Corbyn's triumph. As I travelled around different constituency Labour parties across the kingdom I felt I could see the five stages of grief being played out across the faces of the party's activists.

This was in sharp contrast to the steady-as-she-goes mentality of five years before. The 2010 defeat was a blow but it was expected. It came off the back of the party being in government for a long time, and among some activists there was privately even some sense of relief at the prospect of a spell in opposition. The then Governor of the Bank of England, Mervyn King, had been reported as saying that whoever won the election would have to implement a round of spending cuts so severe that they would be out of office for a generation. Labour had no stomach for that; it was exhausted. In fact, the result was substantially better than many MPs and activists had hoped for. After the worst economic crash in living memory, a 13-year-old government, resignations every other week and a prime

---

* In their case, obviously, it was the Irish Nationalists.

minister who made measles look popular, the party was still left with 258 seats. The party's Scottish heartlands were intact. It had robbed the Conservatives of an overall majority. They would now have to preside over a dire economic inheritance. It would not, it was assumed, be difficult to get back into office next time; perhaps things had worked out for the best.

2015 was of a different order. The surprise of not being back in government had revealed some of the structural weaknesses of the party which had been masked by the unexpectedly decent showing in 2010. The membership began asking some searching questions – it wasn't clear who could answer them. Because if 2010 had buried New Labour then in 2015 the 'soft left' had joined them in the tomb. In two successive general elections, the two main wings of the parliamentary party had been discredited and tarnished with electoral failure. Many began to look elsewhere for answers. As Emily Thornberry was to tell me:

'What I think happened was that we had been triangulating for a long time and the party membership was prepared to put up with it on the basis we were winning elections. But we weren't, we had lost two, so maybe it was time to go back and have a think about what we were doing and where we were coming from and have a period of introspection and not be dishonest. I think that there was a rising up of the membership who just said we want someone who sounds like us and thinks like us, we want someone like that leading our party at last.' In other words, when you've not got much to lose, why not have one more roll of the dice? Why not go for something different?

And how different was it anyway? How much of a push? In policy and political terms Miliband had turned the dial to the left. Who was it who proposed the energy price freeze? Who was it first proposed cutting tuition fees? Who was it first divided businesses into 'predators' and 'producers'? It was Miliband; and policy direction was supplemented by cultural moments that altered the impression we had had of how Labour leaders had come to behave, whether it was telling a man in the street that he was 'bringing back socialism' or turning up to the Durham Miners' Gala, the first leader for decades to do so. All of this came together to help create an ideological and cultural space that Corbyn could occupy and could expand.

Within the party at large too, many believe that far-left drifters, hotly observed and weeded out in the New Labour years, were allowed back in under a laxer Miliband. New parliamentary candidates were also of a leftish hue, as Clive Lewis told me:

'Ed had less command and control on the selection process throughout the country. He worked more closely with the unions ... you were getting to see that some people who were in there who'd come through the selection process weren't from the usual background. So myself, Rebecca Long Bailey,* our politics were a little bit different ... now I remember when Lisa Nandy† got in in 2010 she was kind of singled out as the mad lefty, and she is a good friend of mine, but it just goes to show you how things have changed.'

And maybe the Miliband ideological turn morphing into the Corbyn ideological turn shouldn't have surprised us. After all, the 2015 leadership contest was the first to be fought in the long shadow of the post-crash era. Technically the 2010 election falls into that category, but given much of the crash and subsequent recession took place in late 2008–9, its profound effects had yet to properly soak our politics. I remember, at the time of the 2010 election, thinking a lot about why it was that, in the immediate wake of a crisis of the system of such magnitude, the result of the following election had been so orthodox: huge recession equals Conservative government, a pretty standard result and normal swing between the two main parties. What I realise now is that that general election and the corresponding Labour leadership election a few months later took place not just in the storm's wake but, specifically, in its eye. The political class in Westminster and in the country at large hadn't had time to internalise the profound shock to their long-standing assumptions about the economy, politics, even fundamental philosophies built up since the Thatcher era.

---

* MP for Salford and Eccles since 2015.

† MP for Wigan since 2010.

For proof of this you need only look at Labour Party leadership election results. In 2010, David Miliband, the avowed Blairite candidate, came first in every round but the very last and won nearly 50 per cent of the overall vote. Five years later, Liz Kendall, the Blairite candidate, got 2.6 per cent. Was David Miliband a better candidate? Yes. Was he that much better? No. Rather, the crash, as we've seen, had destroyed the Blairite analysis, the Blairite agenda, the Blairite prospectus. It had reanimated the left's.

Just because Blairism was dead did not necessarily mean that the party was automatically the left's for the taking. But the crash was essential. As John McDonnell later told the *New Statesman*: 'The crash was pivotal in shattering confidence for a period in the operation of capitalism and demonstrating the inherent crisis-ridden nature of the system ... As people sought an explanation for the crisis, they became open to the traditional ideas of the left, ranging from Marx to [John Maynard] Keynes and [John Kenneth] Galbraith, to the modern analyses of economists like Thomas Piketty.' And in this we see, once again, the folly of the idea that the left had died. Rather it is always there, waiting for its opportunity. It is no coincidence that the two occasions in modern history when the left has been at its zenith are the early 1980s and the mid-2010s, in both cases at a point when the prevailing political and economic consensus was deemed to have failed.

And, in this, 2015 finds its closest antecedent in 1994. In so many ways the closest parallel to Corbyn is Tony Blair, and that includes the manner of his election. In 1994, just as in 2015, the Labour Party was recovering from the trauma of an unexpected general election defeat (in Blair's case in 1992). It was also grappling with the tremors of a fundamental economic and political realignment. By the mid-1990s it was clear that the postwar consensus had fundamentally broken down and Margaret Thatcher with her privatisation and pro-market liberalisation of the British economy had shaken up the jigsaw of British political economy, just as Cameron would do (albeit much less successfully) with his regearing of politics towards the austerity agenda. The Labour Party in both cases was in desperate need of a political and moral response to these profound events. In both cases, Blair and Corbyn provided that trenchant, startling rearticulation of Labour values and clear political philosophy to guide their parties through these treacherous and uncertain times. In both cases, they were preceded by leaders of their ilk who started reforms in the direction they eventually took but who were widely perceived as vacillating and neither quite one thing nor the other, by their party and the wider electorate alike. They were just at different ends of the scale. In 1994 and 2015 both sensed their opportunities and they took them.

They were both, also, lucky with their enemies.

On the day before the leadership result was announced I attended Kendall's final press conference of the campaign. It was held at Methodist Hall, just across the road from Parliament. It was an appropriate venue. As Corbyn finished off his 99-stop nationwide tour across the country, surrounded by thousands of joyous, gleeful, optimistic activists and supporters, Kendall's journey ended deep in the bowels of a Westminster venue, surrounded only by journalists who'd come for sport and a cast of Blairite ghosts who'd come for solidarity. Some of the characters there had been with Blair a decade before, and a dozen or so other MPs, special advisers and think-tankers had assumed only a few months or so before that their time had come again. They looked grief-stricken – and none more than Kendall herself. She couldn't then know that the result would be as bad as it was, but she knew she'd lost and would almost certainly come fourth. I watched her take to the stage, resolutely, defiantly, ploughing through her speech, the last act of a career that had barely begun.

As she finished, as she was hugging a few of her aides and supporters, she barely lost her perma-grin. But as I, like the dozen or so other reporters there, interviewed her, you could see as she spoke the enormity of what she was grappling with. The contest marked the last gasp of the New Labour project. She was on the verge of being the new Jeremy Corbyn of the Labour Party. The political ground had given way beneath her feet. And she, like the rest of her wing of the party, had no idea how to get up again.

The summer had started so differently. In the weeks leading up to the election, Andy Burnham and Yvette Cooper had been actively planning a run at the leadership if Miliband didn't make it over the line. Liz Kendall had expected Chuka Umunna to run (so did he, but he dropped out, citing press intrusion into his family and a lack of preparedness to run for the office).

The severity of the result left the party clutching for the thinnest of thin straws. As the world watched a jubilant David Cameron, king of all he surveyed, happily popping down to Scott's in Mayfair for a celebratory slap-up meal with Sam, few seemed interested in the Labour Party. But Labour members, staring down the long, dark barrel of five more years in the wilderness, were looking for answers. Those that came forth were not ones they found especially compelling. In the first days of the campaign, as the activists began to survey the battered political landscape, the party's leading figures provided a strict and tired diet of platitudes about 'aspiration' and reaching out to middle England. Harriet Harman, the acting leader, went so far as to say there were even Labour members who felt 'relieved' that the party wasn't in government.

The main theme of the contest was a profound misjudgement by the other three candidates, Andy Burnham, Yvette Cooper and Liz Kendall, and by the acting leader Harriet Harman, of the mood of the party. They didn't seem to grasp the danger of the moment. They needed leadership and some convincing analysis of what had gone wrong and how to recover. They expected the party membership to respond to a masochist strategy. Their perception was that the party had tried a tilt to the left under Miliband, and now that approach had been found wanting would return to the right course, the only course.

But what course was that? The other three were offering little in the way of anything fresh. Both Burnham and Cooper more or less hailed from the same Brownite wing of the party as Miliband. Their offer was one of continuity; of technocratic Gordonism. In fact, in terms of intellectual engagement with the problems of the left, they were more wanting than Miliband himself. Kendall did offer something different to Miliband but it was an unalloyed return to the politics of the late 1990s, with a relentless emphasis on Mondeo Man and the vocabulary, grammar and political approach of New Labour. She appeared not to like the Labour Party all that much. In their turn, the activists made it clear they didn't like her much back. All three of them appeared worn and tired, especially Burnham and Cooper, both of whom had spent the last decade at the top of politics.

As Jon Cruddas told me: 'In the leadership election, Corbyn looked like the only one with a moral purpose, he looked like the only one who was animated, he looked like he had energy and vitality and passion because of the emptying out of the social democratic tradition. So, it was three or four versus one and they were crawling over the wreckage. The people inspired by Corbyn don't know what lies beneath it in terms of organised factionalism and hostility and the ugliness to that hard-left politics. But he had something.' Cruddas's point is crucial. In that leadership contest, we see the wider political context of the post-crash left encapsulated: the 1990s/2000s 'Third Way' – discredited; the social democratic left – discredited; and the hard left the only one still breathing. It was a microcosm of the travails of the traditional centre left all over the West. Those three were caught in a trap not of their making. For the time being, because of huge forces, their brand of politics had just run out of road.

I feel bad having singled out Evan Davis for calling something so badly wrong with David Gauke, so let me redress the balance. *Newsnight* held the first hustings of the contest. It was in Nuneaton, the seat where Ed Miliband's Downing Street dreams ended. It was must-win and there was a swing to the Tories. Evan called it there and then at the debate: 'The only one who is standing out is Corbyn. The others don't have anything to say.' He was right.

Corbyn offered the members something they wanted: certainty. Moral purpose. That their politics was not only legitimate but *right*. As Angela Eagle, who stood for the deputy leadership and went to many of those same hustings, said:

'I think party members felt that they didn't want politicians to be hedging their bets and talking about pragmatic choices in the context of electoral politics – instead they wanted principles and that's what

Jeremy was doing. I also think that large numbers of party members in that election felt that they might as well be hung for a sheep as a lamb – we weren't going to win the next election so instead they might as well talk in unvarnished terms what their beliefs were.

'They came into Parliament when we were in government, they came in as special advisers (I'm not criticising any one of them, by the way), but they didn't find their voice. I think Yvette started to by the end, but it was too late. So, it's almost like the monkey cage had been opened, and they weren't ready to come out and dance around, whereas Jeremy had been dancing around out of the cage all his career. It's a funny image but it's that – it's saying what you think without thinking about the consequences. All of them raised in twenty-four-hour media, in government, from special advisers, talking about that pragmatism, and the party didn't want to hear that.'

In the years since 2015 one of the principal narratives that has emerged about the rise of Corbyn from the Blairites and much of the PLP, is that the left had spent thirty years on the farthest-flung sideline and were accidentally resurrected by an elixir concocted by the stupidity of MPs in allowing Corbyn to be on the ballot. That is clearly wrong. Another, from the left of the party, is that the years in the wilderness were all part of a long march back to power; the work of the true believers Corbyn, McDonnell, Abbott and before them Benn laying the groundwork for the leftist hegemony we find today. That is closer to the mark but still wrong. Corbyn did not happen by accident. He was the product of a clear trajectory within the party that can be traced back to the 2010 election and beyond. He is also clearly to some extent part of an international trend that has taken hold of many social democratic parties across the West where leftist insurgents challenge the established more centrist orthodoxy, viz. Bernie Sanders in the United States or Jean-Luc Mélenchon in France.

On the face of it though, it's easy to see why MPs cling to the notion that it was an avoidable joke, an accident of history. After all, so much of Jeremy Corbyn's initial election to the leadership was accident and farce. But that is less important than the fact he was able to win and continue to win, within and without. The ascension of the leader is less important than how he does when he is there. In that regard Corbyn has done well, partly because the historical moment is clearly primed for him. The party was changing anyway, with or without Corbyn on the ballot paper, placed there by absent-minded MPs unaware of how the grief felt by their own party members was leading them to experiment with new, untested political medicines.

In all of this Corbyn mirrors another unlikely party leader, Margaret Thatcher. When she became Tory leader, having challenged the incumbent and former prime minister, Ted Heath, for the job in 1975, few gave her any chance. But she triumphed, partly because a fair number of MPs who backed her didn't expect the putative iron lady to triumph. They wanted to send a signal. Just like those MPs who nominated Jeremy Corbyn to 'widen the debate' forty years later, they knew not what they did.

Those Tory MPs who didn't much like Thatcher or her politics failed to reckon with the sometimes profound consequences of apparently mundane political action. It's the political equivalent of chaos theory. A butterfly flaps its wings and somewhere, years later a hurricane forms. In politics, the odd ballot paper crossed in the wrong place can lead to a two-decade dominance of a woman and ideology sitting atop an entire nation and party. The odd nomination paper handed in for a man everyone thought harmless can lead to that same man's name being chanted on every festival field and rally in 18 months flat.

Like Thatcher's, Corbyn's rise did not happen out of nowhere. For a stray flame to start a fire it must have fuel. Just as the Thatcherite flame burned long over decades, so the seeds of the Corbyn revolution were sown long before and the signs were there, if you cared to look for them.

But just why did so many MPs, many of whom had served with him in Parliament for decades, come to fear him so much? Just what had he done? And what does he believe? What is Corbynism? And who are its true believers who have joined the party in such numbers?

Chapter 3

WHAT IS CORBYNISM?

Jeremy Corbyn has repackaged socialism into something essential, something that isn't archaic as we've been told it is for so long.

Maxine Peake, 2017

The mere words 'Socialism' and 'Communism' draw towards them with magnetic force every fruit-juice drinker, nudist, sandal-wearer, sex-maniac, Quaker, 'Nature Cure' quack, pacifist, and feminist in England.

George Orwell, *The Road to Wigan Pier*, 1937

The rebellion of the repentant bourgeoisie against the complacent and oppressive proletariat is one of the queerer phenomena of our time.

Sir Isaiah Berlin, 1972

I spent the summer of 2015 with a mild form of split personality. The journalist in me was in a state of wonderment. After the grim drudgery of the general election with its politically airless days and fetid debate, the explosion of the Labour leadership campaign was thrilling. You couldn't help but look at the other three leadership candidates, standing next to Corbyn, and think to yourself, if the beardy in the cream coat wasn't there, what on Earth would we be covering? Three people who broadly agree chuntering on for three months about Nuneaton and people who want to 'get on'. The crowds, the colour, the sense of an established order falling in on itself was completely intoxicating.

And then there was the 16-year-old Lewis, still inside me, the boy who turned up to Labour Party meetings in draughty community halls and school rooms on wet November evenings. That part of me looked on in horror. Corbyn was part of a world I recognised, one that I had come to know at Oxford and later in London. It was a world of worthy elucidations of the virtues of foreign regimes and the evils of Western ones. It was of eye rolling at crass and ribald jokes that punctuated my house, family gatherings and Sunday afternoon barbecues. Of chilly, sparsely populated demos on drizzly spring days and pop-up stalls in market towns trying to give out 'Stop the War' badges to indifferent shoppers. Of exotic-sounding grains. It was London. It wasn't Longbridge. And although I felt comfortable enough in it after years away, it was not a view I felt confident would sit comfortably with many of the party's most instinctive supporters, including my own family and my old world. In fact, I was certain that it wouldn't.

The next Monday I went into the BBC to find everyone in one of our 'WTF' morning meetings (they became common over that two-year period). The editor of *Newsnight*, the elfin Ian Katz, found me afterwards and said: 'You must be thrilled.' I asked why. 'Well, that's the working-class vote back, isn't it?'

I rolled my eyes and I laughed – probably not a great play to your boss. In fairness, the assumption that Corbyn, because he was more 'left wing', would play better with the working classes was not one that was unique to Ian: it was oft repeated that summer but that didn't make it any less funny. To me it was just another occasion that proved how little the British media understood about much of the British population – and in truth, how little interaction there ever is between either group. It was clear to me that the cultural conservatism of the working class would find Corbyn's cosmopolitan attitudes, his pursuit of esoteric foreign causes, his dalliance with anti-Western forces, his unadulterated London-ness, complete anathema. I felt depressed with the state of politics. Conservative hegemony seemed to beckon, which would be neither fun to report on nor good for politics overall.

I spent the next few days talking to family, my dad, my grandad, my mum. Everyone seemed bemused. They had been no fans of Miliband but had voted for him regardless. A vote for Corbyn seemed to be in doubt; indeed, he seemed to personify and magnify many of the other-worldly elements they had most disliked about Ed. Mum, as ever, provided punchy if not profound analysis: 'Honestly – what is he about, son? Just look at him. He's a mess.' Nan was pithier still: 'They're not going to get in with him, are they, bab?'

Objections in other quarters were more considered. I had a long conversation with Dad about how he could never vote for someone who was against nuclear weapons: 'Look at those Russians, son. Are you telling me now's the time to get rid of our nukes? He just doesn't understand – that system, Trident, is the Rolls-Royce. Crazy.'

Note in that sentence the curious but nonetheless absolute pride that my dad has in Britain's ability to destroy the world – and do it with a really top-notch system to boot. The number of times as a kid he'd tell me with joy that the Americans were desperate to have British soldiers in Iraq because 'they know we're the only ones who can do the job. They don't have a clue what they're doing.' My dad was an altar boy, not a cadet, and the closest he's got to a real gun is going paintballing; but his faith in these simple facts was absolute.

I too then laboured under these assumptions for years. Whether they were right or wrong (they were mostly wrong, God love him), it said something about his profound love of country and, yes, at times, a latent nationalism, which was never far from the surface. These are deep, commonplace impulses about which much of the Labour left (much of the left generally) feels uncomfortable. But he feels much the same about them, summing his feelings up that: 'He'd rather be in someone else's country than ours.'

A few days later, I was in Hartlepool making a piece about just what working-class voters in the party's heartlands made of Corbyn.

It was the same day he refused to sing the national anthem. My heart sank. One man, Trevor, sitting in the Jacksons Wharf pub on the harbourside with his two sons, confirmed my suspicions: 'It's like he's from another planet.'

I feared that Corbyn might well spell the end of Labour, because, although he well understood and epitomised a powerful stream of thought within the party, he ill understood many of its voters. I felt that, irrespective of the rights and wrongs of his particular views, when they and the characteristics of his wider political personality were taken as a whole, the party would suffer because of who he was, of something that he could not help. I thought the very reasons why so many flocked to join the party would be the same reasons why many of its voters would abandon it. I thought of the 16-year-old me, of how much I'd benefited from the huge changes that the last Labour government had brought about. Yet here was an ex-private schoolboy, who sometimes seemed more interested in Belize than Birmingham, who would put the futures of other 16-year-old mes at risk, admittedly with the best of intentions. I confess, it made me angry.

The weird thing was, I was sort of right, but so was he. Because Corbyn and Corbynism have transformed politics and helped to rewrite the rules. Because it turned out that the politics of twenty-first-century Britain was very different to what any of us – even he – thought. He was riding a cultural wave not of his own making but which he perhaps alone was suited to ride. He was not only fighting a different sort of political war but he was fighting it with a very different army. He may have lost some of the old soldiers I cared about, but doing so came with its own reward. We'd never seen a Labour leader like this before. To try and understand him and the movement and ideology that bear his name we have to try and understand not only the man and his beliefs (and the beliefs of his adherents), but also the place Corbynism occupies in the history of the party and the cultural moment in which we find ourselves. In this we see that he presents profound change but also a sliver of continuity, from the unlikeliest of sources.

* * *

Generally Corbyn is spoken about considerably more than 'Corbynism'. Therein lies some of the complexity around this new movement. Because, although there is much sound and fury about the quasi-Marxist beliefs of Corbyn, it has never been entirely clear just what Corbynism as a coherent set of beliefs and ideology is, not least because Jeremy Corbyn's aren't either. The Corbyn project is based on a man whose main virtue is perceived to be certainty of thought and belief. Although this is true in the sense that he has seldom changed his mind about much, the irony is that that certainty, as far as a body of domestic policy is concerned, is less developed and defined than you might imagine.

This is not terribly unusual for leaders of the opposition or successful politicians generally. Now, years after he left office, journalists and historians are still asking what it actually *was* David Cameron believed in. Likewise, Theresa May's fundamental beliefs and even motivations are generally opaque. There is no Mayism and there was no Cameronism, yet that did not stop either of them from becoming prime minister, or leader of their party. The truth is that they remain, like many political leaders, sphinxes without riddles. They don't have any grand scheme, any grand vision, and are fundamentally instrumentalist in their approach to politics; their politics is instinctive rather than programmatic.

But neither of them has built a movement like Jeremy Corbyn has. As far as I know, no one has chanted their names as they arrive at a rally – indeed, I can't quite think what a Cameron or May rally would look like. As far as I know, they've never made anyone cry with joy, as I have seen Jeremy Corbyn do. As far as I know, they've never inspired very many people at all – much less hundreds of thousands – to join their party and flock to their banner. There must be then, surely, something special not only about the man, but about his beliefs?

Roughly, there are four strands of Corbynism as a political project, two of which relate to its external policy prospectus and two to the internal workings of the Labour Party. They are as follows:

Anti-'austerity' economics, more broadly attaching itself to an end of 'neoliberalism' thesis.
An 'anti-war' foreign policy.
Ending Blairism/entrenching a left-wing approach within the Labour Party.
Transforming the Labour Party into a mass-membership and member-led organisation.

The pedigree of all this is easy to spot; there is virtually a straight line from the emergence of the 'New Left' movements of the late 1970s, of which Corbyn was a member, to these four objectives. In particular, the changes to the Labour Party are exactly the same changes that people like Jon Lansman, Jon Trickett, Diane Abbott, John McDonnell and Corbyn himself were evangelising about when they joined the party in the late 1970s. Putting members in charge of Labour's policymaking and internal hierarchies, Corbynism's proponents believe, will embed the left, its beliefs and its style within the party permanently, and the scourge of Blairism in particular will be banished for ever. As John McTernan, a former adviser to Tony Blair, put it: 'Jeremy Corbyn has always wanted one thing – an ideologically pure Labour Party. Theresa May is not his political enemy, she is his political opponent. His political enemies are in the Labour Party, people like me, people like Tony Blair, it's Blairism.'

We will examine the takeover of the party in more detail later; but, beyond the internal world of resolutions, composites and nominations, Corbynism as it relates to the rest of us, to those first two sets of ideas, to the external world of the country, is a muddier affair.

CORBYNISM AT HOME

Corbynism's domestic thinking is a mix of the politics of the counterculture, a dash of the ideological inheritance of bits of the Occupy movement and its close bedfellows, the wider anti-austerity movements, a belief in the virtues of restored public spending to pre-2010 levels, with a few splashes of nationalisation thrown into the mix. At a granular level, it has much in common with the economic agenda and set of policies he inherited from Ed Miliband. The table below shows the similarities and the evolution from one to the other.

Corbyn	Miliband
£10 minimum wage	£8 minimum wage
Similar fiscal rules	Similar fiscal rules
Wholesale energy nationalisation	Energy price caps
Abolition of tuition fees	Reduction to £5,000 per year
No extra taxation on property	Introduction of a mansion tax
Pledge to abolish zero-hour contracts	Pledge to abolish zero-hour contracts

There are plenty of other similarities too; on everything from free school meals, late payments to small businesses, to a new National Investment Bank, Corbynism's domestic policies have generally been an incremental evolution of Miliband's agenda – 'Miliband Max' or, as one commentator put it, 'Milibandism minus dithering'.

Much of the 2017 election manifesto either borrowed directly from or built upon the Miliband offer two years before. There were some distinct Corbynist twists, not least pledges to nationalise certain industries, but the mainstay of the prospectus was more Miliband than Marx. This has especially been the case as Corbyn has become more established; when he was running for leader, more outlandish policies were floated, not least the so-called 'people's QE' programme, whereby the government would instruct the Bank of England to print money for public investment projects. Since that time, however, as Brexit has sucked in political energies on all sides and John McDonnell has sought to persuade big business that Labour is not a threat, much of the economic radicalism from the first 2015 campaign has faded. Some laud this shift, others argue that microwaved Milibandism is hardly the 'new kind of politics' that Corbyn promised. Jon Cruddas is among them:

'To me, given the staleness of what was on hand and the tributaries of defeat in 2015, it had to be detonated in some way and shaken up. Corbyn could have been the detonator, but he didn't create a debate, really. He has brought very little, and that's sad really. The economic policy is reheated, and he's drawing on a lot from 2015, soft Milibandism with a bit of universal basic income thrown in occasionally, some regional policy, green investment bank, which long term have already been Labour policy. So, the lack of contemporary left agenda is disappointing, and the wasted year with the opponents coming up with anything other than saying they're more electable. The question is, what is the guiding modern centre-left public philosophy now?'

The dearth of new economic thinking, in some ways, isn't surprising. The left of Labour does not have the wide network of think tanks, policy thinkers, sympathetic journalists and commentators to incubate and develop policy. The left ascended to the leadership in unexpected circumstances; their detailed policy thinking had been modest. There has therefore not (so far) been the exposition of a sustained, thought-through policy programme of what Jeremy Corbyn's Britain would look like, insofar as to how much it would differ from, say, Ed Miliband's. There has been, however, a significant shift in tone. Corbyn has channelled his (not-so-inner) economic populist, especially since January 2017. This was a conscious decision by his team; Corbyn was struggling and his advisers decided to learn the lessons of the Bernie Sanders and Donald Trump campaigns. Hence in his turn-of-the-year interview with Radio 4's *Today* programme, Corbyn consciously decided to float the idea of a maximum-income cap. There are few inside Corbyn's tent who feel such a policy would be practical, but the signal it sent was important. This was the beginning of a new theme of his leadership. Today, Corbyn is cloaked in the language of economic populism. For example, in November 2017, referring to Morgan Stanley and other city institutions he told his Twitter followers: 'Labour is a growing movement of well over half a million members and a government-in-waiting that will work for the many. So when they say we're a threat, they're right.

We're a threat to a damaging and failed system that's rigged for the few.'

The policies might be the same but the way they are packaged and communicated is totally different. Miliband was desperate to appear sensible and trustworthy, Corbyn is desperate to be seen as radical if not even revolutionary. Corbyn stood on an anti-austerity platform, telling a hustings in 2015: 'In the last election we were offering a form of austerity-lite … It's not good enough to go on the doorstep and say we'll have less cuts than they will, that we'll be austerity-lite.' Yet John McDonnell's plan on public spending and Ed Balls' are virtually identical. Few know that. It's all in the telling.

The ability to sidestep such inconvenient truths, to square circles Miliband could not, lies partly in the simplicity of the narrative, the tale Corbyn and his team seek to tell. He is certain who his enemies are. That is why he doesn't need reams of policy at his disposal, why he requires little explanation of how he will 'de-rig' the system. Because Corbyn has a rhetorical story to tell and Miliband usually didn't. Conversely, as we've seen, New Labour and Tony Blair often did things – the utility company profits tax or the minimum wage – which belied its own narrative, but that narrative was so well articulated and knitted together that what they did was sometimes missed. Corbynism boasts the same characteristic but often in reverse.

Because, in economic terms, his message speaks to a wider truth that the public has internalised: that the most important thing about Corbynism is that it exists at all. Like Thatcherism, it represents the undoing of a consensus, the end of a universally shared set of instincts and attitudes across all parties that the free market is usually a good thing. Indeed, Corbyn himself has an unreconstituted certainty that the private sector is an unalloyed bad in any circumstances. Take this exchange from an interview on the Andrew Marr programme from January 2018:

> CORBYN: Capitalism is a system that has evolved, it's a system that is there.

MARR: Has it got anything right?

CORBYN: Well, it does invest – mainly for its own benefit – but it does get challenged.

This certainty – however sensible or wrongheaded – helps Corbyn politically and is the main nucleus of Corbynism. In this case, he was talking to Marr about the collapse of Carillion, the large private-sector contractor responsible for an enormous swathe of government services and public-sector contracts, which went bust in January 2018. If that had happened under, say, Miliband's leadership, it's easy to imagine the contours of the political debate.

Miliband would have had a sharper intellectual and political appreciation of the issues involved. He would have been forthright in his criticism of the government and he would have called for urgent action. Two things would have then happened. His own political understanding and appreciation of the workings of government would have kicked in. He would have known that it would not be especially practicable or desirable to bring all government services in house. He would have known that tearing up contracts would have resulted in a big legal bill for the government and he would have known that there are many examples of successful outsourcing. He would then probably have called for a review of the outsourcing process and probably a public inquiry into the circumstances of the company's collapse. Information from the National Audit Office on the poor value for money of PFI contracts would have also caused some consternation. Tories would have responded in earnest by asking who was responsible for PFI. The answer would come: Gordon Brown advised by, who else, Ed Miliband and Ed Balls.

Corbyn has neither encumbrance.

His certainty of capitalism's inherent evil means he feels able to say with confidence that it should be banished from the public sector in all its forms. It is simple, it is clear, it is direct and, in an age frightened of nuance, it works. Nor, uniquely, is he encumbered by any of the baggage of the last Labour government's involvement with the private sector. Because his cachet is so great and because he was such a peripheral figure, he is able to disavow anything of which he doesn't approve. So, when an interviewer posits that the last Labour government was as culpable for any given situation as the Tories, Corbyn and his followers are able to say: 'Yes. And we thought that was awful too', just as Blair was able to do in the early 1990s about the Wilson and Callaghan governments of the 1970s.

Corbyn and his supporters are unabashed about presenting themselves as of the left and unembarrassed about its pedigree. Whereas Tony Blair wouldn't have been seen dead at the Durham Miners' Gala, Jeremy Corbyn takes to the stage with a smile on his face. Corbyn may not know all of the words of the national anthem but he belts out 'The Red Flag' with brio. *He* can do this, not only because he is certain of the immorality of the free market, but because his analysis of the sort of country Britain is is different to that of virtually every other Labour leader of the last five decades. Most of Corbyn's predecessors to a lesser or greater extent fundamentally believed that Britain was a conservative country with a small 'c', and if the Labour Party didn't remember that, then it would for ever be that way with a big 'C' as well. The Labour Party, they thought, must therefore do certain things and behave in a certain way in order to accommodate that constraint. Corbyn's analysis is fundamentally different. He and his followers have an implicit conception of a Richard Nixon style 'silent majority' but in reverse, for the left, not the right. Nixon used the concept to refer to the forgotten 'majority' of Americans, uninterested in the countercultural forces of the 1960s, not able to participate in public debate. Likewise, Corbyn shares the concept that the vast majority of Britons are left behind, not by forces of culture especially, but by the unbridled free market and they are seeking a champion who can offer them an alternative. These beliefs have been much burnished by the financial crisis of 2008 and its continuing fallout.

So perhaps the best way of thinking about Corbynism domestically is that it is not so much a set of policies but a mood or a mindset; Corbynism is about self-belief, a semi-populism. The Corbynistas are unabashed and unwavering in their belief that the country has turned leftwards. Some of them go further still and argue that the country has always been receptive to left-wing arguments and it is the failure of the centre left to propose them with sufficient conviction that has led the country to think there's little difference in voting between the parties. Now that there is a proper alternative to vote for, they will come.

Partly as a result of the moral certainty about market forces Corbyn has (and the belief his followers have in his ability to follow through on that vision), he has actually demonstrated considerable flexibility on many aspects of domestic policy and retreated on several important issues. The party has avoided any big pledges to increase taxation; it has become silent on welfare; its policy on immigration has been further to the right than anyone imagined (indeed, by going into the 2017 election pledging to come out of the single market, Corbyn's Labour Party had the toughest immigration policy of any Labour government or opposition in recent history). Where once Corbyn attacked the police, channelling his anti-authoritarian punkish instincts, he is now a supporter of the Met and attacks the government for failing to resource it and its security service counterparts properly (the same security services that in his earlier days he wished to abolish). In other words, he has been sensibly *political*; Corbyn has shown himself a far more dextrous politician than his detractors feared.

Indeed, the policy prospectus we've seen from Corbynism so far has been conservative in two other important respects. The first is that its offer essentially promises the restoration of the status quo ante on public spending bequeathed to the coalition government by New Labour. It is ironic, given Blairite voices in the party argued that Labour should seek to match the Tories on austerity, that it should be a Corbyn-led Labour Party that would seek to restore New Labour levels of public spending and the sorts of programmes latterly abolished by the Tories. It would also seek a New Labour-style restoration of the public realm. Admittedly, it would look to do so through direct public borrowing, rather than through PFI contracts, outsourcing and other private-sector investment as was often the New Labour approach, but the ends would be the same.

It is also conservative in the sense that, in certain areas, Corbynism seeks to re-establish central tenets of another of its predecessors. The nationalisation programme's pledges to renationalise rail, utilities and other private-sector bodies hark back to the Attlee government's economic programme. There is argument about the means of achieving that nationalisation: Corbynistas argue that they're not interested in the 'top-down' centralising model of nationalisation that we saw in the 1940s; they talk about a worker-led, democratising nationalisation. The details, however, are pretty sketchy. Whether or not they can place flesh on that bone, the rationale and thinking behind nationalisation are not much changed from those which Attlee, Morrison and Bevin employed in the 1940s. Moreover, how much actually would come about given wider financial constraints is up for debate. John McDonnell has talked about taking rail franchises back into public ownership only when the franchises come up for renewal, renegotiating PFI contracts on a case-by-case basis, everything in a piecemeal fashion. In that respect, it doesn't exactly sound like the commanding heights.

So when Jeremy Corbyn and John McDonnell talk about creating a 'socialism for the twenty-first century', it is worth bearing in mind just how twentieth century much of its prospectus currently is; an evolution of, rather than a revolution in, recent and not so recent Labour thinking. His approach, a combination of 1940s dirigisme and 2000s public-sector largesse, while an unlikely set of bedfellows and twin set of inspirations, does not constitute a fundamental recasting of British socialism.

But just because Corbynism hasn't shown a deep radicalism in the domestic sphere so far doesn't mean it does not have the potential to do so in the future. A combination of Corbynism's rejection of the free market and more radical iterations of Corbynism developing beneath the surface mean much is still to play for. Corbynism is more than just Corbyn. There are many potential Corbynisms, many paths it could yet take.

Consider, as we have already seen, Blairism's evolution, how different it looked in 1994 compared with 2007. There is a strong possibility that a similar mutation might have taken place in Corbynism as a governing philosophy.

As Clive Lewis told me: 'I think one of the key things for the future of the left and for Corbynism generally is do we just want to turn the fiscal taps on and off. If we want to put more money into the NHS, if we just want to put more money into education, that isn't radical because what will happen is even if you can do that with the economy as it is with a few changes, what will happen is in five or ten years or whatever the Tories will come in and turn the taps off and will continue in the broad direction they've been travelling in. If you want to be radical it's more than just more resources for the NHS, the BBC, giving people more control over aspects of their lives, so that's I think the next stage of Corbynism, but that's all to be debated and discussed … between now and the next election, that's where the philosophy of Corbynism will begin to come through.'

And as a senior source from Momentum told me, that fight is to come: 'There are two strands within Corbynism. One that relies on ideas, mostly from the past that we can sort of rely on and that mostly came out in the manifesto. Traditional, social democratic, but this is the key, very easy to communicate. The task now for the next few years – for my wing of Corbynism, and it is happening in a very satisfying way, is to engage loads of groups across society and Labour members too, to develop the manifesto that is actually revolutionary in how it views the economy.'

You could see the early skirmishes of that fight in February 2018 when Jon Lansman, director of Momentum, decided to enter the contest to be general secretary of the party. He decided to do so despite the fact he would be standing against Unite's chosen candidate, Jennie Formby. Unite and Momentum had hitherto been publicly inseparable, linchpins of the left and pro-Corbyn front. Their politics, however, are distinct. Unite represent the old-fashioned hard-edged end of social democracy. Their ends are straightforward: they want more resources for public services and more state spending – old-fashioned, bread-and-butter Labour politics. Momentum's politics is of a quite different provenance: more radical, environmentalist, experimental; many of its members (including Lansman) see elements of trade union politics as emblematic of the old-fashioned, machine politics they so dislike. Unite would seek to stop nuclear disarmament because they have workers at Faslane; give a trade unionist a choice between 'radicalism' and securing jobs, they'll choose jobs every time. Momentum's politics, by contrast, is at once wider and more rarefied.

There is a battle to be fought and won. Whether Corbynism becomes a traditional social democratic government on steroids or something altogether different is up for grabs. If it's the latter, it will make sense to talk of Corbynism long after the man himself has left the stage: it will outlast him. Right now the disparate strands are united by Corbyn himself and his populist message. The exact nature of Corbynism's soul on the domestic front, partly because the man himself is relatively uninterested in those matters, is yet to be decided. There is another area, however, where it has long been set in stone.

CORBYNISM ABROAD

Corbyn's primary political interest, throughout his career, has been foreign affairs; it is these rather than his views on the economy or international finance or industry that have driven him for forty years or more. It is revealing that the first policy questions he addressed in his first speech as Labour Party leader were the regime in Saudi Arabia, and its then treatment of a blogger, and a campaign on Guantanamo Bay. Here is an extract:

> I've been standing up for human rights, challenging oppressive regimes, for thirty years as a backbench MP.
>
> And before that as an individual activist, just like everyone else in this hall.
>
> Just because I've become the leader of this party, I'm not going to stop standing up on those issues or being that activist.

So for my first message to David Cameron, I say to him now a little message from our conference, I hope he's listening – you never know:

Intervene now personally with the Saudi Arabian regime to stop the beheading and crucifixion of Ali Mohammed al-Nimr, who is threatened with the death penalty, for taking part in a demonstration at the age of seventeen.

And while you're about it, terminate that bid made by our Ministry of Justice to provide services for Saudi Arabia – which would be required to carry out the sentence that would be put down on Ali Mohammed al-Nimr.

We have to be very clear about what we stand for in human rights.

A refusal to stand up is the kind of thing that really damages Britain's standing in the world.

I have huge admiration for human-rights defenders all over the world. I've met hundreds of these very brave people during my lifetime working on international issues. I want to say a special mention to one group who've campaigned for the release of British resident Shaker Aamer from Guantanamo Bay.

This was a campaign of ordinary people like you and me, standing on cold draughty streets, for many hours over many years.

Together we secured this particular piece of justice.

Sitting in the hall, I remember thinking this was a curious way of introducing yourself to the nation. As virtuous an issue and important as the plights of Saudi Arabian bloggers and Guantanamo Bay suspects were, it seemed odd to me to identify yourself immediately – in a scenario where the perception of you was already one of being remote from ordinary affairs, of being rather too north London – to make your first impression, on something astoundingly remote from the lives of ordinary British people. You might as well have started giving a lengthy exegesis on the problems with policing shipping lanes in the South China Sea.

Nonetheless it was authentically him. He was vice-chair of CND, vice-chair of the Stop the War coalition, member and chair of myriad parliamentary groups on recondite campaigns connected with Latin America, the Middle East, Africa and anti-war causes the world over. Consult Hansard and you will see that his politics, before becoming leader, was a mix of the parochial and international, devoted both to the minutiae of the affairs of his constituency, for which it is universally agreed he has been an assiduous and outstanding local MP, and to the affairs of the world, as well as, of course, his repeated criticism of the inadequacies of the West.

It is on matters foreign not domestic that we find Corbyn at his most doctrinaire. Partly this is because it is the subject he knows best – on domestic matters, including Brexit, he quite often defers to close colleagues like McDonnell or Abbott, whose instincts he shares and trusts but who also have better command of the detail. On foreign affairs, his confidence is greatest and his views more fixed.

This is why the big flashpoints (save for Brexit) that have occurred between Corbyn and his party have been over foreign policy: specifically over bombing in Syria and more notably the UK's response to the attempted assassination of Sergei and Julia Skripal in Salisbury in March 2018. We'll see how this fits within broader Labour Party thinking later, but, suffice to say, his view of foreign policy is largely alien to Labour, certainly to the thinking of any Labour leader in modern history.

Corbyn is almost unique in Labour Party postwar history in that you might broadly say that he is neutral about the Western alliance and even the concept of the West itself. He is resolutely anti-interventionist in almost all circumstances; given our recent experiences that is perhaps hardly surprising and is a far more commonplace view beyond the left than it would have been during Tony Blair's liberal interventionist heyday. But I would posit that Corbyn's view on foreign policy is more radical than that. In 1941, George Orwell wrote about his friends on the British left (who are to some extent Corbyn's intellectual antecedents) that they were 'sometimes squashily pacifist, sometimes violently pro-Russian, but always anti-British'. Corbyn is not anti-British in the sense that he wishes to see harm come to the country, but what Orwell meant is that the instincts of those on that strand of the left are highly sceptical towards the actions of their own country and of the broader West all the time. That analysis still rings true for Corbyn, seventy-five years on. The proclivities of Jeremy Corbyn, Seumas Milne (his head of strategy) and Andrew Murray are to assume that, almost whatever the foreign-policy situation, the West will be at fault or to blame. It is the modern embodiment of the anti-imperialist movements of the past. It also explains why that strand of the left tends to find such common cause with fellow leftist (but sometimes undemocratic) regimes in Latin America, Africa, Iran or even non-ideologically aligned regimes like Putin's Russia. If the starting point of your geopolitical thinking is that the West is politically and economically imperialist, then any force that can help check that imperialism is worthy of at least qualified support – and a willingness to look the other way when it comes to some of their more unpleasant characteristics or actions. That is why Corbyn chose to appear on Press TV despite the fact it is the state-backed broadcaster of a regime that if allied to the West would attract Corbyn's scorn. It explains why Corbyn and his part of the left decry Saudi Arabia but support Iran – one is allied to the West and the other is not. The crimes might be similar but the response depends on which side of the geopolitical divide you fall. Corbyn's understanding of power is also at play here; his response can generally be predicted by an assessment of which side appears to wield most absolute power. Given that the West tends to have the upper hand in any given situation, or at least be more powerful on paper, Corbyn tends to view it with suspicion. This 'power lens' is at play in his domestic politics too and leads him to champion some of society's most vulnerable groups and unfashionable causes. These efforts, however, for obvious reasons, are usually less controversial. In foreign policy, the same instincts often land him in hot water.

The Skripal case of March 2018 illustrates this well. Corbyn and Milne were unwilling to do what any other leader of the opposition would have most likely done and offer the government its unqualified support. Instead Corbyn wanted to question the veracity of the claims of the government and the security services. Seumas Milne in an off-the-record briefing with lobby correspondents in Westminster said: 'I think obviously the government has access to information and intelligence on this matter which others don't; however, also, there's a history in relation to WMD and intelligence which is problematic to put it mildly.' There is profound suspicion (some would say well justified, given recent history) about the British state. But so often, it does not seem to be accompanied by a parallel suspicion about the motivations or testimony of the opposing anti-democratic state in question, in that case Russia. This seems especially bewildering given the well-known mendacity of many of the regimes involved. In this respect, as uncomfortable as it might be for Corbyn followers, their leader shares some characteristics with Donald Trump. Consider the absurdity of Trump's performance in July 2018 in Helsinki on the question of election interference, standing next to Vladimir Putin, as he declared that he was inclined to believe Putin and Russia over his own intelligence services. It is not such a stretch to imagine a Prime Minister Corbyn expressing a similar sentiment. Perhaps he would do so for slightly different reasons, but they share the characteristic of being anti-system candidates, suspicious of the 'deep state'. Like Trump, Corbyn would probably, even when assuming a place in the system, indeed becoming the system, find it difficult to change his spots.

Hence Corbyn's semi-farcical insistence that the British government should comply with Russian requests to send chemical samples to Russia. The logical inference of this is that we trust the Russian state as much as or more than our own. It is not a set of beliefs or instincts that sits well with the Labour Party (viz. the furious reaction of many of his backbenchers) or with the British public – as polling data published shortly after Corbyn's response showed; only 18 per cent thought he had handled the incident well. It is unsurprising that throughout the crisis it was McDonnell who called for tougher sanctions on Russia and then attempted to bring Corbyn closer into line with the government. He could doubtless see the political danger and I'm told was flummoxed and frustrated as to why the Labour Party should risk an ounce of political capital over Vladimir Putin, irrespective of the rights and wrongs of the case. He lost that battle – he must worry given the strength of Corbyn's feeling on foreign policy how many more he might yet lose and exactly what the tolerance level of the British public really is for such displays.

It is right to dismiss the claim made by Corbyn's critics that he is somehow 'anti-British' or unpatriotic. In early 2018, when various right-wing papers attempted to suggest that Corbyn might have been a Soviet Czech informant, the accusations rightly fell flat. But his base political reflexes are most certainly suspicious of the British state and nearly all its statecraft in the international arena. There is a legitimate question mark as to how someone with those beliefs could reasonably be expected to sit atop the vast security deep state, which Corbyn would have to protect, defend and administrate as prime minister. It was oft remarked during the 2017 election campaign and during the Skripal affair that the public was far more tolerant of Corbyn's more exotic views on foreign affairs and terrorism than were the Westminster political and media class. His allies (rightly) point to the fact that his colourful connections with the IRA seemed not to damage him a jot. Nor did his speech on the link between terrorism and foreign policy, delivered in the shadow of several terrorist attacks, considered unthinkable by many sage hands. They therefore posit that moments of exposure on Russia (and episodes like it) will similarly go over the public's head. I think they're wrong. They misunderstand the fact that those counterexamples are not analogous: for anyone under forty and on the British mainland, the Troubles are as remote as the Battle of the Boyne itself. After two decades of foreign adventures that have too seldom appeared to deliver any dividend but expended plenty of blood and treasure, the public is more tolerant of an alternative analysis on the causes of terrorism at home and abroad. Neither means that Corbyn is invulnerable: if a new threat emerges, like Russia, the public may be less forgiving of a leader whose instincts are muddied. They have forgotten the distant Soviet past, they have not forgotten the Putin present. Corbyn's global views represent severe vulnerability for the Corbyn project and an unknown in government.

In the 1980s, Nigel Lawson, the man who gave Thatcherism its intellectual ballast, attempted to define the creed that he had helped to make. He said this: 'Free markets, financial discipline, firm control over public expenditure, tax cuts, nationalism, "Victorian values" (of the Samuel Smiles self-help variety), privatisation and a dash of populism.' Lawson did this with the benefit of hindsight, when both he and Thatcher had left office, Thatcherism's deeds done. So perhaps it's unfair to try and do the same with Corbynism before the fact – but let's give it a whirl.

Corbynism is: controlled markets, state intervention, anti-austerity, anti-imperialism, international neutrality, anti-interventionism, a dash of multiculturalism, limited nationalisation with a strong dose of identity politics.

And it's that last one, Corbynism's identity politics, which is more important for the ideology's future success and failure than all of the others.

Chapter 4

THE 'A-WORD'

We don't walk by on the other side.

Jeremy Corbyn

'I'm so inspired, I just want to go out and start knocking on doors!'

Over tea and Jaffa Cakes, I watched a Labour Party activist, clipped up on the evening news in Manchester, on a September evening in 2006, in the front room of a girl I had long hoped to make my girlfriend (but never quite succeeded). Maybe the reason for that lay in the reason I was in the front room in the first place. I was crashing at her parents' house in Oldham because at the age of 17 I was attending my first Labour Party conference, which was taking place just down the road in central Manchester. This probably didn't do too much to help my cause.

Worse still, I did nothing to hide my glee. Far from it, I was buzzing. That activist had been inspired and so had I: by a speech we'd both heard that day at conference. I remember it so vividly because I devoured every bit of news coverage I could about that day. As sad as it is, it was tremendously exciting.

If you ever want to see the definition of fanboy, just google Tony Blair's conference speech in 2006. It was his final turn as leader and his first stab at defining his own legacy. He'd been forced to announce the timetable for his departure by the martialled forces of Gordon Brown only a couple of weeks previously. It was a masterclass of oratory and sparkling speechmaking. But, in that quintessential Blair way, it wasn't easy to remember exactly what he'd said. It's now probably best remembered for a joke made early on, when he'd thanked Cherie for all her love and dedication, followed by the perfectly delivered quip: 'At least I don't have to worry about her running off with the bloke next door.' The background was that Cherie, never one to keep her feelings to herself, had been overheard by a journalist watching Gordon Brown's speech in one of the darker corners of the conference centre. When Brown said: 'It's been such a pleasure to work with Tony,' she is said to have retorted: 'Well, that's a lie.' The joke instantly defused what had become a major row while simultaneously acknowledging what had really happened. The hall was in stitches.

Well, it seemed funny at the time. And if you care to watch that speech, then you might see one smiling, long-haired, bespectacled figure in a stand-out dark-tan jacket and grey-striped shirt, which for some reason I thought was a good look. If you can't spot that, I'm the one clapping like a seal and laughing like a drunk. I'd been chosen by someone in the party to be one of the fresh-faced (and entirely unrepresentative) cadre of smiling mannequins who used to sit behind party leaders for big speeches like this, as was fashionable at the time. I was beyond excited. Seeing this man, who had been prime minister for virtually as long as I could remember, appear on the stage was thrilling. I sat in awe.

The hall lapped it up. The charm, the self-deprecating lines, the firm arm gestures, the furrowed but vital brow, the pastor-like fervour interlaced with flashes of a boyish grin – the Blair magic still worked. Maybe it was because they knew they'd never see the wizard's tricks again. Either way, the hall lapped it up.

'But, in the years to come, wherever I am, whatever I do. I'm with you. Wishing you well. Wanting you to win. You're the future now. Make the most of it.'

I'll confess something to you. Part of me thought he was talking to me. Yes, a part of my stupid, juvenile, hormone-swamped, underdeveloped, absurd 17-year-old brain thought, Yes! That's me! I'll be the next prime minister (or maybe next but one – even my enormous teenage ego didn't think it particularly likely that I might overcome the Brown political machine and pip him to the post).

Yet as unlikely as that might have seemed to anyone at the time, it probably was only just a little less likely than him, entirely unknowingly, speaking to Jeremy Corbyn.

Nine years later, I was sitting in the crowd at Jeremy Corbyn's first conference speech in Brighton in 2015. The mood was quite different. Many of the activists, both supporters and detractors, were stunned. While in 2006 the party was wrestling with what to make of its recent past, in 2015 many wondered whether it even had a future. Now a journalist, with a very different set of priorities, I was among their number.

It's hard to believe it was the same conference and the same party. We've seen what happened to New Labour, but it is its deep symbiotic connection with Corbynism that is most intriguing. Indeed, you cannot understand Corbynism without understanding their deep interconnection.

If you ask the average Corbynista what Corbynism is, they generally say something along the lines of it's returning the party 'back to its roots'. Perhaps that's why, during the campaign, T-shirts started cropping up with the slogan 'Old Labour New Start' under a picture of Corbyn. In case you're interested, they are still available in all sizes and a variety of colours.

It is at best, however, a half-truth. Corbyn was absolutely a new start, the biggest change in the party's modern history; precisely because of that, what he most certainly was not was 'Old Labour'. Nonetheless, the belief that Corbyn is in effect Charles II* at the head

* A parallel that I'm sure neither man would enjoy.

of a 'Restoration' of the Labour Party, displacing a Blairite (Cromwellian) interregnum, is ubiquitous and a key component in explaining both (a) Corbyn's rise within the Labour Party and (b) the genetic makeup for the beliefs of Corbyn's followers.

In a nutshell, the idea is a simple one we've already encountered: that Blair was an aberration, that he was not really Labour at all, and that Corbyn's ascension represents a return to true Labour Party values. This is the nucleus of Corbynism.

Blairites have no one to blame for this but themselves – it is a myth of their own making. The branding strategy and conceit of 'New Labour' was a potent one and served a purpose in the mid-1990s as an attempt to signal a clean break with the dog days of the late 1970s and early 1980s. But decades after its inception that clever trick had an unforeseen consequence. By necessity, any talk of New Labour meant there must be an 'Old Labour', against which the new entity could be judged and from which it could be differentiated. New Labour's practitioners spoke as if everything that came before could be placed in one amorphous blob. That blob included the militant-Bennite fringes with the more middle-of-the-road, electorally successful social democratic policies and attitudes of Labour in the 1960s and 1970s and before.

The effect of this has been to allow Corbyn to cloak himself in the pedigree of the party's past, something to which in reality his wing of the party had little right. Let's take just a few examples of ways in which Corbyn is not 'Old Labour', some of which we've already encountered, but are worth recapping:

1. **Unilateralism:** No Labour prime minister has ever been in favour of abandoning Britain's nuclear weapons. With the sole exception of Michael Foot (itself a source of enormous controversy), no Labour leader has either.* Lest we forget, it

* Neil Kinnock's views 'evolved' on the subject. Although he started his time as leader of the opposition in favour, by the time of the 1992 general election he had abandoned the idea.

was a Labour government and, in particular, a Labour foreign secretary, Ernie Bevin, who moved heaven and earth to ensure that Britain did have its own independent nuclear arsenal after the war. As Bevin said: 'We've got to have this thing [a nuclear bomb] over here whatever it costs. We've got to have the bloody Union Jack on top of it.'

2. **Anti-NATO/Americanism:** Corbyn's general anti-American stance, which has even extended to his suggesting we ought to leave NATO and be a neutral state, is unprecedented. Once again it was a Labour foreign secretary, Bevin, who designed the postwar international architecture for peace, including NATO. Likewise, every single Labour prime minister since the war has sought to ensure an extremely close Anglo-American alliance and, in particular, a close relationship with the incumbent president. Nor would any Labour leader in the past have entertained some of the more exotic foreign connections with which Mr Corbyn has been associated. His response to the murder attempt on Sergei Skripal and his daughter, Julia, in Salisbury in March 2018, and his perceived criticism of the intelligence services, could only be his.
3. **Ireland:** No Labour leader (or UK prime minister full stop since partition) has publicly supported the policy of a united Ireland.
4. **Mixed economy:** Every Labour leader since Gaitskell has been committed to the mixed economy and some degree of private enterprise. Corbyn was asked what, if anything, was good about capitalism and he struggled to think of anything. He starts from the premise that the private sector is bad in virtually every setting, which is on the outer edges of where most Labour leaders have been in the same way that Blair was on the outer edges in assuming the market was always good.
5. **Marxist:** Both Corbyn and John McDonnell have openly flirted with Marxism. Virtually no leader since the birth of the party would have done so.

Another T-shirt has become ubiquitous at Momentum rallies and at party conferences: 'What Would Clem Do?' As we see from that list, what might be somewhat unsettling for its owner to accept is, the chances are, Clem would have invaded Korea, purchased atomic missiles and resisted the nationalisation of private schools (Old Harrovian as he was). Indeed, if you fancied getting a few boos at any Labour Party gathering you might wonder aloud if Corbyn's policy positions sit at least as uncomfortably with much of the trajectory of his predecessors as Blair did with his. The outlying positions are just different ones for each man.

Nonetheless, despite being ahistorical, the conceit of Corbyn as true inheritor to the party traditions, of Labour 'coming home', is enormously effective. Just recently, I heard a speaker at a local election rally, Martha Osamor, a long-standing north London activist (and mother of the shadow cabinet minister Kate Osamor), say: 'We're on the verge of something historic: a Labour government which lives up to our Labour values.' Enormous cheers followed.

This is the ultimate victory of the left of the modern Labour Party. They have effectively, in a way not achieved at any other point in the party's history, managed to establish themselves as the sole arbiters of Labour purity, the ideological and political inheritors of the only other government that in their rhetoric lives up to those same standards, 1945. They have drawn a straight line from Attlee to Corbyn. This is consistently juxtaposed with its opposite, the New Labour governments. While this has been a fillip for the fortunes of the Labour left, it has come at a cost to the party's wider reputation.

As one Blairite MP put it to me: 'They have been implicit with the endeavours of the right and the right-wing press to destroy the reputation of the Labour government which on almost any measure has the right to be considered at the very top tier of governments throughout the twentieth and twenty-first centuries.'

Without the destruction of the New Labour government's reputation (which, it must be said, some of its architects, including Blair himself, have done little themselves to defend, by either their words or deeds), neither David Cameron nor the Labour left could have won nor sustained their power. Because Corbynism is, ironically enough, not just about the 'ishues', as Tony Benn used to say. It's about identity.

THE PECULIAR CULT OF JEREMY CORBYN

Not many things make me feel proud to be a Brit. But he makes me feel quite proud.

A 19-year-old Momentum activist, talking about Jeremy Corbyn, York, summer 2016

August 2016 and I was knackered. We'd just had the Brexit referendum, a change in prime minister and now a second Labour leadership contest in a year.

Yet, as I followed him around, Corbyn's energy, unlike my own, was undiminished.* Over 170 of the party's MPs had signed a vote of no confidence in him only a few weeks before. Every single political journalist I knew thought he would have to go, myself included.

But it didn't take long for the old Corbyn songs to start making the troops dance once again. As I stood waiting in York for the latest Momentum rally, one of dozens staged that summer, I couldn't believe the push-back had not been greater. I stood in the middle of the city's old, twee streets, surrounded by hundreds of under-35s, students and middle-class professionals. I'd have eaten my microphone if more than 1 per cent of them had voted Leave. Dozens of them waved small EU flags, one young woman even had an EU flag painted on her cheeks. I found the disconnect hard to process. Jeremy Corbyn was not to blame for Britain leaving the EU – that will be firmly inscribed on to David Cameron's tombstone (and the ulterior motive in his

---

* When I remarked upon Corbyn's ostensible zest during that campaign to a prominent Remainer MP, he waspishly said: 'It's not that surprising. He's been in bed during most of the referendum.'

team's efforts to say culpability lies with Labour is obvious). But there is no doubt that Corbyn hardly campaigned with great vigour and that, when the history of the period is written, historians will judge that he had some part to play.

Yet very little of this appeared to affect Corbyn with his troops. That disconnect speaks to a wider truth, something profound about the sort of politics that characterises the early twenty-first century, when political life is at least as much about the sort of person you are as the sort of society you want.

When he appears, there is no doubt as to where the centre of gravity in the room is. Alan Clark once wrote about Margaret Thatcher that when she walked into the tearoom 'You could sense it. A change in the surrounding magnetic field.' Corbyn has only become 'magnetic' in the last few years, but now its force is awesome. And unlike the awkward, painful, computer flowchart interactions of Theresa May, Corbyn enjoys the attention. It's something that many misunderstand about the man. His reputation as a mild-mannered, gentle soul belies his confidence and his presence.

I've watched May turn up at community centres, shopping centres and factories on the stump. She is almost too polite, crippled by shyness and the pressures of overthought social formality. I don't think it's snobbishness or distaste for ordinary people but, if anything, pure embarrassment. Her interactions with voters can be painful to watch, punctuated with long, barren silences. She often doesn't say anything to the person to whom she has been introduced, I think out of embarrassment that they ought to speak first because she doesn't want to be impolite and overbearing and disrespectful. The person she is meeting, by contrast, is meeting the prime minister and usually can't think of much to say because they feel, naturally enough, a bit overwhelmed. Seconds ensue which feel like hours. She is a textbook introvert.

Corbyn, by contrast, is the opposite – someone who is entirely comfortable in his own skin. More than that, for all his talk of disliking 'personality politics', there is no doubt in my mind he takes satisfaction and pleasure from the lavish, if not occasionally cultish, attention that he now receives anywhere he goes, from all of those who think of 'Jeremy' as not only a political ally, or hero, but a friend. Who can blame him? After decades when no one much cared and no one much listened, it must be delightful. Upon stopping for the umpteenth selfie at a campaign event I ask one of his close aides if Corbyn ever finds the attention annoying or gruelling. The aide smiles and half rolls his eyes: 'Never. He loves it.'

The attention the man does not enjoy is the media's. Only a few months before, in February at the Scottish Labour conference in Perth I earned his wrath for asking him three times whether he would definitely lead the party into the next election. On the third time of asking he exploded: 'Listen! I've given you a very, very clear answer! All right?' and walked away. The clip then proceeded to be picked up by all the papers and anti-Corbyn websites. At that time, neither of us knew just how close the next election would be. In Perth he appeared almost broken, under enormous pressure having just lost the Copeland by-election. Only six months later, as he began a summer-long tour of marginal constituencies in the Western Isles, I joined him in Scotland once again. But in the time and space between Stornoway and Perth he had become a man transformed.

It's a mark of how far he has taken the party that he even started that summer in Scotland. All but moribund a few months before, thanks to some Corbyn-style CPR, Scottish Labour had a pulse again. It now has seven seats and is in striking distance in twenty more across the country, including that one on the westernmost fringes of the kingdom. I followed him around the Harris Tweed factory, a local school, a community centre. It was all standard fare. But something wasn't – the set-up wasn't changing but the man seemed to be. For a man who has earned his reputation as a straight talker, a set of views set in stone, it was no longer the case.

It was the week after the appalling events in Charlottesville, where President Trump had said there was wrong 'on all sides' – i.e. both the Nazis and anti-Nazi protests and protesters. After a long conversation at our hotel in Stornoway the night before with producer Zach, we'd decided it would be fruitful to ask him about his personal reaction to what had happened. We reasoned that we could get an easy newsline out of him by asking him not only to condemn Trump personally, but also whether he thought that the president was a white supremacist, as many in the Democratic Party and the wider American left were saying. This would be a perfectly mutually beneficial interview, the ideal for us in the trade. We'd get a newsline and he would get a chance to throw some catnip to his supporters. It's increasingly hard to predict anything about politics, but it doesn't take a bucketful of political nous to make the assessment that there's not a single Corbyn supporter who doesn't loathe Trump or think he's a racist.

What happened next surprised me. Sitting surrounded by Harris Tweed coats (I noticed out of the corner of my eye that his wife, Laura, was trying a few on), Corbyn refused to engage in any direct condemnation of Trump. He declined on multiple occasions to rule out a state visit (the very least I expected him to do), and although he condemned Trump's remarks, he wouldn't condemn the man or confirm that he might be a racist or a white supremacist. When I pressed the point, he fixed me with that famous geography teacher stare, nostrils flaring slightly wider, raised his hand as if to a naughty schoolchild and said with a full stop so firm I could almost see it come out of his mouth: 'Listen – I'm not going to get into labelling people.'

I was surprised. There is no doubt in my mind that the Corbyn of 2015, the no-hoper renegade running for the leadership, would have condemned Trump as a thoroughbred racist. It is surely what he thinks. I suspect the Corbyn of pre-June 2017 would have said it as well. And that's when it finally hit me that this was quite a different man. This was a leader who was starting to do precisely that which he always said he found so distasteful: bend. He had changed.

Walking down a street after a school visit later that afternoon, I put that point to him. Again, he gave me short shrift: 'I really admire your powers of psychiatry … Lewis "Sigmund" Goodall, you're doing really well … I tell you this, I'm proud of leading the Labour Party, I'm proud of what we put forward in the election and I'm very proud that Labour is going to win the next election and bring about social justice for everyone across the UK.' With that definite slap-down we went our separate ways.

On the plane back to Glasgow (nicknamed 'the boneshaker')* I reflected on our odd exchanges; the new chemistry of Corbyn's politics. I thought about what would have happened had I been walking down that street in Stornoway with another Labour leader, with Kendall or Burnham or Cooper, or certainly with Blair or Brown, what the reaction might have been if they'd refused to condemn Trump in Corbyn's shoes. I don't doubt that, rather than equivocating as Corbyn had about personally condemning Donald Trump after the ugliest week of his presidency, the left would not have lost a second in condemning a Labour leader. I've not much doubt either that among their number would have been Jeremy Corbyn.

Yet as the story went out, there was almost no condemnation, apart from of me for asking a series of stupid questions. No counter-reaction from the grassroots, not a word on Twitter.

The whole episode was revelatory in two ways: first, I concluded that Corbyn was preparing for government and for being prime minister. In those days of the 2017 summer, with the Grenfell row raging and Theresa May at her weakest, power seemed tantalisingly close. He was hedging his bets at the prospect of having to deal with Trump as prime minister, potentially within months. Although he didn't get into this with a view to crossing Number 10's threshold, it became clear to me then that he wants it now and so do the people around him. And who can blame them? After decades in the wilderness a taste of power must be potent.

But it also says something about his standing and cachet within the Labour Party. Corbyn has total latitude with his base. He is of the left. He is one of them. They trust him. They have a fundamental (and at times fundamentalist) faith in his motivations, in his instincts in a way that a more moderate or right-wing leader would not enjoy, even if they were parroting a leftist policy prescription or political position word for word. Corbyn and Miliband could issue

---

* I soon understood why.

the same statement and the political reaction from many of the grassroots and even voters would be different. Corbyn is their man. He is them. Only Nixon could go to China. Only Corbyn could sidestep Trump.

Corbyn, in other words, has the A-factor, the word that now dominates our political life, increasingly the only thing that seems to matter: authenticity. Whatever you think about him, he is thought to be himself. He is said, as Tony Benn before him said of himself, to 'mean what he says and [say] what he means'. His longevity on the left, the rigidity of his past intellectual vision and the prestige with which it imbues him allow him to make compromises and fudges that might fatefully undermine another Labour Party leader. Indeed, it allows him to gloss over the fact that in reality Corbyn almost certainly wasn't shedding any tears that Britain left the EU: he dropped his long-standing opposition because, like a politician, he recognised that it was a battle he could not fight with so much of the Labour Party being in favour. His authenticity allows him, just sometimes, to be inauthentic. As George Burns once said: 'Sincerity – if you can fake that, you've got it made.'

When I put it to another young activist in York, a Remainer, that Corbyn had let him down over the EU vote, he said he believed that his leader had tried his best, that it was the media and his opponents who were using it to undermine him but that, in any case, even if he hadn't cared that much about the EU, 'He has the policies I agree with, an end to Trident, and bringing an end to austerity and increasing investment in our infrastructure because a lot of people are struggling and *Jeremy knows best for people like me*.' That is a remarkable statement not least for the degree of trust it puts in a man who is, after all, a politician – it is hard to imagine anyone saying such a thing about Theresa May. But trust is a currency of which, unlike other politicians, Corbyn has an apparently inexhaustible supply with his own people.

But it's not authenticity alone, because it's not just about him. Corbyn is the vehicle but there are hundreds of thousands of drivers, because Corbynism is just as much about the people looking at the man, as it is about the man looking out at them. And when we get down to it, we all care about what our vehicle looks like, what it says about us and our status. Supporting Corbyn has much the same moral and political signalling power as driving around town in a Jaguar adverts to economic prestige.

To support Jeremy Corbyn says something about you in a way it would not of any other contemporary politician. It's a meme. A code. A signal of your values and your place on the cultural spectrum. He is the political equivalent of getting into vinyl. When the throngs are chanting 'Oh – Jeremy Cor-byn', they're not just adoring the man – they're letting everyone know which side they are on and what it says about them. This is not to undermine the importance of his emphasis on change and a new type of politics – it's crucial. As one of his introducers says: 'I used to think politics was about centrism, about compromise, breaking down and selling out your morals. Jeremy Corbyn, this brother, showed me it wasn't so.'

His phenomenon fuses hope, the politics of possibility, with the politics of identity and self. It is, for a man who so fetishises the idea of the many, opposed to the few, a peculiar cocktail. But it has proved potent.

To 'stand with Jeremy' is to say that you care, that you have had enough of war, that you want change, it denotes virtue and a mood of thought. Walking around London I've seen people holding tote bags, wearing T-shirts, even tattoos, all sporting Jeremy Corbyn's face. He is the titular commander of one side of a culture war.

Which is lucky, because that's exactly what we're in.

Chapter 5

CORBYN THE CULTURE WARRIOR

I have met a couple of Tories who were genuinely really anxious for me to see that they weren't horrible people and really believed putting everything into private enterprise will achieve better results. Whatever type they are, I have absolutely no intention of being friends with any of them. I go to Parliament to be a mouthpiece for my constituents and class – I'm not interested in chatting on.

Laura Pidcock MP, August 2017

Rise like lions after slumber, in unvanquishable number, shake your chains to earth like dew, which in sleep had fallen on you – ye are many, they are few.

Jeremy Corbyn, quoting Shelley at Glastonbury, 2017

Protesting is the new brunch.

Placard, anti-Trump protest, 2017

How do you feel when you read the words 'blue passport'?

Proud? Wistful? Angry?

It was certainly something about which my dad felt strongly. We talked about it over WhatsApp:

Hey Dad what did you think about the blue passports story? Do you want blue passports back?

Son the blue passport was a English/British passport it gave us individuality so yes I voted brexit so blue passport for me

But why does it matter Dad?

because we were a blue passport nation before the common market the red or burgundy when we entered europe and now we are leaving we should go back to blue we are British by birth but english by the grace of god

Serious note we had blue passport prior to the common market so let's go back to blue it's our heritage.

I could spill a thousand ounces of ink analysing the state of contemporary Britain but I don't think any selection of words could be bolder on the page than those few exchanges.

And, you know, when I had that conversation, the scary thing is this: I have no idea why he thinks that. It seems so patently and utterly ridiculous to me, to the point of being comic. The idea that flipping the passport back a few shades on the colour palette might somehow strike a hammer blow for sovereignty, that it might be of actual value to anyone, seemed preposterous. The sort of thing I know that many friends of mine would guffaw over. How silly, how ill-informed, how trite and glib. But to my dad it wasn't any of those things. It was axiomatic, obvious, common sense. He wouldn't necessarily have put it like this but he would have absolutely agreed that it was part of making Britain great again.

We're not the first father and son to look at the world a bit differently. My politics might have always been a bit different to my dad's. A bit more pluralist, a bit more open, internationalist, less sentimental and nostalgic. But I'd thought we'd had at least a lot of the same starting points. He's only fifty. When I left for university, I would have said that, broadly speaking, we weren't a million miles apart.

In the interim between his dropping me off at St John's, something had changed, like I'd become rewired, fused differently. A decade on from that nervous late September day on St Giles Road in Oxford, something had happened to our political sight. It was like one of those colour-blindness tests where some people can see the shape and some can't. Even the terms of trade with which we talked about politics seemed disparate and disjointed. His talk of nation and Englishness and heritage was now enough to make me annoyed or frustrated, even angry. I had the sad realisation that my own dad might have been one of those middle-aged men or women at whom I and my producer, in the middle of England somewhere, vox-popping in the street, might have quietly rolled our eyes.

It reminded me of the night of the Brexit referendum itself. He'd started off a reluctant Remainer, having been a Eurosceptic for years, but was worried about the effects it might have on industrial jobs like his. By the end of the campaign, after a Remainer effort that spoke to his head but left the rest of him cold, he changed his mind. 'OUT, OUT, OUT,' he texted me, followed by three Union Jack emojis. I should have known then that Leave were going to win.

On the night, as I left a friend's referendum night party, full of twenty-something journalists and TV producers, finally enjoying a night off after a long campaign, not long after the close of the polls, the word went out that Nigel Farage had conceded that Remain had won. A cheer went up around the room. It was the only cheer of the party, which swiftly became a wake. As the night wore on, the room sobered up, in every sense. Most of us slipped away by the wee hours, not factually certain of the result – but in our bones, we knew. As the sun rose, we knew that it was doing so on a new world, not just for me, but all of us. And not just because those of us there who worked at *Newsnight* knew that we weren't going to have the post-referendum lull we'd hoped for. And not because we knew or cared that we wouldn't be in the Customs Union any more, or Erasmus or the EU Atomic Agency, but because the cosy and unquestioned assumptions we'd had since adolescence were vanishing before our eyes.

When I was a kid, I was given a Dorling Kindersley *History of the World*. It was divided into different sections, 'The Bronze Age', 'The Renaissance', 'The Age of War', and then the final pages, signposted '1991–', were called 'One World'. Its words told a story of a new global society emerging from the darkness of the Cold War. Optimism shone through and its story was of a new world characterised by freedom, co-operation and of liberal democracies joining together in harmony and peaceful co-existence. It suggested that politics had ended, in a way as had history itself.* Nationhood, buttressed by economic and political globalisation, was becoming less and less important. It was coated in the language of post-politics but, looking back, I see it was intensely political. When I wasn't buried in a history book, I spent a lot of my time (too much time) watching *Star Trek*. The united, peaceful world of the twenty-fourth century and the Federation didn't seem so implausible. We were in the early stages – for sure, but history was going in one direction. This was the ideological and cultural inheritance that the world bequeathed us after the fall of the Berlin Wall – we, Generation easyJet – of working in London, weekends in Paris, clubbing in Berlin, beach-hopping near Lisbon, a spouse from Stockholm and friends in Barcelona and everywhere in between – the ultimate triumph of Western political and economic liberalism. 2016 taught us that history had other ideas. The cultural and political world we had thought was inexorable and endless was, in fact, finite. If you reprinted that Dorling Kindersley book now, you might write an end date for the 'One World' after all. For British millennials, in a sense, it came to an end in the early hours on 24 June.

---

* This, though I could not have known it, echoed the Fukuyama 'end of history' thesis gripping political science at the time.

But as we mourned and questioned everything we thought we'd inherit, there was another man who was more than happy to see us move into the next chapter. The next morning, I received a text from Dad. He was jubilant: 'Son, we should all be happy. You went to sleep a European and you woke up an Englishman.' My girlfriend, by contrast, spent much of the evening weeping.

I know my dad is one of the best men you could ever hope to meet. But I also know that if I'd showed that text even to some of my friends they would assume my dad is a racist, a bigot, a nativist. I know that's what some of you will be thinking right now.

But that's not right. He, you, me – we're all part of a transformed and transforming political settlement. Because with every day that goes by our politics is moving, crawling at first and now sprinting, away from a politics of reason to a politics of feeling and belonging. A politics of heat and fury and identity. A culture war. A politics not about economics, but about how you think I should live and vice versa.

Look at this list.

- Toby Young is offered a place in the Office for Students by the government, an office designed to promote students' welfare.
- The *Daily Mail* is banned on Virgin Trains.
- Furore over the President's Club dinner.
- Row over BBC equal pay – the BBC's China editor, Carrie Gracie, resigns from her position in protest at the corporation's treatment of its female staff and lack of action over the gender pay gap.
- Jeremy Corbyn supports the inclusion of trans women on all-female shortlists for parliamentary seats.

Does each one get your blood burning? Or are you not too fussed? I suspect if you're reading this and you're angry about one, you're angry about them all.

They are all stories that dominated the headlines in a single month: January 2018. I probably popped up on your TV screen somewhere (usually on mute in gyms) talking about every one of them at some point or other. In fact, when I think about covering my job now and what generates the most interest, what gets retweeted the most, what gets people writing to me, is nearly always something about who we are, our identities, rather than about the subject that has dominated politics largely uninterrupted since the war: what's in our pockets. We are in the middle of a political reformation.

Let's take the Virgin Trains example. Virgin came under pressure to stop stocking the *Daily Mail* on its trains. In November, an internal memo was circulated among company staff saying that 'considerable concern' had been raised about the *Mail*'s position on issues such as immigration, LGBT rights and unemployment. The memo added the paper was 'not compatible' with the company's beliefs.

Leaving aside the contention that a company has 'beliefs', which would have struck some of its antecedents as peculiar, clearly staff members felt they just couldn't abide a newspaper of a certain political hue being sold on the company's trains. This was despite the fact that there had been no pressure from the public to do so (they presumably sell next to no copies in any case).

This followed a number of other examples. Towards the end of 2017 Paperchase not only ceased advertising in the *Daily Mail* but apologised for doing so, saying sorry for running a promoted advertising campaign over the course of a weekend. When the apology came, it was as profuse as it was earnest:

> @FromPaperchase
> We've listened to you about this weekend's newspaper promotion. We now know we were wrong to do this – we're truly sorry and we won't ever do it again. Thanks for telling us what you really think and we apologise if we have let you down on this one. Lesson learnt.

Reader, I confess to you: I'm not fond of the *Daily Mail*. But anyone would think from this apology that Paperchase had been caught investing in blood diamonds as opposed to advertising in the biggest-selling newspaper in Britain. It did so after a little-known group, 'Stop Funding Hate', tweeted the following message at the company: 'After a torrid few weeks of divisive stories about trans people, is a *Daily Mail* promotion really what customers want to see @FromPaperchase?'

This was not a tweet that took the online space by storm. It was retweeted 250 times. But Paperchase decided that it had to pick a side out of fear. And it reckoned (probably rightly) that more of its customers were urban, cosmopolitan and liberal: in other words, not readers of the *Daily Mail*. They had more to lose by ignoring it. In short, even companies are being forced to pick a side in a culture war that is transmuting our politics to an American-style values-based fight.

A few months later, with the *Financial Times*'s scoop exposing the antediluvian practices of the President's Club, Great Ormond Street Hospital put out a statement making clear that not only would it not accept this year's donation but in the light of the exposé it would be returning money for the last three years' fundraising. It made that decision in the space of a few hours. There had been no Twitter storm or calls for it to do so. Meanwhile David Walliams, who was hosting the event, issued a statement that he was appalled by it and that he would not be accepting his fee. He emerged unscathed.

That is by contrast to the escapades of Toby Young. He has some unpleasant views. I've interviewed him and confess I am no great fan. He was probably unqualified for the job. But the position in question was for the lowly body of the Office for Students, an organisation of which I'd say the vast, vast majority of people have not heard. It dominated the news for days. Had Toby Young been at the President's Club, do we think that he would have escaped so lightly as Walliams? Or is it because Walliams was on the 'right' side? That he was 'one of us'?

These are only ripples from an enormous series of waves, minor disturbances in a much larger storm. Every week, every day, it washes over us and tears our country apart and separates me and my dad and, maybe, you and yours. It makes us think the very worst of each other, that people with whom we disagree are not just wrong but pernicious. It's bigger than Brexit – although Brexit has put it on steroids – and without it Corbyn and Corbynism would not be the force that it is.

The questions are: what is it, where does it come from – and why has it helped Corbyn?

Politics used to be so simple. It was about left and right. You either wanted a bigger state or you wanted a smaller one, you wanted more money taxed from the rich and given to the poor or you didn't. You were either wealthy or you weren't, and which of these you were was the best predictor of your voting intention. As the American academic Peter Pulzer once said: 'Class is the basis of British party politics; all else is embellishment and detail.'

Today we have no such certainties. The left–right axis has been bisected at least a couple of times. Now we can add open vs closed, young vs old, educated vs uneducated, city vs small town. All of which today tends to give a better indicator of your politics than your class. Questions of identity and culture now occupy the centre of our national debate, especially among elites. When I was at *Newsnight* we used to joke about the daily 'identity politics' slot, the space every night when we'd debate the latest development or controversy over gender or sexuality or race. And it came, almost without fail. Such discussions would have been unimaginable probably even a decade or so before.

It's been a long time coming and is the result of a culmination of huge political and sociological forces that have been at play for decades. Indeed, you might argue that we're living in the end-state of the counter-cultural revolutions of the 1960s and 1970s when, basic economic questions of sustenance being largely (if not entirely) quashed by Labour's postwar welfare state (and those of similar institutions across the West), the development of the first modern 'youth culture' pushed questions of individual identity to the fore. It can be overstated – much of the British and wider Western youth culture was only slightly less conservative than its forebears. But there was frenetic activity at the margins, especially in the universities (a theme that continues in today's politics). Tony Judt, the late historian, had a better understanding of these intellectual currents and flows than anyone:

> Social justice no longer preoccupied radicals. What united the '60s generation was not the interest of all, but the needs and rights of each. 'Individualism' – the assertion of every person's claim to maximised private freedom and the unrestrained liberty to express autonomous desires and have them respected and institutionalised by society at large – became the left-wing watchword of the hour. Doing 'your own thing', 'letting it all hang out', 'making love, not war', these are not inherently unappealing goals, but they are of their essence private objectives, not public goods. Unsurprisingly, they led to the widespread assertion that 'the personal is political'.
>
> The politics of the 1960s thus devolved into an aggregation of individual claims upon society and the state. 'Identity' began to colonise public discourse: private identity, sexual identity, cultural identity ... However legitimate the claims of individuals and the importance of their rights, emphasising these carries an unavoidable cost: the decline of a shared sense of purpose.[1]

This emphasis on individual rights and self-expression, born in the 1960s, developed over subsequent decades and sat increasingly ill-at-ease with the social conservatism of much of the working class. But you can see a direct line from this 1960s intellectual rebirth to many of the vexed social questions of our own age and the politics that accompanies it.

Politics has become at once bigger and smaller. It has become bigger because the worries, concerns and problems of more groups and more people have entered the discourse and been acknowledged for the first time. Questions over equal pay, sexual discrimination, racial diversity, gender identity, gender relations are only really now being grappled with properly. But they are usually questions of the rights of the self, or of smaller groups of selves. It has become harder and made less sense to talk of a politics of the common good because politics has become dominated by discourse over the interests of ever-smaller competing groups or the violation of individual rights. This has even descended into the endless debate over offence: that individuals' own moral and perceptual universes must be protected against transgression by ideas or notions which that individual finds damaging. Hence the debate over so-called 'micro-aggressions' and 'no-platforming'. Now the ultimate political virtue is achieved by being seen to observe and protect those rights, and the ultimate sin is to transgress or question them. The idea that the 'personal is political', which began in the 1960s with the liberation of society from stultifying social and political norms, was apparently culminating in the twenty-first century with the development of insulated cultures for tinier and tinier groups and even individuals; it was becoming an endless contestation of what the correct way of living and even speaking should be, as well as a celebration of the 'diversity' and perceived atomisation of natural cultural life and relegation of their own importance as the dominant cultural/radical/political group. All of this flows from the rights-based political culture of the 1960s and 1970s. Many ordinary voters feel alienated from this sort of political settlement – 'political correctness gone mad', 'you can't say anything these days', etc. – and it helps fuel the rise of populist or anti-system political parties.

A few things have intensified those trends. The first were the breakdown of the postwar consensus in the 1970s and the development of the new right and their victories of the 1980s. As we've seen, the collectivist and statist model of the postwar period to a lesser or greater extent began to break down across the West; figures like Margaret Thatcher and Ronald Reagan used the opportunity to 'roll back the frontiers of the state' and forge a new pro-market consensus, in which the individual and choice were king. This was a project imbued with deep irony. What is not commonly appreciated about the new right and Thatcher in particular was that she had no interest in a purely economic enterprise. Though she deeply believed in a smaller state and open, freer markets, she had a grander vision. As she was to say towards the end of her premiership, weirdly echoing Marx, 'the method is economics, the point is to change the soul'.

What she meant by that is that she assumed that by shrinking the scope of the state she would force people to become more self-reliant and autonomous, but that in so doing she would restore a lost Victorian morality and ethical code. That society would inevitably return to the uncomplicated moral strictures of the Grantham of her 1930s childhood and away from the social illnesses induced by the 1960s permissive society: restrained, Christian, patriotic, conservative, with a strong degree of social conformity.

She couldn't have been more wrong. She and others failed to appreciate the truly breathtaking and extraordinary power of the market; that the privatisation of the economy would not stop in the public sphere but instead extend its tentacles into the private. That greater choice of how to spend our money would lead to greater choice and diversity in how we lived our lives, in the people we could be and identities that we could adopt. She failed to appreciate that liberalism, once out of its bottle, couldn't be contained or aimed only in one direction.

These trends have reached their apogee with those of my own generation, Generation Y, or the Millennials. But in other ways we are not liberals either. Our social liberalism is profound and non-negotiable – but our tolerance for alternative ideas that might disrupt our own rigid world view, of the values of the so-called open society, is low. Ironically, my generation's politics and those of others on one side of the culture war is a liberalism fused with a deep moral code. And that moral code was inculcated, developed and formalised almost universally at university.

THE RISE OF THE GRADUATEOCRACY

Britain has never been better educated. Even that sentence would probably ignite a mini-culture war – imagine the guffaws and howls from the *Daily Mail*'s letters page with tales of perfect recall of logarithms and being able to recount every capital city of the world while being simultaneously birched by the headmaster. Whatever they would say, it's true. As of mid-2017 there are over 14 million graduates in the UK; that's 42 per cent of the workforce. Even when compared to relatively recent times, that's a lot of people whose heads have been graced by a mortar board. As recently as 2002 the figure was only 25 per cent; less than a decade ago, in 2009, the figure was 30 per cent. Go still further back and they were a mere residuum. In 1964 Gallup wanted to check how graduates intended to vote in the upcoming general election. They had to give up on the idea because at less than 5 per cent of the population it was too difficult to find a sufficient sample number when conducting phone surveys.

Today we talk about 'graduates' as a significant political entity, a demographic in their own right. We are right to do so. It has become a cardinal characteristic and predictor of voting intention. As Matthew Goodwin, professor of politics at Kent University, has pointed out: 'Whether you look at the vote for Brexit, the vote for Trump or for Marine Le Pen, education was the biggest predictor of whether somebody would vote against the mainstream centre option.'

The arguments around this are complicated and disputed and we don't quite know what the relation is between university and broader political behaviour. But my point is wider – that a greater percentage of the workforce having been to university has generally led to a liberal and cosmopolitan world view that is at odds with the conservatism and social stickiness of many older, less educated voters. That seems to me to be indisputable.

The best sociological explanation of this comes down to the introduction of a second dimension in how people choose to vote. This is a big simplification but, broadly speaking, in the immediate postwar period there was left and there was right. People placed themselves on that spectrum and then judged which of the parties best adhered to that position and picked that party at election time. That held for a few decades but in the seventies, a second dimension emerges, a 'post-materialist' dimension, so-called because it alludes to Judt's idea that the material concerns, the conflict over resources that was at the heart of postwar politics, had been quelled through affluence. The second dimension was essentially a libertarian/authoritarian one, based on our social values, going from liberal to conservative. Hitherto no such axis existed because questions of identity were extremely muted. Western societies were remarkably homogenous and such questions did not therefore arise, in the main. But over time the two axes flipped in importance.

Universities led the way in the creation of the new-left movements Judt was speaking about. Despite the fact that at that time a much smaller proportion of the population enrolled in higher education (and far fewer still in the elite liberal institutions that formed the locus of these movements), they proved a motor of social and political change. These movements focused on issues of individual freedom and empowerment and breaking-out of social strictures, on sexuality, the environment and self-expression. As that generation filtered through and into positions of prominence, they began to drag left-wing political parties to the upper left-hand corner of the chart.

So if politics is now a compass, it's not just a question of going west to east but also north-west to south-east. And right-wing parties across the world are able to gain political advantage by emphasising to voters that they have more socially conformist ideas. Richard Nixon, with his talk of the 'silent majority' and tough rhetoric on crime and race, was the first right-wing leader to truly capitalise on this shift. That was the start of a trend, the beginning of an American political journey which would culminate forty years later in some of the US's poorest states voting for a plutocratic multi-billionaire. Not because he might be where they are on the first axis but because that axis barely seems to register any more. It is the second, the culture axis, that matters. And once you achieve cultural dominance, you can begin to change minds on the economic. Hence why some of the most hitherto progressive and redistributionist states in the United States, like Kansas, are today deeply libertarian.

Left-wing parties have struggled to adapt to this new world. They may still have been roughly where their voters were on the left-right scale but millions of voters across the globe have made a calculation that they are closer socially to a right-wing/conservative party. In short, as Chris Hanretty, professor of politics at East Anglia University, told me: 'University graduates fucked everything up, and pulled left-wing parties away from where they need to be.'

Recent research by French economist Thomas Piketty confirms this view. It shows that after the war right up (in Britain and America's case) to very recently, you were far more likely to vote for the left-wing party if you were less formally educated. If you were more educated you'd vote for the right. That has changed: today the more educated you are the more likely you are to vote for the left. Piketty shows that much of the transformation of our politics and the rise of populism is linked to the rise of graduates and the clash of cultural values that has flowed from it, arguing that many of those low-education voters (my family and those around them back in Birmingham) have been left unrepresented in modern politics: In the 1950s–60s, the vote for left-wing (socialist) parties in France and the Democratic Party in the US used to be associated with lower education & lower income voters. It (the left) has gradually become associated since 1970s–80s with higher education voters, giving rise to a multiple-elite party system: high-education elites vote for the left, while high-income/high-wealth elites for the right, i.e., intellectual elite (left) vs business elite (merchant right). Other groups might feel left behind [which tends to] populism?[2]

So often then, voters who don't share this common, university-derived understanding and way of talking about the world are dismissed as vulgar and uneducated. No better example of that could be the 'gammon' incident of early 2018, where Twitter was set alight with 'left-wingers' dismissing Brexit-voting white (but rosy-skinned) middle-aged men, written off as a joint of pinkish meat.

They did not have a place in the new identity politics. Yet they are, many of them – men like my dad – decent just, kind people, but who sit outside the new 'progressive' politics. Yet if a left is to mean anything, how could they so easily be discarded, practically or morally?*

One way or the other, with so many more now being proud owners of degree certificates, graduates' outlooks are a huge driver of the politics of now, especially on the progressive left.

But the vicissitudes of the culture war wouldn't be possible without the atomisation of our culture itself.

TECHNOLOGY AND LOST 'SHARED CULTURE'

What do you do on your Christmas Day? You might find yourself bingeing on Netflix. Maybe Charlie Brooker's latest *Black Mirror* offering.

Maybe you watch *Mrs Brown's Boys*? If so, you're not alone: it's the most watched TV programme on Christmas Day. My family love it.

---

* This new politics, which prizes culture and identity above class, manifests itself in all sorts of ways. A simple one by way of illustration: when I was at the BBC, I used to get into a state of apoplectic frustration with our policies around diversity. It was a corporation-wide aim to increase the number of women and ethnic minority voices on air – quite right too. However, I grew frustrated at the hamfistedness with which this was applied. There seemed no understanding that diversity might be about more than just what our political culture then prized – diversity you could see. I once emailed my editor asking if a northern working-class man was inherently less diverse (and interesting) than an Asian public-school-educated woman who lived in London? Whether all our diversity problems would be solved if 100 per cent of our guests went to one school and lived in the capital but were of different ethnicities and sexes. Finding it harder and harder to get stories commissioned about working-class issues, especially housing, while seeing running order after running order devoted to matters of culture, I felt my anger rising. It was, for me, the product of a bizarre wider political and cultural settlement.

You might be wincing at those words. I remember when it first came out. I was home for the weekend and my dad said: 'Hey, son, have you seen that new comedy, *Mrs Brown*? It's fantastic.'

'No, Dad, is it good?'

'It's brilliant, son,' my mum agreed, reverently nodding.

My dad put it on. You've probably guessed the rest.

I just did not get it. The jokes were hammy and you could see them coming a thousand miles away. The main character was like something from a 1970s variety show. And not a very varied one. I've seen Philip Hammond deliver better gags.

Yet I looked over to see my mum and dad in hysterics. I started laughing not out of embarrassment or at the jokes but because they found it so funny. We had a laugh about it.

I think if I showed my mum *Black Mirror* she would (a) not understand it, (b) find it disturbing, (c) wonder why anyone would want to watch something like that. Kind of how I felt about *Mrs Brown's Boys* really.

But here's the thing. I know that virtually everyone, most people of my sort of age in my social group, will like the one and dislike the other. And I bet you can guess which way round it is.

Go back thirty years, to 1986, and there's no doubt what we'd all have been doing on Christmas Day – watching *EastEnders*. It's astonishing to think now, but on Christmas Day 1986 no fewer than 30 million people (more than half the overall population) tuned in to watch Dirty Den give Angie their divorce papers at the back of the Queen Vic. Ten years later, 24 million – me and Mum included – were still tuning in to Tiffany being knocked over in the street. The year before, 25 million watched Del Boy sell that famous pocket watch and finally become a millionaire.

I remember these things vividly. And even though I'm not exactly an avid viewer of *EastEnders* myself these days, certain cultural moments stick in the mind. I've spoken about them to people of my own age. We've even pulled up Tiffany's scene on YouTube and had a good laugh about how she's somehow killed by a car clearly moving at about 10 mph.

The point is that you don't have to go back that far to find culture littered with shared moments, memories and mutual understanding. It still made sense to talk of a popular shared culture.

Does it really now? Even on Christmas Day, the time of year we have most opportunity to all sit down and do the same thing, *Call the Midwife* got about 9 million views in 2017.* You could count the number of programmes throughout the year to get over 10 million on fewer than ten fingers.

There is more choice than ever before. In 1986 you barely had four channels to choose from. Save from the occasional repeat if you missed it, you missed it. Today not only are there hundreds of channels but also TV viewing opportunities that aren't even on channels: Netflix, Amazon Prime, Apple TV. Far from being restricted, the choices are overwhelming. I can guarantee I'll have at least one conversation a week with a friend who asks: 'Have you seen xyz on Netflix?' Almost certainly I'll have missed it in the interim and watched something else, which I'll recommend to them and which they, likewise, will have missed. We both say we'll make a mental note to watch the other's recommendations. We seldom will.

And it's not just television. The digitisation of culture and explosion of choice have reached every arena of cultural life: how many number ones are now a must-buy? How many soundtracks to the summer are there? How many films mean everyone goes to the cinema? With the packaging up and Balkanisation of sports rights, how many sporting events can all of us even enjoy if we don't have the right TV box at home? They are all few and far between. These days we don't always share even the communal experience of the public world with the people immediately next to us on the street, or on the train or bus, because we're too busy enjoying the private experience of our digital lives through our phones, narrating the world as we see it ourselves through a plethora of different online media platforms.

---

* And that's the consolidated rating, i.e. after iPlayer, recordings and on-demand services have been considered. The number who watched it live was lower still.

And it's not hard to see the effects of cultural self-selection on my trade either. Today the apps for both of my main employers, Sky and the BBC, offer a service where you see only the news most likely to interest you.

So culture is going through the same process of hyper-individualisation that the public services and the state and market experienced a quarter of a century ago. The idea of an individualised culture might ostensibly seem an oxymoron but it is the clear direction of travel. A friend in another area of the BBC told me that work was being done on dramas with multiple endings, in which the user controls the plot, and it could potentially go in several different directions. Not only would we be consuming culture at different times but potentially with different conclusions, powered by our own preferences too. But, for the moment, culture is being consumed by groups, with fewer formats and programmes proving to have genuine cross-demographic/class/age appeal. In these circumstances, it's easy to see why the Labour MP Stella Creasy has argued that, culturally, we are 'a nation that is becoming ships that pass in the night'. We are drifting further and further apart, and with fewer uniting shared reference points and experiences our shared understanding declines and the propensity for cultural conflict increases.

WHY DOES IT MATTER?

The effects of the culture war are manifold. But for our purposes I'd say they break down into three broad areas:

1. **'Alternative facts':** It's not hard to see the link between self-selecting cultural experience and the culture war and some of the difficulties Western democracies have experienced recently. With the hyper-individualisation of cultural experience it is easy to see why the successful operation of the democratic space and public realm more generally has become fraught. Healthy and well-functioning democratic polities

require some commonly if not near universally accepted truths, and at the very least impartial places to exchange competing ones. Americans have played this game for longer than us. Cable news and talk radio began to cater for different political persuasions and hues decades ago. The result has been a fractious and frankly debased political discourse where each side either trusts only its own sources of news information (be it Fox or MSNBC) or none at all. The internet has accelerated and intensified this process with the endless new and often unhinged 'news' websites, like Breitbart or the Canary, peddling factual relativism and misleading, inaccurate or 'fake' news, and hearsay.

2. **Accelerated social change:** We are undergoing a revolution in manners and attitudes, especially on social affairs. Many of the arguments are long overdue and many represent a clear evolution of our mores. For example, the revelations over Harvey Weinstein have provoked welcome deep introspection about the nature of gender relations and relative power between the sexes. But the endless domination of discourse by questions of identity has clearly alienated often less educated and less liberal sections of the electorate. That has left space open for the right – who are often keen to fight a culture war of their own – to try and bring these people into their political orbit. Brexit and Trump are a series of revanchist counter-reactions in that culture war.
3. **Left-wing malaise:** Cultural atomisation makes it harder for the left to succeed. The lack of shared experience, the hyper-individualisation of culture and consumption, must almost by definition pose problems for the left. The left side of the political spectrum relies on a modicum of shared experience to exist, to encourage empathy and solidarity in the face of adversity. The breakdown of solidarity, of mutual interest within society, poses a much greater problem for the left than for the right, which could deal with the rise of nationalism in a way that the left could not. Certainly, when I started writing

> this book, that was a major diagnosis for the travails of the left not only in Britain but around the West. It was a given that with the breakdown of class loyalties and affiliation that the left was struggling to retain the traditional working-class voters it needed while at the same time alienating them through a focus on social liberal issues. As Nick Pearce told me before the election: 'There are lots of reasons why the left finds it hard to do identity politics. It seems to be clear that in the last decade the expressive dimension of people's politics has become more powerful … you're trying to replace a class identity with something else, then national identities are there to be used and remain potent sources of affection and belonging. The left hasn't found it easy to contest that terrain.'

And certainly, this was the principal analysis that existed before the general election result of 2017. Across the West the pattern was the same. Social democratic parties were becoming stronger with better educated voters in urban centres but they weren't replacing their more traditional blue collar voters who felt socially alienated from their old parties, whom they were losing by the bucketload. There didn't look to be much of a way around it.

I don't want to get into the weeds of the 2017 general election result, we'll save that for later. But suffice to say this: Brexit turbo-charged the culture war in Britain, accelerated its progress and provided Corbyn with a lifeline. It was coming anyway, but it's telling from Piketty's analysis that Labour had in fact managed to do better than the French Socialists or the American Democrats in maintaining its hold on lower education voters. Brexit changed that. Its introduction provided clear comprehensive camps and tribes of which we could be members, and new cultural identities of 'Remainer' and 'Leaver' to boot. Polling shows that we feel greater emotional and political connection with those terms than with political parties or even ideologies. Its fusion with cultural dislocation gave Theresa May an opportunity. She sensed Labour's weakness in dealing with questions of identity. May made a direct pitch to those voters in the general election. No one anticipated that there would be a cultural counterattack in the form of Jeremy Corbyn. A bourgeois coalition of the liberal, the educated and the European internationalists had had enough of being kicked around and kicked back.

This is the best way of understanding the appeal (if not the content) of Corbynism. It is the end game of the old foundations of left-wing politics and the beginning of the new. It is a political response to the financial crisis but it is also a British form of generational bourgeois cultural counter-reaction to Brexit and populist forces. It is a populism for the educated middle class and their liberalism, derived and cultivated through a common education; while for its younger members, it fuses with frustration – a vehicle of protest at not enjoying the fruits of the bourgeois life their parents had enjoyed, despite having the same or better education. And Corbyn is lucky – the left has for decades been screwed by that second dimension on the political compass pulling them off course. It is possible that now, with so many millions of graduates in the workforce, sharing a more liberal world view, that the numbers are there in the population to at least make viable a winning political project based around a politics like Corbyn's. Once you understand that, you see not only why these new forces have sat so uncomfortably within a traditional social democratic, technocratic political party but also why Corbyn won and why candidates like Cooper and Burnham now seem hopelessly out of date. Identity is what matters and that is why Corbyn, whose personal identity is so secure and in whose political identity it is so easy to share and bask, has done so much better than expected.

In an era where values and authenticity are considered the ultimate virtues and the messy business of compromise and middle ground are so reviled, the idea of a man who has on the face of it held true to his own beliefs is so appealing. In an era where your opponents aren't just wrong but ethically and morally compromised, where their actions and beliefs inexorably lead to the subjugation of others, there is no public value in compromising with the other side. Purity is everything. This is not a war that Corbyn started but it is the territory on which he now fights and from where he draws much of his appeal.

It is why Corbyn's opponents were wrong. He has proved to be the perfect vehicle for the politics of now. In much the same way that Corbyn would not have been successful in the 1990s, likewise Blair would not be successful in the late 2010s. Even supporters like Clive Lewis accept Corbyn's appeal is new: 'I mean if Jeremy Corbyn had stood five or ten years ago he would have gone down to a defeat; he didn't, he stood in 2015 and he was in the right place at the right time and history is often about people being in the right place at the right time.' Because he has managed, curiously, to channel the hyper-individualised politics of millions of followers and through him it is refracted as a politics of the common good. Many millions were attracted to his vision of social justice, many millions more were attracted to him out of desperation that their lives hadn't been what was promised to them, but many more were attracted to him because he had accidentally become the leader of their tribe and crucially had given their tribe meaning and some coherence. Saying you're a supporter of Corbyn on your Instagram or Facebook page, or sharing Corbyn memes of the 'absolute boy', says something about yourself and about your social virtue. It is the ultimate symbol that you're on the right side of history and of the war.

The irony of all this is that I suspect it is a vision of politics that neither Corbyn nor his senior lieutenants necessarily share. It is probably still just class, not culture that is the base unit of their political thought, especially for those like John McDonnell, a self-described Marxist who no doubt shares his materialist conception of history. They are thus unwitting warriors of the culture war. But inadvertently they have become its prize fighters. In so doing they may yet discover that the working classes aren't cheering them on – worse, that they have even switched sides.

Chapter 6

A CLASS APART

Poor Evelyn Waugh. It was certainly not the Festival of his Britain. For those sections of the upper- and middle-classes of whose subconscious anxieties he is the curator the Festival marked the climax of a decade in which almost every single act of government had been inimical to their immediate interests. Festival Britain was the Britain of the radical middle-classes, the do-gooders; the readers of the News Chronicle, *the* Guardian, *and the* Observer; *the signers of petitions; the backbone of the BBC. In short, the Herbivores, or gentle ruminants, who look out from the lush pastures which are their natural station in life with eyes full of sorrow for less fortunate creatures, guiltily conscious of their advantages, though not usually ceasing to eat the grass. And in making the Festival they earned the contempt of the Carnivores – the readers of the* Daily Express; *the Evelyn Waughs; the cast of the Directory of Directors – the members of the upper- and middle-classes who believe that if God had not wished them to prey on all smaller and weaker creatures without scruple he would not have made them as they are.*

Michael Frayn on the Festival of Britain

If you've never been to the Durham Miners' Gala, you should add it to your summer 'festival' list. A more joyous jamboree of politics, of anything, does not exist. Every year, tens of thousands of people descend upon that jewel of the north-east, packing into its narrow, cute streets to celebrate kith, kin and a way of life long gone. Intricately woven banners depict collieries closed long after the men and women holding them aloft were born. It is the Glastonbury of the labour movement – the 'Big Get Together'.

The gala began in 1871, when the Trimdon Colliery branch miners marched from Trimdon to Durham. Their descendants, marching under the same banner, are still making the same journey from Trimdon 146 years later. In July 2017, I went with them. At 8 a.m. – yes, 8 a.m. – it felt like the whole of the north-east was in the pub. The sun beat down and bacon and sausage sandwiches were being served, washed down with … pints. It's at times like that I remember why my dad (hailing from just down the road) can – and always will – drink me under the table.

As the summer heat rose, we marched, slowly but surely, around the streets of Trimdon, mums, dads, kids, nans, grandads, families and friends. People were emerging from their houses, in their dressing gowns, pyjamas and sometimes not much at all, and waving as we went by. At the village green, everyone just stopped and held hands.

There was no order of service, no programme, no one in a high-vis jacket telling everyone what happened next. There was a simple shared understanding, a mutual recognition of patterns and rhythms passed on from one year to the next. And now was the moment to mourn. To remember fathers, sons, brothers and uncles lost long ago beneath their feet and in the darkness. As the hymn came to its end, a priest stepped forward, bellowing at the top of his lungs for all to hear, setting the march on its way: 'We give thanks for their labour, their sacrifice, for daring to dream of justice and opportunity as we prepare to march, in memory of yesterday, to strike open the path of our fathers as we prepare to bring about the hopes of today.'

It was deeply moving. As the muted horns played, I looked over and the women who had walked to the end of their gardens were weeping.

In a world where working-class people are so often depicted as feckless bingers, the Miners' Gala is a part of life, a part of England, you don't often see. When you think of the village green, you think of the *Bake Off* tent, of cricket whites, of old posh Penelope Keith-type ladies, carrying trays of Pimm's and cucumber sandwiches. But this is a no less quintessentially English scene, bringing together the social history, work and social pleasures of ordinary people.

When we arrived in Durham, I chatted to David Gibson, who arranges the trek down from Trimdon. He is a former miner himself and for him the day is a melancholy one: 'We have a lot to celebrate but it's mixed emotions up here. We've got no industry left. You've seen the state of the communities through having no industry. But we're celebrating what we *had*.'

But this year there was something new to celebrate. The gala came only weeks after the general election. What could have been a wake became a belated victory party. David was a happy man: 'Jeremy Corbyn – crackin' lad! We should have had him years ago.'

On the Old Elvet road in the city, the County Hotel balcony is the traditional spot where the labour movement's top brass take in the parade. For the past few decades most Labour leaders have politely but firmly declined the invitation. Corbyn had no such compunction. As my producer and I tried to work out a way we could sneak into the hotel to try and get an interview, we watched him, out of the corner of our eyes, beaming, almost regally waving at the crowd below.

But the thing is, I'm not sure how many people were that thrilled to see him. At one point, outside the hotel, a few people chanced their luck: 'Oooooh, Jer-e-myyyy Corr-byn!' they cried. I waited. There were a few echoes. But there was no roar, no guttural, joyous wall of noise. Most of the families and their kids barely noticed; they were too busy laughing, dancing, waving at the smiling faces beaming back at them from the parade. Days before, Corbyn had had another engagement: headlining at Glastonbury. There, among the tens of thousands of faces, his name ricocheted from body to body, an endless verbal percussion.

These sounds of the summer, in their own ways, say something about the changing electoral base of the Labour Party, and about Corbyn's unique brand of populism. The middle-class twenty-, thirty-, forty- and fifty-somethings shouted louder and with passion, easily beating the clamour of the colliery crowd.

Because – whisper it – for all the talk of the downtrodden, the dispossessed and the down-and-outs, the beating heart of Corbynism – its primary proponents, its foot soldiers and many of its beneficiaries – is the middle not the working class. It is an outfit of the professionals, the culturally immersed, the Remainers, the urban.

Go to any Labour Party meeting today and you will find a great many worthy and engaged people. In some constituencies you will find truly enormous numbers. Some CLPs like Haringey and Brighton now boast thousands of members. They are also likely to be cut from a very similar cloth – and it is not from a cloth cap: 77 per cent of the party's members are drawn from ABC1 groups, or the professional classes, in other words. For all the talk of a membership that is broad-based and a cross-section of Britain, that percentage is only slightly lower than the figures for the Conservatives or Liberal Democrats. And the members aren't all Remainer youngsters either. The average age of Labour Party members is 53 and they are still more likely to be male. You do meet a lot of returnees who rejoined the party after having left over Iraq.

And the very top of the Labour Party too is similar. Seumas Milne (son of a former Director-General of the BBC, Alasdair Milne), Director of Communications and Strategy, is an Old Wykehamist,* as is James Schneider, a prominent Corbyn aide, and Corbyn himself went to the voluntary-aided Adams Grammar School. The top of the Labour Party is populated by many posh boys (and they are mainly boys) with a penchant for hard-left politics.

Sometimes, just sometimes, talking to some of the new recruits to the party, you can't help but feel that if they met an actual working-class person they might find it a deeply dispiriting experience. It's a

---

* i.e. a pupil of Winchester College.

feeling I share with a fellow Brummie, Jess Phillips MP: 'Thing is, the problem with the Labour Party right now is that we're generally sneery middle-class elitists and that's a fact. That's not true, I have to say, of the PLP. The Labour Party is a different thing. But the party has become sneery. It's not all of them. Most of them, lots of them, are lovely. But this sort of righteousness. Righteousness is the prize.' She goes on to say that the dominance of posher people in the party makes campaigning and winning votes harder for the party right now:

'Literally go to any Constituency Labour Party. And speak to anyone who is comfortably off in a meeting. And have them talk about poor people who should have stuff done at them. It's always like: we have got to help these people! These people are nothing and have no agency. Their idea of women's rights is not to think about advocating leadership or that women self-advocating is the thing. No, it's that we've got to help you. Look, poor women. We have to turn up and wring our hands. About how awful it is, about this or that, about being women. We never empower or do anything, and that is not what the Labour movement was. It was the empowerment of a mass of people. Now it feels like a pitying of a mass of people. I don't want to be pitied.' The voters seem to have responded to all this, and it doesn't make for happy reading for a party wishing, as Corbyn said, to return to its 'working-class, socialist roots'.

Paula Sturridge's constituency-by-constituency analysis paints a picture of a party, far from reconnecting with its working-class base, accelerating its decoupling. Sturridge's analysis showed comprehensively that the more working class a constituency was, the more it swung to the Conservatives. Specifically, she found that for every 10 per cent more working-class voters in a constituency, there tended to have been a fall of about 3 per cent in the Labour vote and a rise of about 5 per cent in the Tory vote between 2010 and 2017. Sturridge makes a broad sweep over the party's performance too, examining its results since 2010. It shows that, far from the party recovering ground in its base since 2010 and 2015, the 'bourgeoisification' has intensified. She finds that since 2015 the party has lost support from non-graduates and voters in ethnically homogeneous areas. At the same time, it has gained support, relatively speaking, from the reverse. In other words, Labour's traditional base likes Corbyn's Labour less and its new coalition likes it a bit more.

There are a few things to say about this. The first is that, in and of itself, you could argue: well, at least it worked. Corbyn may have done worse than Miliband with the party's traditional base, but (a) it's much, much better than many predicted only weeks before the election, and (b) it's still a better overall performance than Miliband ever achieved. There is such a thing as the Corbyn coalition, a genuine social and political base that exists in the country, and it came out to vote for him, inspired by his brand of politics. You can't say that about everybody.

But the party that was born, made and designed to represent the interests of working people should not rest easy as its traditional working-class support bleeds away. Nor can we know how contingent the coalition was on the Brexit result, nor how sticky a voting base determined by age and demography can be in comparison to a politics based on class attachment, which we know has been enduring. Things have also got worse since the general election, with some polls in the summer of 2018 showing that the Conservatives had taken the lead with C2DE (working-class) voters.

There's another irony too. With the Labour Party becoming increasingly culturally bourgeois, you might argue that Corbyn is continuing Blair's work; indeed surpassing him. The entire ethos of the New Labour project was to attract the middle classes to the Labour flame. Corbyn is achieving that at levels Blair could only have dreamed of. It is one of the many reasons why no matter how much pressure he receives to reverse his stance on the abolition of tuition fees and invest the money in early-years or sure-start centres, Corbyn never will. The policy is catnip to his new middle-class base. Middle-class graduates are now to Labour what pensioners are to the Conservatives. Corbyn knows where his sourdough bread is buttered.

When we take all of this in the round, we have a much fuller idea of what Corbynism has become, what it has evolved into if not by design but by a combination of circumstances, the peculiarities of the historical moment we are in. It is a bourgeois force in a working-class party with a potentially revolutionary leadership.

Chapter 7

THE TAKEOVER

Afterwards I went to North St Pancras Labour management committee. Terrible. Constantly passing mad motions denouncing the government, if ever the party – and government – is really controlled by these middle class, left wing neurotics, who represent and are typical of nobody but themselves, then that is the end of either the labour government or of Britain.

Bernard Donoghue, *The Downing Street Diaries*, 1977

We've got our party back.

Neil Kinnock, 2010, upon hearing that Ed Miliband had defeated David

Alfriston isn't the sort of place you might imagine a former Labour chancellor of the exchequer to live. It's a sleepy, dreamy, rolling East Sussex village, right in the middle of the glorious South Downs. It's one of those places you walk through safe in the knowledge that, save for the cars and the contents of the shop windows, it remains proudly unchanged from fifty years ago, will be so in fifty years' time, and you sigh and you breathe and you smile, because that's one of the glories of living in a country as philosophically and physically eternal as

England. And so perhaps, after all, it's exactly the sort of place you might expect to find Denis Healey, a man with England in his bones.

When I met him, on 1 July 2015, my twenty-sixth birthday, at the front door of his glorious 1930s house, Pingles Place, perched atop the highest hill in the village, those bones hadn't long left. He had just celebrated his ninety-eighth birthday and I was going to interview him about the seventieth anniversary of the 1945 general election, in which he, as Major Denis Healey, was the Labour candidate for the Otley division, just outside Leeds.

As I knocked on Healey's door, the sun beating down, I heard nothing. It suddenly occurred to me that I hadn't phoned ahead. I'd booked in the date weeks before. I began to castigate myself: of course, he's forgotten, he's 98, how could I have been so stupid, his children have probably taken him out for the day. He could be in hospital. He could just be asleep.

And then I heard it. Singing. Muffled at first, then louder. I looked around and realised it was coming from inside the house, scratchy but a perfectly formed lilting melody. I peered inside the small fuzzy window and could see a patchwork of distorted colours, mainly tans and light blues and beiges, shuffling towards the door.

When it opened, I saw before me one of the giants of twentieth-century British politics. A crumpled giant. Like an oil painting left out in the sun too long, a faded picture of the man I'd seen in a score of documentaries and books: he looked made less of flesh than of paper. His legs were extremely thin, painted with indigo bruises and markings. I was glad that the air was still, for if not he might have blown over.

As he stood there, wearing shorts so short that for one horrified moment I wondered if he hadn't worn any trousers, I didn't quite know what to say.

'Hello!'

'Hello, Lord Healey, I'm here from the BBC.'

'Have you paid?'

'I'm sorry?'

'Have you paid?'

You could tell he was an ex-chancellor. I lied and said we had. He relaxed instantly and invited us inside.

He was entirely alone in that big sprawling house, but was more or less living in one room. A room full to the rafters with VHS tapes of ballet and opera and theatre performances, and books of poetry, and paintings. It was clear that his trademark hinterland was as broad as ever. But alongside the Keats and the Shelley there were a few reminders that this old man, this former chancellor of the exchequer, defence secretary, colossus of his time, was still just an old man, like all the other old men, sitting in their chairs, looking out of the window thinking of times past, next to old copies of the *Radio Times* with programmes circled in biro, half-empty pill boxes and wine gum packets. The room's walls were scattered with yellow Post-it notes, presumably written by his nurses, with messages like: 'REMEMBER: Drink seven glasses of water – PER DAY!' and 'REMEMBER: Keep your feet up!' I asked how often they visited: 'Every two days.' Aside from that, with his children abroad and his beloved wife Edna dead for five years, he was alone.

He was a bit forgetful about the recent past, especially the very recent past – he asked us to remind him why we'd come at least three or four times and often forgot he'd just made the point before making it again, but his long-term memory was just fine. I wondered afterwards why this is so often the case with old people. Instinctively, you'd think it might be the other way around. I'm sure there's a biological reason but part of me wondered whether it was the body protecting itself; after all, who wants to remember the recent past, the last few weeks of being alone and old? Decaying, the endless days stretching out without form ahead of you. Better, instead, to live in the days of past glory, of vigour and excitement and wonder. For me, he was a treasure trove. I asked what he thought of Wilson, of Castle, of Callaghan, of Benn. I'd mostly heard him say it before in the interviews and documentaries I'd watched, or read in numerous accounts, but it was still a thrill to hear him say it. He hadn't lost any of his wit either. I tried to ask if, were he a young man in 2015, he would have gone into politics. He cut me off as soon as I got to 'if you were a young man':

'I am a young man, what the fuck – what the fucking hell are you talking about?'

He then flashed the widest toothless grin.

Inevitably I asked him about his battles with the left in the 1980s. He spoke of his antipathy for Tony Benn and told us how, in later life, both widowed, they had reconciled and become friends once more. But, he said, he could never understand his doctrinaire approach, right up to the end. He asked us if he could read a section of his memoir, *Time of My Life*, to camera on the subject. We readily agreed. This is what he read, a section from his 1959 Labour Party conference speech in Blackpool, where he was chastising the left, who were arguing that the party's recent defeat had been due to its not embracing a sufficiently socialist platform:

> There are far too many people who want to luxuriate complacently in moral righteousness in Opposition. But who is going to pay the price for their complacency?
>
> You can take the view that it is better to give up half a loaf if you cannot get the whole loaf, but the point is that it is not we who are giving up the half loaf. In Britain, it is the unemployed and old age pensioners and outside Britain there are millions of people in Asia and Africa who desperately need a Labour government in this country to help them. If you take the view that it is all right to stay in Opposition so long as your Socialist heart is pure, you will be all right, Jack. You will have your TV set, your motorcar and your summer holidays on the Continent and keep your Socialist soul intact. The people who pay the price for your sense of moral satisfaction are the Africans, millions of them, being forced into racial slavery; the Indians and the Indonesians dying of starvation.
>
> We are not just a debating society. We are not just a Socialist Sunday School. We are a great movement that wants to help real people living on earth at the present time. We shall never be able to help them unless we get power. We shall never get power unless we close the gap between our active workers and the average voter in the country.[1]

At the time, I had no idea how searingly relevant that speech would once again become to the Labour Party's future in just a few months' time. Neither did Healey; he said he didn't pay much attention to politics any more – he found it dull – and he died just a few months after we met. We'll never know what he'd have made of the Corbyn takeover of the party and its success in the 2017 election. Either way, back in those hazy summer days of 2015, he told me that he didn't think the battles he'd fought so vigorously in the 1980s, against the left, would ever be repeated.

In one sense, he was right. There is no battle now. The picture is entirely different from his day. Because the left have comprehensively won.

It's important to get a sense of how big and how unprecedented the scale of the takeover of the Labour Party by the left is. It has never, ever happened before. Today for the first time the Labour left controls every organ of the Labour Party: the leadership, the trade unions and the National Executive Committee.

This is curious because, as we've seen, some of the real cultural power of the Corbyn project is derived from the idea that the party was, in some respect, going back to its roots, that it was becoming 'authentically' Labour once more. In particular, Corbyn is fond of saying that under his leadership the party has returned to being a 'socialist' party. But the truth is that certainly in the postwar period, and arguably ever, the Labour Party was never truly socialist and the left was never in control. Not in the 1980s, not in the 1960s, not in the 1950s, not in the 1940s.*

---

* Nor did it wield significant influence at the party's genesis. A survey of the favourite authors and writings of the first generation of Labour MPs in the early twentieth century revealed a bibliography that wouldn't have seemed terribly out of place to an average reformist Victorian gentleman. The list contained works by Dickens, Thomas Carlyle, John Ruskin, William Morris and – crucially – the Bible. As Harold Wilson famously put it, the party 'owed more to Methodism than to Marxism'.

You can think about the Labour Party as being comprised of – broadly speaking – four separate strands: the Blairites (very relaxed about free markets and especially in their delivery of public services), the old right (who were broadly social democratic but very pro-defence and often socially conservative, epitomised by figures like James Callaghan), the soft left people like Neil Kinnock, Ed Miliband, or Harold Wilson, and then the hard left, which would take in most famously Tony Benn and now Corbyn and those around him. Generally speaking the party's leadership has alternated between the right and the soft left, as the chart below shows:

Clement Attlee (1935–55)	Right/soft left
Hugh Gaitskell (1955–63)	Right
Harold Wilson (1963–76)	Soft left
James Callaghan (1976–80)	Right
Michael Foot (1980–83)	Soft left/left
Neil Kinnock (1983–92)	Soft left
John Smith (1992–4)	Right
Tony Blair (1994–2007)	Blairite
Gordon Brown (2007–10)	Blairite
Ed Miliband (2010–15)	Soft left
Jeremy Corbyn (2015–)	Left

Every leader since the war – indeed nearly every leader since the party's birth* – has been on the right or centre or soft left of the party. Occasionally, leaders have sung from the leftist hymn sheet and have greatly irritated left-wing members of Parliament by quickly or slowly shifting in outlook, of whom Harold Wilson and Kinnock are good examples. Corbyn's ascension therefore represents a new start for the party, in that it (a) has an avowedly left-wing leader and (b) has a left-wing leader who seems determined to remain that way.

* With the possible exception of the brief and lamentable leadership of George Lansbury in the 1930s.

It is also the first time the party has had a leader of the New Left, i.e. of the political and cultural responses to the changes of the 1960s and 1970s. This important distinction is not widely understood. It is one of the reasons why, in the wake of Corbyn's first victory, a lot of ink and bytes in cyberspace were wasted on both sides with the incorrect claim that the party had returned to the 1980s. This was nonsense. True, some of the characters are the same – Corbyn himself was a minor player in Tony Benn's outer circle. Jon Lansman was doing what Jon Lansman still does, arguing for more Labour Party democracy (Denis Healey's memoir recalls Lansman in 1981: 'Jon Lansman, a twenty-three-year-old unemployed graduate, was a key organiser for CLPD'). Other players, both local and national, are also the same, creating a sense of continuity. But, in terms of leadership, its success, its moment in history and its ideology, what we've seen since 2015 is of an entirely different order to the 1980s.

To start with leadership, Michael Foot, with whom Corbyn has again and again been compared, was a quite different political creature and not a left-winger as we understand the term today. He was not 'outside the tent', in any respect. Foot had been a distinguished cabinet minister throughout the 1970s Labour governments. As leader of the House and deputy prime minister he gave a virtuoso parliamentary performance on the night of the Callaghan government's last stand in its vote of no confidence, leading the debate and the defence of the government. He had also been employment secretary under Wilson and had held a string of junior ministerial posts before that. He was a machine insider. By 1980 he'd run for leader twice and deputy leader too.

Michael Foot was of the left but not a Bennite. He was a romantic, a man of letters, never happier than when discussing the works of Jonathan Swift within the world of literary reviews. He was, essentially, the last of the old Hampstead socialists, probably more at home in the 1880s than in the decade and century in which he found himself. What he was not, what he could not be, was part of the hard left that Tony Benn and later Jeremy Corbyn came to epitomise.

Indeed, the idea that Foot's leadership in any way mirrored the so-called 'hostile takeover' of 2015 is risible. In 1980 he was the candidate of the majority of Labour MPs. He was chosen over the more electable Denis Healey because it was perceived that the abrasive and truculent Healey might be too divisive; Foot, by contrast, was a more emollient if wan candidate. This could hardly be a greater contrast with Corbyn, who carried the support of at most 10 per cent of the party's MPs. As Healey was to tell me three decades later: 'They [Labour MPs] wanted an easy life. They thought they'd get an easier one with Michael, than they thought they would have done with me. They were right. But I should have worked harder for it.'

Moreover Corbyn, by contrast to Foot's senior status, spent over 30 years on the backbenches. Until his spectacularly rapid elevation, Corbyn's biggest claim to fame had been his record of defying his party whip over 500 times. And in terms of ideology Corbyn, by any stretch of the imagination, hails from a more doctrinaire wing of the party. As former deputy leader of the party Roy Hattersley told me: 'The situation now is altogether different and worse by comparison to the 1980s. Not least because I think Corbyn is much less reasonable and susceptible to reason than Michael Foot was.'

By this, among other things, he means that, reasonable or not, Foot was not a pacifist. Although he did believe in abolishing Britain's nuclear weapons capability, he supported the Thatcher government in its prosecution of the Falklands War; it would be unimaginable to think Corbyn would do the same. He was not interested in so-called 'command and control', nor in promoting the hegemony of one faction of the party. He was not a sectarian. It's why he immediately made Healey his deputy leader in 1980. He was furious with Tony Benn for attempting to wrest it from him. He begged Shirley Williams and David Owen not to split from the party and was desperate to preserve a big tent approach, with no one tradition destroying the other. He ought to be seen, then, not as an active partisan on the battlefield but rather, in the recent tradition of Wilson and Callaghan, as a leader who did his best to mediate between the different wings of the party. Jeremy Corbyn (like Tony Blair before him) is not of that school of thought. His project is about ensuring the Labour Party remains in the hands of people like him, permanently; indeed, it is his cardinal aim. In any case, today's Corbynite left aren't keen to claim Foot either. As Paul Mason has written: 'Michael Foot was a dire leader not because he was too old or too left wing (or wore a duffel-coat), but because he was a compromise candidate, constantly torn between the interests of the unions – who were largely on the right – and the membership, which had moved left.' It's something about which Tony Blair agrees, telling me:

'It's worse than the 1980s ... for sure it's worse than the 1980s. For one: at no point in the Labour Party in a hundred years has the left ever taken the leadership. I mean Michael Foot wasn't on the far left and was unlikely to become prime minister, I mean he was deputy prime minister of the Labour government. First time I met Michael Foot I was the lawyer, the young lawyer for the Labour Party and he was my client and the issue was the expulsion of Militant. Today you've got the Labour Party leadership which is trying to encourage these people into the Labour Party not throw them out. So, no, that is a lot more serious. And secondly: the world moves faster so I think this is a pretty existential crisis for the Labour Party.'

Although Foot's rather hairshirt style and pleasant demeanour might prompt superficial comparisons with Corbyn, they are only that.

THROUGH THE LOOKING GLASS

Besides, the comparison with the 1980s doesn't give Jeremy Corbyn and his team nearly enough credit for the scale of their political achievement. The left of the 1980s would give their hind teeth to wield the sort of power that their modern counterparts now enjoy. Then, while the left was strong on the party's National Executive Committee and within many local parties like Birkenhead and Lambeth, they remained relatively isolated. It thrived best in small, isolated parties that had been allowed to decay by the central party and become moribund, and therefore were easier to infiltrate.

The most successful infiltrator of them all, the Militant tendency, the great bogeyman of early 1980s politics, at most controlled two councils (Liverpool and Lambeth) and could boast only three Members of Parliament. Shadow cabinet elections meant that the shadow cabinet was largely controlled by moderates. The left couldn't even secure the deputy leadership in 1981. Tony Benn lost by a hair's breadth to Denis Healey, by less than 0.2 per cent ('or half a hair on half an eyebrow', as Healey was to later put it), but lose he did. The unions were also much more evenly divided between left and right than they are today. Despite entryism, at that time it was widely perceived that ordinary Labour Party members were suspicious of Bennism. Certainly, the members' representatives on the party's National Executive Committee tended to return moderate candidates. After their defeat for the deputy leadership in 1981, the power of the left gradually receded. Once the catastrophe of the 1983 general election was out of the way, the story of the Labour Party was one of gradual shuffling, and sometimes sharp lurching, to the right. The leftist insurgency lasted for a few years at most. It was a tale of weakness as much as strength.

This is not to undermine or undervalue the strength of the battles waged in the party in the 1980s. They were poisonous and bitter. They inflicted scars that never healed, on both sides. The left was more powerful than it had been for many decades, but it was a burst of light across a sky that faded quickly. Contrast that with the situation today.

In the 1980s the hard left couldn't win the deputy leadership. Arguably, it had never truly won a leadership contest in the party's history.* By 2016, it had won two in twelve months. Likewise, control

---

* Purists will point out many examples of candidates who arguably ran on leftist platforms. Of course, Foot, whose leftist genealogy I've addressed, but also Harold Wilson, who ran as the left candidate in 1963. My response to this would be that Wilson, though nominally on the left at the time, acted as leader and as prime minister in a very different way. He was clearly not of the hard left and simply used it as a convenient way to ascend to the leadership. It seems unthinkable that Jeremy Corbyn would act in a similar fashion today.

of local parties is much stronger today than it was then. Corbyn garnered support from hundreds of CLP nominations, from a real and sustained mass movement in the style of other grassroots organisations, like Podemos, in other European countries.

And that isn't surprising when you consider the very different historical and political currents at work in the 1980s and now. Too often we (and journalists are the worst of all for it) look for historical parallels and expect them to play out in the same way in our own age, 'first as tragedy, then as farce'. But in fact, the past can at best provide a script with half the stage directions missing. An echo, rather than a score.

So it is today. Bennism and Corbynism, although related and similar, have walked on to the stage at entirely different historical moments. Bennism was a political and even moral response to the breakdown of a leftist consensus, the slow decline of a postwar era, the contours of which had been set by Labour governments. Benn and his followers argued that the answer was to embrace a hard-left approach, both within the party and in the country, adopting a siege economy and mass democratisation of Labour, centralising control in the hands of local management committees. Thatcherism and Bennism, doctrinaire, draconian, extreme, were both intellectual responses to a period of profound British decline. But there was only going to be one winner. The right was intellectually dominant through the West, it was, in happenstance and history, the right's turn. Corbynism, by contrast, is the same thing but at a time when a consensus founded by the liberal right is (to some extent at least) in retreat. It is perhaps no surprise, then, that it has a more popular basis within the party and the country. As Paul Mason, who was around in the 1980s, recalls: 'Once we had revived our local Labour ward in Sheffield in 1980, its monthly attendance rose from the twelve pensioners and councillors that had kept it alive under Callaghan to maybe thirty, one-third of whom were Trotskyists or sympathisers of the Communist Party. And that was it. We achieved stuff – above all in supporting Sheffield City Council when it resisted cuts. But ultimately the social forces that were driving Thatcherism were stronger. Thatcherism was the main event.

'The main event of 2016 – in England and Wales at least – is that 300,000 people have joined the Labour Party. Sure, some of the same people are still around, including me, but it feels like a much bigger moment than the Benn insurgency. Anybody who thinks it is being driven, or "twisted", by re-enactment groups from twentieth-century Marxism is going to the wrong meetings.'

That movement, as we know, has been driven by hundreds of thousands of new joiners to the party. One bit of that party which could not be swamped with new members was the Parliamentary Labour Party. It remained beyond the reach of the new regime. It was the last significant pocket of support that Corbyn did not control. Fortunately for the leadership, MPs put a gun to their own heads.

THE PYRRHIC VICTORY OF THE PLP

One instructive way to think about how dramatic a transformation the Labour Party has experienced over the past decade is to consider the evolution and changes in the composition of the Labour and Conservative Party leaderships over that period. The Conservative Party in 2018 is not enormously different to the one that went into the crash in 2008. Much of its leadership are the same today as then. Theresa May was in the shadow cabinet. So were Philip Hammond, Chris Grayling, Liam Fox, David Lidington, David Mundell, Michael Gove and Jeremy Hunt, who at the time of writing are in the cabinet.*
Boris Johnson too was bestriding the national scene, having just been elected Mayor of London. The cast of characters were essentially the same, and their ideas, more or less, were too.

Contrast that with the Labour Party. Looking at the list of Gordon Brown's cabinet ministers in 2008 is like looking at a roll call of the political dead. Not a single one remains: Alistair Darling, the Milibands, Jack Straw, Jacqui Smith, Des Browne, Alan Johnson,

* David Davis was also there and was about to resign. Some things never change.

Douglas Alexander, John Hutton, Hazel Blears, Ed Balls, Geoff Hoon. The list goes on. Indeed, of the 22 names on the list, only four even remain in the House of Commons. Astonishingly, the clearout continues further down the ranks. By my calculations, of the whole Labour front bench of that time (including those far below cabinet level), some 120 or so ministers, you would find only two of those ministerial behinds gracing the same Labour benches today.* Sure, it's ten years ago; yes, some have left Parliament, but all the same, it is a stark turnover. The Labour front bench is 99 per cent entirely new compared to only a decade before – and it represents as much an ideological changing of the guard as a physical one.

But the backbenches have proved stickier; and that's why before 2017 the organ of the party where Corbyn was weakest was the PLP. Today they are almost entirely impotent. There has never been an occasion in British parliamentary history when a parliamentary party has been led by someone the vast majority of MPs did not want. That is because it is simply alien and anathema to the way our constitutional processes developed. The leader of a party was the person who could command the support of his or her colleagues. The leader of the biggest party was the prime minister. It was simple. The Labour Party's tinkering changed all of that. But, as we've seen, whatever system it had used, the eventual winner had usually been someone that the party could live with. Not so with the newest incarnation of the system.

Unlike the rest of the country and political journalists, his fellow parliamentarians knew Jeremy Corbyn. He'd been around since 1983. He'd been a reliable member of the Socialist Campaign Group, the Campaign for Labour Party Democracy and various other left-wing phalanxes within the parliamentary party. As we've seen, he had a reputation as an assiduous constituency MP and for being unfailingly courteous. He tended to stick with his own faction within the party.

---

* For those who care, the two remaining are the great survivor Nick Brown, still in the same post of chief whip (after a lengthy interregnum), and Dawn Butler, also at the time a whip but in 2018 in the shadow cabinet.

A former deputy leader, Roy Hattersley, who crossed over with Corbyn for nine years in the Commons told me: 'I've racked my brains but I just can't for the life of me ever remember meeting him.'

But because they knew him better than anyone else, many felt they must be living in a parallel universe. Every MP you ran into at the time wouldn't have to say much before one common word escaped their lips: 'Surreal.' Even some of his eventual allies couldn't believe it. Emily Thornberry, who knew Corbyn especially well as they were both Islington MPs, told me:

'I had no idea it would happen, I mean I found it particularly difficult because Jeremy has been my northern neighbour ever since I was elected as an MP, we've known him as Uncle Jeremy, and it's really difficult to get your head around, that idea of Uncle Jeremy being leader of the party, I mean it's funny but there we are, so I just lacked the imagination to work out how it was going to work.'

Others were less kind. One MP told me: 'He was in way over his head.' Another who was to serve with him initially in his shadow cabinet said that he felt he had got into something and had no idea where it would take him, and not for the first time implied his strings were being pulled by others: 'He was utterly shocked by it, I think. It was like getting on a surfboard for your first paddle into the sea and being picked up by an enormous wave and suddenly discovering you'd won the world surfing championship. I mean, it was the wave that propels him.'

Initially, it was chaos. It took him days to perform a reshuffle. MPs from different wings of the party implored Corbyn not to make John McDonnell his shadow chancellor. MPs, including Tom Watson, impressed upon Corbyn that such a move would be extremely divisive. Corbyn, wisely, ignored these entreaties. He knew that in a Parliament with precious few allies, with almost no one wishing him to succeed, he had to keep his most loyal lieutenant close. Moreover, as one insider put it to me: 'Jeremy, with the best will in the world, economic policy, detail, isn't his thing. He needed John. Also, frankly, it was a massive fuck you to the PLP.' More moderate MPs agreed: 'It was an act of war.'

But it was the first of many occasions that exposed the PLP's misunderstanding of the hard left and Corbyn's strategy. They expected him again and again to play by the old rules. He was never going to. Leaving aside the fact that Corbyn wanted to repay his old comrade and friend and that strategically he wanted to keep his allies close, he had not just become the first leader from the Left in the party's modern history only to diffuse his own power by spreading the spoils across different wings of the party. This was never a project about balance, this was a politics about transformation. It was a statement of intent that was to set the tone for things to come. Corbyn had his mandate from the party members and it was from this that he derived his legitimacy. The support of his MPs was desirable but his eyes were wide open – it was unlikely to come and it was not essential.

The reshuffle also set the tone in a more unfortunate way. It was a total shambles. They felt that their leader didn't have the chops for running a whelk stall and nor did his team. After he appointed his shadow cabinet, all three great offices of state – shadow chancellor, shadow home secretary and shadow foreign secretary – were filled by men. This caused much consternation on the backbenches, which had hoped to see Corbyn appoint the party's first female shadow chancellor – especially given that many were (rightly) smarting that their party had once again rejected the opportunity to elect its first official female leader, despite the presence of two credible women on the ballot paper. When Corbyn's team realised the flak they were receiving, they attempted to wind back. Simon Fletcher, one of Corbyn's key lieutenants, was overheard saying: 'We are taking a fair amount of shit out there about women. We need to do a Mandelson. Let's make Angela [Eagle] Shadow First Minister of State. Like Mandelson was. She can cover PMQs.' Minutes later, all lobby journalists received a text saying that Eagle was shadow first secretary.

Anyone who has participated in or observed politics up close cannot fail to be struck by how much of it and the decisions which affect nations are made up of sustained incidents of low farce, but in that first year, for many of his own MPs, the Corbyn leadership seemed beyond a joke. He failed to sing the National Anthem, he put in a series of weak performances at Prime Minister's Questions, where David Cameron dominated the chamber; John McDonnell thought it would be funny if he threw a copy of Mao's Little Red Book across the dispatch box; Corbyn failed to sack Hilary Benn as shadow foreign secretary despite having briefed the media that he would. Then, during the Syria debate, the public endured the ludicrous spectacle of seeing Jeremy Corbyn, as leader of the Labour Party, open the debate by opposing military action only for his own shadow foreign secretary, Benn, to close the debate by urging MPs to vote for Britain 'to do our bit'. The Labour Party had not one but two positions on matters of war and peace. It was risible.

The public made it clear what it thought. The Conservatives opened up a clear lead over Labour in the polls, increasing their vote share on their 2015 performance. In the local elections of May 2016, Labour lost seats.

One shadow cabinet minister said they thought that Corbyn was simply overwhelmed: 'I think for anyone in those circumstances, having been a backbencher for all these years, to find yourself as the leader of the Labour Party, it's not described as the most difficult job in British politics for nothing, I think it was an enormous change, he was at sea.'

Speculation mounted about a leadership challenge. One was always going to come. One senior left-winger told me: 'Look, I think a challenge was inevitable. The PLP weren't going to accept him long term, we knew that, they knew that, it was just a question of when.'

In the end, MPs' hands were forced by an issue no one had even seriously thought about in the Labour Party for decades.

BREXIT BEHEMOTH: LABOUR AND THE EU

The European question had dogged the Conservative Party for a generation but by 2016 it was exposing Labour's more limited divisions too. Somehow events had conspired to produce a situation where Labour MPs – who were overwhelmingly pro-EU – and

Labour members, who were also overwhelmingly pro-EU, were being led by one of the tiny number of MPs and members who happened to be a Eurosceptic.

This is contentious stuff, but there can be no doubt about Jeremy Corbyn's pedigree on this subject. He represented a holdover from the party's deeply Eurosceptic past. It is often forgotten now that it was the Labour Party which was the Eurosceptic force in British politics, right up to the late 1980s. Many Labour MPs saw it as a free-market racket, a capitalist club designed to create a continent-wide free market and diminish the power of national organised labour. It is why many of the trade unions were against membership and the Attlee government, after some hesitation, decided not to join the embryonic EU (in the form of the European Coal and Steel Community) in the late 1940s. With some low farce of his own, Herbert Morrison, chairing the cabinet in Attlee's absence, shrugged blithely: 'the Durham miners wouldn't wear it.' Ernie Bevin, the foreign secretary, was less prosaic but more prescient: 'If you open that Pandora's Box you never know what Trojan Horses might fly out.'

Ted Heath finally took Britain into the European Community, as the organisation had by then become, in 1973. Heath usually gets the credit but the spurs ought really to belong to Harold Wilson; it was his quicksilver brilliance and political skill that cemented Britain's presence in Europe for the next five decades. By 1974, Labour was as riven with division as Cameron's Conservatives had become by 2016. These were nullified by Wilson, via a masterful political performance. As with all things Wilson, his true motivations are obscured by layers of political intrigue (themselves wrapped in a film of cunning), but it's reasonably clear that he had been anti-market yet gradually softened, and had ultimately decided he wanted to stay in,* even though many of the party's powerbrokers wanted to leave. He set about renegotiating the terms of entry (sound familiar?). But the difference between Wilson and Cameron was that Wilson was a

* He said, you might think presciently, that if the anti-marketeers won, 'all the wrong people' would come to govern Britain.

better player of the game, a man who understood the impulses and instincts of Britain, rather than a small, rarefied stratum. As Ben Pimlott, Wilson's biographer, noted in the early 1990s:

> The real issue was not the Wilson terms as opposed to the Heath terms, but whether the large body of opinion in the Labour Party which favoured non-membership would win the day. In the end, the outcome depended on fickle public opinion. The question was how to maximise the chances of a 'yes' vote, without doing irreparable damage to the government and the Party in the process.
>
> This was to become one of Wilson's most remarkable achievements; perhaps the greatest triumph of his career. Since 1931, the nightmare of successive Labour governments had been another crisis in which senior ministers, activating the national interest as they perceived it, found themselves dependent on other parties and opposed by the Labour Movement. Such a possibility existed over the common market. In 1974–75, however, Wilson brilliantly succeeded where Ramsay Macdonald had failed. He created a national consensus in favour of his cabinet's policy and overrode the declared wishes of the Labour Party and many of his own ministers, yet avoided either a government collapse or an irreconcilable split within the Movement. At the same time, he turned the referendum, which the Left had backed because it saw it as a clever ruse for taking Britain out of the Common Market, into a means of legitimizing once and for all, the decision to go in; and did so in such a way that it was impossible for anybody except die hard antis to argue that he had acted unfairly.[2]

It was the slenderest tightrope on which to walk and Wilson danced across. Cameron thought he could perform precisely the same trick decades later. He fell off.

In any case, as Pimlott said, the matter was largely settled within the country and within the Labour Party. But a few kept the torch aloft. Chief among them, who else but Tony Benn. On referendum night in 1975 Benn said that 'When the British people speak everyone, including Members of Parliament, should tremble before their decision and that's certainly the spirit with which I accept the result of the referendum.' But a few years later he was arguing for a unilateral withdrawal without a new plebiscite. He and his protégés continued to argue against the EU for the next few decades. He wrote, in the years after he had been a minister, of his experiences sitting in the Council of Ministers representing Britain: 'I came to realise that the EEC – far from being an instrument for the political control of multinationals – was actually welcomed by the multinationals, which saw it as a way of overcoming the policies of national governments to which they objected.'[3]

He was to become progressively more isolated. The rest of the Labour Party not only grudgingly accepted the result of the 1975 referendum but, over time, came to embrace Europe. The turning point was probably the address by the European Commission's president, Jacques Delors, to the TUC conference in Bournemouth in 1988. His vision of a social Europe, which protected workers' rights across countries from one corner of the continent to the other, won the movement's hearts and heads. By the end of his speech, the Congress broke out in a spontaneous rendition of 'Frère Jacques'. Apparently, it brought a tear to the wily old Frenchman's eyes. It probably made Margaret Thatcher cry too but not for the same reasons. It is no coincidence that, inversely, Euroscepticism began to rise within her at around the same time.

But, like his mentor, Benn, Jeremy Corbyn never lost his dislike of the *grand projet*. He voted against membership in 1975. He went on to vote against the Maastricht Treaty in 1992* and voted against the Lisbon Treaty of 2009. His was a relatively lone voice on the Labour

---

* In fairness, that was the party whip's position at the time. Labour was cynically choosing to vote against it because it was trying to use the vote to destroy John Major's government. Nonetheless it's virtually certain that if the party position had been to vote in its favour, Corbyn's position would not have changed.

benches consistently and persistently speaking against the European Union and virtually all its works. Here are a few of his top European hits:

- 'Does my hon. Friend recognise that the imposition of a bankers' Europe on the people of this continent will endanger the cause of socialism in the United Kingdom and in any other country?' – Hansard, 13 January 1993, Maastricht Treaty debate.
- 'Do we think that this is a cri de coeur? Well, yes, it is. It is a cri de coeur for democracy and for the right of people to elect a Government who can decide what goes on in their country' – 15 January 2015, Hansard TTIP debate.
- 'What powers do we have to do anything about the fraud in EU institutions? Much of that money seems to find its way into the hands of the Mafia or into grandiose, unwanted and often badly-built construction projects that are of no use to anybody.' – Hansard, 30 March 1993, Maastricht Treaty debate.
- 'The project has always been to create a huge free-market Europe, with ever-limiting powers for national parliaments and an increasingly powerful common foreign and security policy' – article, deleted from Jeremy Corbyn's website.

No wonder at one point Nigel Farage said of Corbyn that 'Jeremy Corbyn is showing his true Brexit colours. He's almost a proper chap.'

It was of little surprise to anyone, then, that in the early stages of the 2015 leadership contest Corbyn expressed his Euroscepticism quite stridently. Now almost entirely forgotten, in July 2015 Corbyn said that he was uncertain as to how he would vote. Asked at a hustings in Warrington whether he would rule out campaigning to leave, he said this:

'No I wouldn't rule it out … Because Cameron quite clearly follows an agenda which is about trading away workers' rights, is about trading away environmental protection, is about trading away much of what is in the social chapter.

'The EU also knowingly, deliberately, maintains a number of tax havens and tax evasion posts around the continent – Luxembourg, Monaco and a number of others – and has this strange relationship with Switzerland which allows a lot of European companies to outsource their profits to Switzerland, where tax rates are very low.'

Pro-Europeans sensed trouble. Alan Johnson, who was to head the Labour Remain campaign, issued a statement that said: 'The Labour Party ditched its anti-European stance in the mid-1980s, at the beginning of our long march back to electability. The membership has a right to know if any leadership candidate wants to take the party (and the country) back to its isolationist past to the detriment of British jobs, growth and influence in an increasingly interdependent world.'

Corbyn had to clarify his position, and by the weekend he had changed his public stance: 'Labour should set out its own clear position to influence negotiations, working with our European allies to set out a reform agenda to benefit ordinary Europeans across the continent. We cannot be content with the state of the EU as it stands. But that does not mean walking away, but staying to fight together for a better Europe.'

Nonetheless, his parliamentary colleagues were well aware of Corbyn's political lineage and had little doubt about what they thought were his true feelings. When I asked a close colleague what he *really* thought about Europe – and even, indeed, how he voted, they said: 'Honestly … I really don't know; you'd have to ask him.' Others say that he is not as anti-European as some believe but rather that he is consistently indifferent to the subject.

This is the background to Jeremy Corbyn's performance during the 2016 European referendum, which remains a femur-sized bone of contention within the Labour Party. Talking to those involved in the happenings of those fateful months is to listen to comprehensively different histories of the same events. Even issues as basic as requests for Corbyn to appear as part of the campaign are disputed. Senior figures in the Remain campaign tell me that repeated requests for Corbyn to campaign, or at least coordinate events, were ignored. Senior figures in Corbyn's team insist that no such messages were even received, that the Remain campaign, ultimately, 'was being led by Craig Oliver and a bunch of Tories who weren't interested in us'.

Whatever the truth (and I don't suppose we'll ever know for sure), Corbyn certainly didn't behave as if his political life depended on it. When he was asked how much he cared about the issue on a scale of one to ten on a popular chat show, he replied: 'Seven … seven and a half.' For many MPs, it summed up his tepid support for the cause. Ben Bradshaw spoke for many Labour MPs when he told me:

'Well, all that I can say is we did more canvassing in Exeter for the referendum campaign than probably anywhere else in the country and our canvassing data confirmed exactly what a number of data polls showed right up to the eve of the referendum – which was a significant number, around 40 per cent of voters, did not know what Labour's position was and I would've thought that one of the basic tenets of leadership is to ensure that your own voters know what your own position is. I was warning before the referendum, even to Number 10, that the referendum will be won or lost on Labour votes and that as things stood we were going to lose … It wasn't a huge margin in the end and I think if the campaigning had been better all round and if the Labour campaign had been better we would have won.'

Corbyn's team entirely reject that assertion and argue that much of Labour MPs' reaction plays into Cameron's hands. Cameron and his acolytes, they say, have been seeking to write a revisionist history of the referendum and blame the Labour leadership for what was in fact a wrong-headed and inadequate Remain campaign, devised, orchestrated and executed from Number 10. When I asked if a different leader who was more instinctively pro-Remain would have made the difference, Emily Thornberry rejected the idea: 'I don't know, I suspect it wouldn't have because Labour campaigned, I don't think the campaigning would have been different. I think Jeremy giving Europe a seven out of ten was an honest response and reflected what most people felt.' She did say, however, that she wouldn't have given the seven-out-of-ten assessment:

'No, I wouldn't actually, but perhaps I would have said seven out of ten slightly differently. I'd have said that it was far from perfect but we are better in than out. I don't think that result would have been different, I mean sixty-seven per cent of Labour voters voted to remain; we got more of our people to vote that way than the Tories and on a par with the Scots Nats.'

A source close to Corbyn agrees: 'People like Hilary and Alan Johnson and Chuka, they have this great belief in themselves and they thought Labour voters would follow. But if you want to get Labour voters out you have to paint your enemy and they wouldn't do that because they were too busy sharing platforms with Tories. So when they lost, they felt so upset they tried to blame Jeremy for not doing more than he could, and they didn't want him anyway. The rewriting of the EU campaign is hilarious. I mean, Jeremy had a very pragmatic approach, he just wanted to keep everyone happy, it was not his big issue.'

On the accusation that Corbyn could not be brought out to campaign, the same source said: 'It is like a revisionist history. I've got email chains which prove it. It's just bullshit. There was an element, towards the end, when everyone was like, you guys [the Remain campaign] have led it so far so just carry on. They didn't have a very good analysis of it, the problem with that campaign was that although it had a strong leader, it was run by Craig Oliver. It got to the stage where I started changing the ringtones on my phone of people who were working on it to the *Eurotrash* theme tune, because I'd get rung by one of them from the official campaign and one from Labour In and they would both say the same thing to me, with only ten minutes of separation.'

Whatever the rights and the wrongs, it was the reddest of red Labour rags to the Parliamentary Labour Party's bull. The 2015 general election defeat had left them dazed, the 2016 referendum defeat left them incandescent. As one Corbyn aide put it to me: 'There are certain people in the party, like Chuka [Umunna], Europe is their socialism.' There was a feeling that after a lamentable referendum performance and with his clear insouciance towards the subject, they could not allow Corbyn to continue; that with big Brexit decisions looming and negotiations to begin, they could not risk allowing him to inflict further damage.

But what to do about it? Corbyn's election had left the PLP wounded and its power much diminished. But MPs still had one bullet left in the revolver: the chance to force another leadership contest. One MP told me: 'The working assumption was to give him eighteen months to two years. After that we could say to the membership, look, it's not working, the polls haven't moved, he doesn't want it, let's try something else. The referendum forced the issue.'

The 'coup' of July 2016 is the moment when dislike, antipathy and suspicion between MPs and the leadership degenerated into outright contempt and open warfare. An uneasy truce had simmered for a year, with fires frequently doused if not completely extinguished. Both sides remain largely unrepentant and stick to their own side of the story. Corbynistas say that MPs had been looking for an excuse to remove Corbyn all year and this was it. The MPs say that Corbyn had underperformed in the referendum and that they felt someone should carry the can for that and that their motivations were principled and heartfelt. Those two views aren't necessarily mutually exclusive. MPs didn't like Corbyn, true. MPs were angry about the referendum result and blamed Corbyn: also true. MPs thought he should pay the price. Frankly Corbyn had not helped himself throughout the campaign, nor in the hours after the result when he called for Article 50 to be triggered immediately.

What MPs were guilty of is once again misunderstanding Corbyn and the hard left, their conception of politics and power, and, crucially, underestimating their resolve. As the resignations came in, one after the other, a coordinated drip, drip, drip, they assumed that Corbyn would behave like any normal leader of the Labour Party, like any normal leader of any political party, and resign.

As Hilary Benn, ringleader of the resigners, told me: 'Well, in normal circumstances if eighty per cent of the people of the team you are leading say it's not working, we have to have confidence in you, then the person would have to go. I mean, it was an extraordinary event and I don't know whether he came close to it or not.'

Ben Bradshaw agrees: 'I don't think that it was a mistake. I think given the circumstances at the time … the leadership had let the party down and the treatment of Hilary Benn, especially, the treatment of those individual ministers who had tried for a whole year to make it work. What I think surprised me in any democracy is that the leadership lost the confidence of his or her parliamentary colleagues and didn't just resign or walk away voluntarily. It was extraordinary. I think that it was the right thing to do and the necessary thing to do. I don't think it was a mistake, it was inevitable given the trauma given the aftermath of the election.'

But he wasn't dealing with a normal leader. The hard left once in power do not give it up without blood on the walls. There was, however, at the time some suggestion that Corbyn, demoralised, destabilised by his overflowing inbox of resignation emails, was close to quitting. One MP who resigned on the phone told me: 'McDonnell did all of the talking, all of the begging. Corbyn barely said a word. You got the sense that he was on the edge.' Corbyn's camp deny any suggestion he even considered throwing in the towel: 'He never even considered it. And I can tell you that because I was in the room the whole time. Why should he?'

And Corbyn and his allies, as so often, seemed to derive strength from siege. As one of his aides told me: 'I stood next to him the night of the PLP vote of no confidence and I stood back, the acid response he got from MPs, literally foaming at the mouth, he was utterly calm. I walked up to him at the end and I was like, "You all right, JC?", and he was like, "It is going to be fine." He has got that strength to him, people don't see it, the thing was that you don't understand people like Corbyn, the moment they put that motion of no confidence in, he was never going to back down … the idea he was ever going to back down was bollocks. I know because I was close to it. The moment that tipped it for him was that confrontation, that confrontation was literally an adrenaline shot.'

When I asked an aide close to Corbyn and McDonnell whether or not the shadow chancellor was ever worried that his old ally was going to throw in the towel, the aide dismissed the idea: 'No, they are quite close friends, so there is always a situation of knowing what the other is thinking. I think they thought above all that the whole project here was to build for the next generation. To be honest, I think that John quite liked it, liked the robust nature of it, and I think he quite enjoyed it.' Corbyn and McDonnell, as so often, came out fighting when their backs were against the wall. But this is what the left is. Its instinctive way of thinking, its most base reflex, is that the rest of politics, from within and without, is seeking to destroy it. This 'coup' was vindication of that belief; power, then, must never be surrendered willingly.

No finer proof of that theory could exist than the thinking of those around Corbyn at the time of the general election, when they were mulling the possibility of heavy defeat. Months later, I asked a senior Corbyn aide if he thought Corbyn would have quit had he lost seats: 'I don't think there was ever going to be a reason as to why you would quit after a year of being re-elected for the second time.'

When I asked how low the number of seats could have gone before he had yielded (*170, 160, 150?* I speculated), a stony stare greeted me by way of reply: 'He wouldn't have gone.'

I'm not sure if any other Labour leader would have shown such bravura (or arrogance) in the face of such heavy defeat. Blair, Miliband, Brown, etc. would all have gone (indeed, some went over less). But none hailed from Corbyn's wing of the party – and that's just not how they think. If they fail, they look to bigger structural problems, the media, the Tories, the wealthy: it's a structural analysis born of deep (if occasionally justified) paranoia. The job to do in the case of defeat would be rebuilding the party from the ground up, in the left's image.

Fortunately it was a problem that never arose. But when we think about the attempted coup with that in mind, it's clear the MPs' cause was lost before it even started: Corbyn was never going anywhere. As one resigning shadow minister told me: 'They were telling him, we've got our hands on the steering wheel, under no circumstances you should let it go.'

Either way, in holding a vote of no confidence, with Labour parliamentarians voting against Corbyn by a 172–40 margin, MPs had used the last weapon in their armoury. Corbyn's fate would now, for the second occasion in twelve months, be in the hands of the membership.

Matlock in Derbyshire is typical Corbyn territory. Prosperous, semi-rural, relatively well-educated and well-heeled; the perfect retreat for a weekend break. Exactly the sort of place where you won't find many Labour MPs but you will find plenty of committed activists, on that same weekend, traipsing up the streets happily knocking on doors, talking to residents, canvassing the opinions of people who will generally receive them merrily and then go and vote Tory at the next election anyway.

They were similarly welcoming and kind to me. In an era when so many in politics and especially in the Labour Party are viscerally wary of the media, it was nice not to be treated with McCarthyite suspicion. That night hundreds of party members travelled from across the sprawling constituency to Matlock Town Hall, nestled on the hilly climbs of the East Midlands spa town, to support their embattled leader.

As I spoke to them about their thinking, what surprised me was how little the European question featured and how often the inner workings of the constitution of the Labour Party did. Part of me felt a little frustrated: the country had just had the political equivalent of a heart attack and all they wanted to talk about was the Labour Party rule book and who had a mandate from whom and for what and for how long; the tyrannies of minute differences.

But it neatly illustrated something else the PLP had just not understood. Corbyn had already been successful. He had realised a long-cherished left-wing aim. He had made the party think that its power structure was almost entirely horizontal. There, in Matlock, was the clash of visions of what the Labour Party is writ large; a difference, you could say, of emphasis between those who focus on the idea that Labour is a traditional party and those who prefer to use the phrase 'the Labour movement'. Or, to put it another way, a disagreement about Clause 1, article 2, of the Labour Party constitution: 'Its purpose is to organise and maintain in Parliament and in the country a political Labour Party.'

The MPs are of the belief that the emphasis should be on the first bit of that clause and, not unforgivably, of the view that they ought to be at the very centre of the Labour Party's thinking and efforts. The representation of working people in Parliament is, after all, specifically why the Labour Party was founded. It was not established to be a pressure group or a debating society, they say, its only aim was and ought still to be to swell the ranks of Labour MPs on the green benches and eventually to get as many as is required to form a government.

The Corbyn high command – and many of the new members who have joined to support them – are firmly in the movement camp; as were many of the people in that grand old oak-panelled room in Derbyshire. As Andrew Botham, one of the councillors, put it, anger flashing in his eyes: 'Just because a small minority of the party, which is a small majority of a faction of the party which are the MPs, are against does not mean he should go.' When I put it to him that MPs were more than just another faction of the party his nostrils flared and his eyes rolled:

'No! They are a faction of the party. They *are* a faction of the party. And if you want to listen to the party and you want members to be involved in the party and you give them the right to join the party or even just pay £3 to have a say in the leadership, you cannot just take that away from them because you don't like the decision they've made.'

The genie was out of the bottle. The conception of what the party was had been altered. If you think about the Labour Party as a flowchart, then the two sides had just come to see the flow and order of that chart differently; MPs see themselves at its apex. Corbynistas do not. In the 1980s that had been the case too, but enough of the membership and trade unions supported MPs' primacy. Now they did not.

Any anger that there had been towards Corbyn and his European escapade had been dispersed by MPs' perceived treachery. The chair of the local youth branch was especially forthright: 'If the Labour MPs feel the leader of the Labour Party is unrepresentative of their views they're perfectly within their rights to refuse the Labour whip.' The chair of the CLP, Rosemary McKenzie, was similarly angry with the party at Westminster: 'The failure of leadership was the people around Corbyn because from the very beginning there were so many media leaks and little bits of things about him not being suitable but how can you say he's not suitable? His vision is excellent – it's why so many of us followed him in the first place.'

There were a few lone voices of dissent. But they were gentle, at best. It was telling they didn't feel comfortable expressing much open hostility to Corbyn, or else feel that there was much point. That night there were three motions in favour of the leadership or condemning the rebels; all three were overwhelmingly carried.

Just as everyone in Westminster was getting excited about a closer contest this time around, every single person in that room thought that Corbyn would win again, even those who didn't intend to vote for him. Even among his detractors there was little enthusiasm or warmth for the two putative leadership candidates, Angela Eagle and Owen Smith.

As soon as their names were mentioned, someone shouted: 'We don't want New Labour again!' Smith hadn't even been an MP at the time; indeed, he'd first been elected 18 years after New Labour's first victory – but it didn't matter. Corbyn's secret asset as beneficiary of that old Labour inheritance to which he didn't belong was once again key.

Fundamentally, perhaps unbelievably, opinion throughout the party hadn't changed. The same desire, yearning for a bolder articulation of social democracy, remained. A few weeks later I travelled up to Elmet and Rothwell, near Leeds, to visit another CLP that had nominated Corbyn in 2015 and had just done so again. By that time,

Smith had been confirmed as the moderates' candidate. The members there didn't think much of him and were still just as taken with the Corbyn vision. Marie Lynch, the treasurer, was unrepentant: 'Why should I be interested in Smith? What does he even have to say? Jeremy's message and conviction has not changed in twelve months. I voted for him twelve months ago and I'll do so again.'

The coup gave Corbyn a chance to do what he does best. Campaign, go around the country rallying his supporters and talking about social justice. Try as Smith might, he could not make the Europe song sing, despite the shock of the referendum result. That shock probably helped Corbyn – Article 50's triggering still a long way away, politicians taking the summer off, Europe, perhaps incredibly, seemed a relatively peripheral issue, Brexit's contours hard to see. Certainly nothing by comparison to the convulsions it was to reap in the summers to come.

Added into that mix were some members who didn't care for Corbyn that much but were annoyed at the PLP attempting to subvert their democratic rights. One member, Luke, told me: 'I think there's a lot of members who might not have supported Jeremy last time but on the principle of democracy in the party will be supporting him now, because frankly there's a feeling that democracy has been undermined.'

Somehow the PLP had managed to put their leader, once again, in the position he liked best: the underdog.

At the time, plenty of journalists went along to London Labour parties and picked up their ire and thought it was replicated across the country – it wasn't. That was important for Corbyn. London had proved a real power base for him in his first leadership run, but second time around there was genuine anger with him there and a real bleeding of support. No fewer than 16 of the 50 or so CLP nominations Smith received were from the capital, some of which, like Richmond or Lambeth, supported Corbyn in 2015. But he picked up more support from the Midlands and in particular the north-west and Yorkshire, which had been redoubts of Andy Burnham and Yvette Cooper in 2015.

In these places, they may have voted Remain, but in truth they were probably closer to Corbyn's position of 7 out of 10 than the maximal position of someone like Chuka Umunna. And even if they weren't, many of them lived in and represented heavily Leave constituencies. They were extremely wary of Smith's position of unilaterally reversing or stopping Brexit, expressed in the campaign in an attempt to halt its slide. They thought that Corbyn's more equivocal position would be best for them.

Either way Smith failed to impress. After a campaign where he was criticised for a number of gaffes, not least an incident where he said he would 'like to knock Theresa May back on her heels', no one seemed especially excited, even those who supported him. One Labour MP was to call him 'the wrong man at the wrong time with the wrong policies'. It was hard not to agree. Corbyn defeated Smith by 61 to 39 per cent.

In retrospect, the Corbynistas couldn't believe their luck. But it might not have been so easy. One senior Corbyn aide told me:

'My big fear – and I still to this day don't know why they didn't do it – was them nominating more than one person against Jeremy. What we would have had then was a really right-wing candidate and then potentially someone coming through the middle. I know Labour members and I knew what would happen; we might not get to 50 per cent on the first round and there would have been transfers. Angela would have probably come bottom, Owen would have come second and her transfers might have pushed him over the line.

'I thought that was the only way they could win and when they put only one person up I thought, "Thank you very much", it's so easy. All I had to do was paint Owen, which we did quite easily at the time, as the Blairite candidate. He's not a Blairite but it was quite fun doing it. We could do that easily in a two-horse race because he's basically the opposite to Jeremy, but in a three-horse race, all that would have happened was Angela would have come out being the cheerleader for the right, we would have been out there being extreme and Owen would have been there being like: guys, let's all be together, let's be friends. Even with his incompetence he could have done that and put through modified versions of our policies and he would have probably done enough to get second in the vote. You only need a third of the vote and then get fifteen per cent/twenty per cent.'

Another insider agreed with that analysis: 'I have worked on lots of elections, I have worked in Scotland during the referendum, I've done lots of different things, the hardest thing I have even gone through was that coup, in that sort of two-week period we were so close – their tactics blew it.'

We'll never know if that third candidate might have made the difference.

The effects of the coup overall remain extremely contentious. The position of many key figures in the leader's office is that it was this, not Corbyn's lacklustre leadership over the previous nine months, which damaged the party most. One insider reflected to me that 'If it wasn't for the coup I genuinely believe we'd have won more seats at the election, we'd have been level pegging with the Tories if not ahead.'

Is there any evidence for that? Corbyn had been doing badly in the polls in the period after he became leader. But it is true to say that in the immediate few months before the referendum he had closed the gap a bit. Does this prove that he had begun to turn the tide? It's far from a watertight case. Corbyn's personal ratings remained dire throughout the period and the gain was negligible, only a couple of points. Labour did badly and lost seats in May's local elections. At the same point in the cycle Ed Miliband's Labour gained hundreds of seats, which is what you'd expect an opposition party to be doing at that stage.

If anything, the polls show that the narrowing comes as much from (i) declining Tory support as the referendum neared, probably because of Tory divisions over Europe being brought into the cold open air with cabinet ministers taking opposing sides, and (ii) UKIP gaining support, soaking up Tory Eurosceptic sentiment as Europe became a dominant issue on the airwaves. If you were being uncharitable to Corbyn you might even suggest that Labour gaining a point or two was a result of his relative invisibility and other Labour figures stepping forward.

So, it is not as if the coup disrupted growing nascent Corbyn support out in the country. The charge that it did enormously tarnish the party's reputation is more credible. As the party descended into civil war, its ratings did start to sharply decline, right at the moment when the Tories' rose.

It would be silly to think that the coup didn't contribute to that. However, I suspect much of it would have happened anyway. Theresa May was a new leader and seemed, however briefly, the right woman at the right time. In swiftly adopting the 'Brexit means Brexit' line that she did, the Conservatives absorbed a sizeable proportion of UKIP support, who instantly faced existential angst the moment the referendum result was announced. All of this would have happened regardless. And it's not as if Corbyn had enjoyed an especially stellar year before the referendum. He had struggled and the public knew it.

None of this has stopped Corbyn's allies from being angry about the coup and its perpetrators – and they still are. Emily Thornberry told me:

'I was very angry at the challenge. I mean, given the huge cultural, economic challenge that we had been thrown by the British people the last thing we should be doing is turning in on ourselves. I really felt it was our job as the opposition to work out what should we do now. I was very angry at that, it was a distraction we could do without; he had only been leader for about a year and was elected with an overwhelming majority and I think it's time that people figure out what this party is and it is the party of the membership.

'I'm bored and I'm fed up with the irreconcilables ... with those who cannot be reconciled with Jeremy and think there is some good to be had with the Labour Party continuing to snipe at him when he is leader when he is getting on with it. I have a lot of respect for people who didn't think he would be a good leader, were involved in the coup, and who have decided there is no point in fighting, let's help Jeremy be the best leader that he can be, let's make the opposition the best party they can be, we owe it to the country to be an alternative. I have no respect for the others.'

Thornberry is right; Corbyn had been damaged in the eyes of the public and Labour appeared entirely unelectable. At a moment of national peril Labour was looking inwards, not outwards. On the other hand, had Corbyn campaigned harder the issue might never have arisen. We will never know.

Either way, in purely internal terms the coup sealed Corbyn's dominance. The one threat to his leadership would come from the House of Commons. After the second leadership contest, they would never be a threat again. After all, what could they do now? Resign? They had demonstrated for all to see their own impotence. A few trickled back to the front bench, more still languished. Even if some among their number had wanted to come back, they were not asked. One figure in the leadership took great pleasure in seeing these enemies put in their places, telling me: 'The best thing about the coup was seeing what happened to all the egos, they thought they were the masters of the universe. It was great to say, well cheerio! The thing I like to do sometimes is look at the back row, like Rachel Reeves, Chuka, Yvette. They believed their own hype, they thought they deserved to be the leader of the Labour Party. But who are these people? These are yesterday's people.'

Another was equally damning of the old guard and in hindsight pleased that the coup had forced out the last of them. When I asked if the leadership perceived them to be in any way a threat, they grimaced and replied:

'Not particularly, at the moment they are perfectly positioned, no one cares. They go off and head a select committee, no one cares what they do. No one cares that these people are struggling to make themselves relevant. They have some level of access due to their connections within the media but aside from that they are just a small group.'

Not only did the coup seal Corbyn's dominance around the shadow cabinet table and remove any significant dissenting voices, but it was also positive for Corbynism. As one insider told me: 'I think the coup was good because it freed us, there were so many things that we had to accommodate people on, from there on in we did our own thing.'

It's easy to forget now how relatively mixed Corbyn's first shadow cabinet was in terms of ideological makeup. Despite his crushing victory in the leadership election, he had felt the need to offer many shadow cabinet seats to the old guard: the old Blairite Charlie Falconer was shadow Justice Secretary, Angela Eagle at Business, Michael Dugher at Culture, Maria Eagle at Defence, Lucy Powell at Education and Hilary Benn at Foreign Affairs. They were a visible and real constraint on Corbyn's freedom of action. Today they are all gone and their views largely immaterial.

Did the PLP misplay their hand? If they did, perhaps it was a forgivable error given they had very few cards to play. Strategically, it was probably the only thing they could do. If they hadn't challenged at that moment, when Corbyn was theoretically at his most vulnerable with the membership, then when would they? Their big mistake was in the first place underestimating their leader and his thirst for power (again), and then nominating Smith alone.

However, the bigger problem was more familiar. Mainstream social democrats struggled in 2016 ultimately for the same reason that the mainstream social democratic bit of the Labour Party struggled in 2015, for the same reason they struggled in 2017 and struggle today: they still had little of interest to say and an uninteresting way of saying it.

Smith said he was just as radical as Corbyn but was more electable. He felt he had to ape Corbyn's policies because his wing of the party was so devoid of its own and still lacked any convincing or compelling analysis or narrative of Britain's troubles or ways to ameliorate them. In running as a better vehicle or salesman of those ideas he fatefully underestimated what had propelled Corbyn the first time around. He was appealing not just because of his ideas but because those ideas were authentically his. The prospect of a man who worked for Pfizer and who once said he agreed with Tony Blair about pretty much everything coming along and saying he was as radical as Corbyn was the antithesis of what could have worked.

But it was Smith because it was no one else. The PLP did what they thought was right. But in so doing they exposed their own intellectual and political bankruptcy. Corbyn didn't have to take over the PLP now – he just didn't need them.

And when the dust settled? Relations since have been very difficult but were initially ameliorated by the general election in two key senses.

The first was that there just wasn't time to fight each other. There is nothing so tribal in any democracy anywhere in the world as a Labour MP at election time. Even those who loathe each other still both loathe a Tory more on general election day. They had to get on and fight for survival. Momentum diehards fought in the trenches alongside Blairite old-timers against a common enemy. Secondly, the general election allayed any immediate fears of deselection. There wasn't time to deselect; the snap election meant that all sitting Labour MPs who wished to stand again were automatically the candidate.

The peace, however, didn't last long. In the spring of 2018, rows over Russia, anti-Semitism and tensions over May's Brexit Chequers agreement reignited merely suppressed tension. As for the selections issue, now there is a pro-Corbyn majority on the NEC there will be an attempt to make deselection easier. Corbyn sources tell me, however, that it is unlikely to be centrally mandated but it will happen organically: 'It'll happen locally. Look, if you're an MP substantially to the right of where your local membership is and you're very vocal about it you have two choices: either get on board or get out. There are smart ones who are more political about it and some are just bloody-minded. That's fine but then you should expect a reaction.'

Perhaps that's the sign of ultimate victory and a sign of how far the scales have tipped. Whereas once there was warfare, now the guns on one side are so small that the victor barely even notices when they fire. They've moved on to bigger and more important battles.

Many of the grassroots, however, have not. But who were these thousands of people flooding into the party?

'WE GOT THE BIG MO'!'

The Corbyn footsoldiers

Momentum, the internal pro-Jeremy Corbyn pressure group founded by his allies to support his leadership, has received a lot of attention. It is comprised of the most die-hard Corbyn-supporting members, a 'party within a party'. Earlier I explained how a huge proportion of the appeal and reach of the Corbyn project was in its perceived left-wing credentials. What we know about the members who have joined since 2015 confirms that hypothesis, especially the Momentum members. They are, vis-à-vis the general population, unsurprisingly, very left wing. However, in surveys of their views, interestingly, they are not significantly at variance with the opinions of members who were in the party before Corbyn's rise. We know the party was drifting further to the left in the Miliband years but I suspect you could have polled members in Blair's time and the results would have been much the same.

The intriguing thing is this: the new members think they are more left wing than the old. The ERSC Party Members Project asked new and old Labour Party members to place themselves on an ideological spectrum from right to left. The new members place themselves significantly to the left of the old. When Momentum members are isolated they put themselves even further along the spectrum. Remember that this is despite the fact that they are all more or less in complete agreement about the issues involved.

The new members clearly see their left-wing status as a key part of their social identity, and are more likely to do so than the old members. That is what attracted them to Corbyn in the first place, someone who not only inspires them but reflects their own self-perceived politics and virtue back at them. They see themselves within the movement as a leftist vanguard.

They are also considerably more likely to be graduates, and, of those, considerably more likely to be graduates earning less than the average salary of around £25,000. The proportion of graduates among Labour members earning less than the average salary is ten points higher among new members than among older ones (51 per cent vs 41 per cent). And a considerable gap also exists between pro-Corbyn (54 per cent) and anti-Corbyn (41 per cent) new members. This led one of the authors of the research, Monica Poletti, to speculate:

'Relative deprivation theory suggests that people tend to make comparisons between what they expect out of life and what they actually experience, looking at people who are rather similar to themselves for cues as to what to expect. Thus, university graduates tend to derive their expectations from looking at other graduates and risk frustration if these expectations are not met. Did a sense of relative deprivation trigger some graduates to join Labour in the hope that the Corbyn leadership would help render their actual economic conditions closer to their professional expectations? Possibly so.'

In other words, many of the sorts of people joining the party in 2015 and 2016 for Corbyn weren't rabid Trotskyites, nor wandering returnees coming home hankering after a rerun of the fights of the 1980s (though there were some of them). Instead, many of the new joiners were a foretaste of exactly the coalition who were to rally to Corbyn in the general election: the socially liberal, the middle class, educated but dispossessed.

Corbyn and the Labour leadership are rightly proud of their enormous achievement of expanding the party's membership. It can now boast more party members than every other party put together. It is probably the largest in Western Europe. Central to the Corbyn thesis has been a different way of doing politics: that a broad, mass-membership organisation, through sheer numbers, could spread the gospel and outnumber and outgun a hollowed-out Conservative membership.

This is self-evidently an advantage. Parties derive moral and political legitimacy from a wider membership. They provide ammunition and warm bodies at election time. Getting down to brass tacks, they have been enormously beneficial in helping the Labour Party extricate itself from a dire financial situation. Labour now receives over ten times the revenue from membership fees as the Conservatives (some £14.4m compared to £1.5m). Half of that money is directly attributable to the Corbyn surge. Financially, it has saved the party, which a decade ago was at the point of bankruptcy. Today it is £11m in the black.

However, the new members have not proved a silver bullet, either within or without. Despite the Conservatives having less than a fifth of the members of the Labour Party, they still won sixty seats more than Labour and one and a half million more votes in 2017. That is partly because, as a result of their relatively narrow social base, Labour's members are concentrated in certain places. Places like Haringey, in north London.

There are few locations in Britain that better exemplify the shift in Labour Party power than Haringey. If you're from the rest of Britain you're probably largely unfamiliar with it, save for the horrors of the Baby P scandal in the late 2000s. If you're from London, you've probably never visited it.

But you'll hear about it a lot more soon enough. In effect it has become the UK's first Momentum Council. That isn't to say that Momentum control it directly, but it is nonetheless the first council in England where Corbynistas are, if you like, in government.

Yet only a few years ago it was the most 'Blairite' council in England. Its transformation tells us something about the Corbyn project, where it has been successful, where it hasn't, and about the wider ideological torrents within the party.

Haringey: Planet Corbyn

If there were a place tailor-made for Corbynism you'd be hard pushed to do much better than Haringey. An outer-London borough, centred on the Wood Green, Crouch End and Tottenham areas in the north of the city, it has that perfect mix for a Corbynite cauldron: a large middle-class bourgeois base, many of whom work in academia, the public sector or the arts, and significant pockets of deprivation and poverty.

Haringey has always been solidly Labour (the council has been nothing but Labour since its foundation in 1964), but in the Blair years the party struggled, especially in the leafier, more intellectual pockets of the borough. Unhappy with the Iraq War, the introduction of tuition fees and the wider Blair project, the party bled support to the Liberal Democrats. By the time of the 2010 London local elections, the Lib Dems had come close to snatching control from Labour for the first time, winning 26 seats to Labour's 30. It was a picture repeated all over neighbouring boroughs, like Islington and Camden, with the Lib Dems mopping up the disaffected votes of the intelligentsia. At the 2005 election, the party took one of Haringey's parliamentary constituencies, Hornsey and Wood Green, with a majority of over 2,000. In 2010 it repeated the trick, but with an increased majority of over 6,000.

Today the Lib Dem bird's wings have been well and truly clipped. The party's involvement with the coalition was exactly the sort of shabby political compromise many of its new Haringey voters had disliked in the first place. In 2014 Labour almost entirely neutralised the Lib Dem threat, reducing its presence on the council to nine seats. In 2015 Labour won Hornsey constituency back at a parliamentary level with a majority of 11,000. In 2017 the Labour MP, Catherine West, won an enormous, tubthumping majority of over 30,000 votes.

That's the sort of majority Labour used to get in Lancashire mill towns and Yorkshire pit villages, not suburban London. But in 2015 and 2017 Haringey was fast on its way to becoming ground zero of some of the vast sociological and demographic forces shaping Britain as the party under Miliband and then Corbyn became more urban, more bourgeois, younger and, eventually, Remainer. But it was at the centre of the party's internal strife too.

Although the coalition was shunting Haringey back in Labour's direction, clearly Corbyn was an asset here. It was, after all, his back yard, the next-door borough to his own Islington. He was also a councillor in Haringey in the 1970s. When Corbyn ran for leader in 2015 local membership went through the roof. Today it stands at around 7,000, probably the largest of any constituency Labour Party in the country. By one measure, as many as one in fourteen of local voters are members of the Labour Party. It is, as one councillor there told me, 'at the heart of the Corbyn revolution. I mean, you go to the shops in Haringey and the *Guardian* sells out. Where else in the country does that happen?' One senior councillor reflected on the change: 'My local ward branch meetings, not even CLP or General Council meetings of the whole constituency, I'd get over a hundred people turning up. Before 2015 I'd be lucky to get a dozen.' Who were all of these people? My source explained:

'With us there were four groups. Now we're a bit unusual in Haringey because of the sheer numbers, but nonetheless from what I've seen it's a good approximation of the new members across the country. First of all you had the middle-class Marxists, people who demographically should be Tory but who were now being drawn back into the cause; before, most of them had buggered off to the Lib Dems. Then you had the left-wing students. They're pro-Corbyn but not especially doctrinaire, more normal. Third you had a small but noisy group of mainly older men, trade union types who had gone off to the Socialist Workers Party or other splinter groups. They're usually the nastiest and most militant. And then fourthly a mix of mostly middle-class, middle-aged folk on the soft left/left who started trickling in during Miliband but arrived with a bang. They just generally think Corbyn is a good thing and they wanted to support him. They're probably the least committed, most amenable and also the least likely to be involved with Momentum.'

From everything I'd seen around the country that seemed to be a good barometer of what was happening nationally.

My source went on: 'The biggest thing was, you could sense a huge difference between the new members who had joined before 2015 and those after. After 2015 and especially after the failed coup in Parliament in 2016, there was just a different attitude. Those new members had a zeal for a purge.'

And they were to find the perfect mechanism.

The Haringey Development Vehicle, or HDV, doesn't sound like something that would make grown men and women scream at each other. But then funny things go on in north London.

It's unlikely you came to this book to read about the finer points of London local government's attempt to regenerate its housing stock, so I don't propose to get into the weeds of this here. Suffice to say, it was a controversial initiative started by the members of Haringey's then Labour cabinet to try and build new houses and regenerate the ones the council already has. They did so because Haringey, like most local authorities, had precious little cash. After 2010 it was forced to accept a 40 per cent reduction in its budget. It moved out of or sold twelve of its buildings and cut 45 per cent of its staff. Yet the burdens placed on the council's shoulders became heavier each year. At the same time, their estate, their stock of council houses, declined in quality, desperately needing investment. One senior member of the council put it to me like this: 'Look, we had a choice. Either we accepted decline, accepted that there would be no new council houses, accepted that we couldn't afford to put new heaters in people's homes, or we had to think creatively. Clare [Kober, the leader of the council] and the rest of us just weren't prepared to accept managed decline.'

On the contrary, many among the Haringey leadership were ambitious – very ambitious. Unusually for the leaders of a local authority they were young, mostly well under forty. Many had cut their teeth as student politicians in Blair's heyday and their remedy for the council's woes was one of which the old master would doubtless fully approve. The thinking was that because the council was asset-rich but cash-poor, it would pool most of its £2bn assets with a private company, Lendlease. In return, Lendlease would provide cash upfront for 7,000 new homes and the renovation of many others. Lendlease would then develop other land for commercial purposes and attempt to commercialise other council buildings, and thus in the long run, it hoped, return a profit. Some of those assets included council houses.

This was not, as you might imagine, uncontroversial, and the scheme generated much resistance locally. Not all of it was from the left either. David Lammy, the MP for Tottenham, which falls within the borough, expressed his concerns. So did some other councillors not aligned with the left internally. From my impressions, Kober and her team did not always behave well towards either their new or old members, acting in a secretive and often high-handed fashion. They did not wear their ambition lightly.

But the incident is instructive for us about wider trends within the party, not least its organisation. Momentum showed its organising muscle. Within a few weeks, no fewer than a third of the entire council had been deselected or had stood down, knowing that if they had stood then they would have been deselected. Momentum's strength was impressive. As Councillor Nate Doron, elected in 2014, choosing not to stand again in 2018, told me:

'You'd arrive at the meeting, and greeting you at the front door would be a couple of Momentum activists, handing out leaflets with instructions as to how you should vote on resolutions, who you should vote for selections, this way, that way and this way. I'd never seen a slate before Jeremy Corbyn became leader. What happens now is they hand it to you and tell you who to vote for. They'd be phone-banking members. How are you supposed to compete with that? It was just a different Labour Party in 2013 when I got in. I used to look forward to Labour Party meetings. We'd all go down the pub afterwards. Now we go to our pub and they go to theirs.'

Momentum and the left, for their part, say that the deselections and the acrimony were purely about the HDV. They say that if it weren't for that, there would have been no problems. Those deselected disagree. Alan Strickland, until 2018 the housing member on the cabinet, is in no doubt: 'It's a Trojan horse. This was coming anyway. They just wanted control. They might not have been as successful without the HDV but they would have got rid of most of us anyway.' National commentators agree and seized upon the developments as proof of an impending wider purge. John McTernan, former adviser to Blair and Brown, declared: 'It's the Keyser Söze* approach to managing the party. It's Maoist – one executed, one thousand educated. If you're a moderate in local government and want to achieve change, winter is coming.'

---

* Me neither. Apparently, it refers to the crime lord in the 1995 film *The Usual Suspects*.

Momentum and the left have pointed out that while Haringey has been full of deselections, there have been very few in the rest of London. Surely if there were some mass purge going on, they would be taking place in (at the very least) the boroughs next door. There's a fair amount of truth in this. The HDV clearly stirred up real feelings and to some extent that was reflected in the local political activity.

But Haringey councillors had another big disadvantage: they were selected much later than everybody else. A senior councillor in another borough told me at the time: 'If I'd had my selection when Haringey did, I'd be fucked. So would most of my cabinet.' Most London selections took place in the period immediately before June 2017, i.e. before the general election. This was a time of unusual weakness for Momentum and Jeremy Corbyn personally. He languished at the bottom of the polls and was perceived to have performed extremely poorly during the European referendum, an issue particularly close to the hearts of Londoners and London Labour members in particular. Corbyn's faction within the party were therefore less able to fight their corner and pick fights over selections. They were also distracted by supporting Corbyn in his second leadership struggle. This was the case for most councils across England standing for re-election in 2018.

Haringey, however, did not select until autumn/winter 2017, long after the general election was over and when Corbyn had not only re-established his reputation and authority but had become unassailable. New members poured in. The writing was on the wall. This is probably why Jon Lansman called for nominations across the whole of the city to be rerun.

Moreover, Momentum and the Labour left are not strong everywhere. This is something that everyone misses because they expect some sinister organisation embedded everywhere with the all-knowing Sauron-like figure of Jon Lansman watching and pulling the strings. They have 40,000 members – a big number, but not nearly enough to influence the debate in every contest. In boroughs without much Momentum presence there has been little activity. Where there are lots of them, as in Haringey, Lambeth, Redbridge, Ealing and Manchester, there has been much more.

So, what Haringey does partly represent is the clock catching up. The vast majority of elected Labour Party officials across the country, from the Parliamentary Labour Party down, were selected and then elected when the internal Labour Party constellations were much different. As Nate Doron said to me, when he was chosen, 'It was a different Labour Party.'

In some ways, deselection will become less important than sheer natural wastage. As sitting councillors and MPs, chosen in the Blair, Brown and Miliband years, retire for the myriad reasons that people do, then slowly their replacements will be chosen not by the party membership who selected them but by the new order. That lag in time and space between party members and elected officials will gradually lessen. We already got a taste of that in the 2017 election. Centrist MPs deciding for whatever reason to stand down were often replaced by more Corbynite candidates. The 2017 PLP is therefore already to the left of the one elected in 2015. That process will continue throughout the country at council and parliamentary level in the years to come. Haringey was just on accelerated development due to timing and local politics.

Frankly, that is the way it always has been. If one faction, united by a common set of beliefs, brings more people to a room than you, out-organises you, wins over enough people with a set of common beliefs, and all rules are obeyed – well, in a democracy and a democratic party that's kind of … tough. It has always happened. Whichever faction is in the ascendancy within Labour Party history tends to dominate. That is often painful for those who are more established, to watch a party to which they've given so many years be taken from before their eyes by new recruits. Unfortunately, those are the party's rules.

Nonetheless, a few things present themselves. Firstly, in the Labour Party, the rules are the rules right up until the point that they are no longer the rules. The left isn't standing still but using its new-found dominance to permanently alter the balance of power within the party. Some of this has happened already, with an expansion of the number of places available on the NEC for members, and other innovations. Most is still to come – by the time you read this the party's internal 'Democracy Review', ordered by Corbyn in 2017 when enjoying the full spurs of his election comeback, will likely have reported and been accepted by the party's structures. This will include direct election to party official positions, election of local council leaders by party membership (not councillors) and the reduction yet further of the threshold of MPs required to place a leadership candidate on the ballot paper. All of these measures are designed to embed Corbynism within the Labour Party's structures permanently, to ensure that Corbyn, whenever he finally goes, will be replaced by another Corbyn. Momentum will be at the centre of all of this – arguing for a Labour Party that is, in their view for the very first time, truly bottom up. Haringey too gives us a few clues to what might come next in other councils across the country as Momentum gathers strength. That will be especially the case if the Parliament runs the full five years up to 2022. As councils continue to hit the buffers, Labour local authorities will have no choice but to continue to experiment and innovate with how they provide their services. It is clear from Haringey that if that does not meet certain expectations of how they think a Labour council ought to behave, then there will be trouble. As one councillor told me: 'It's really frustrating. It's right we were challenged over the decisions; groups of people have genuine concerns. But some who just hated us, who wanted regime change, latched on to the issue. That's going to happen elsewhere.'

Some also believe that Jeremy Corbyn's office was directly involved with the selections. Cabinet members have alleged to me that the day before selections were due to begin the interview panel, who comprise the initial stage of the process to become a candidate and vet who can be put forward for the next stage, was changed. To do so at the last minute is quite unorthodox. Cabinet members say that only an intervention from the leader's office could have precipitated such a change. Corbyn's office has not commented.

We'll never know whether that is true. But it would fit a pattern indicating that Corbyn and those around him took a particular interest in Haringey. Corbyn himself made an oblique reference to the HDV in his 2016 party conference speech. And after the Corbynites took control of the NEC in early 2018, the body flexed its muscles by making an unprecedented appeal to the council to stop the HDV. This led to the resignation of the leader, Clare Kober. Corbyn's office is, in many of these cases, a shadowy but powerful force.

As councils square up to their second decade of austerity, the gap between the ideals of what the new members want and what can be achieved might grow all the greater, creating more Haringeys across the country. Except of course that having seen the political slaughter in the borough, those leaders will be much more careful about exactly what they do. That, the pro-HDV councillors have told me, is the real tragedy. Nate Doron: 'There is a big disconnect between the members and the realities. We have to be pragmatic. We don't think the HDV is ideal but we're not going to stand by and see people suffer just so we can be ideologically pure.' Another long-standing local member, who left the party over the issue, agreed:

'I think it's profoundly immoral. I think you've left some of the poorest people in the borough – and in the country, because it's Tottenham – languishing in really bad accommodation. Crime hot spots, drug dealers on the stairwells, damp, mould, people scared to walk through there in the evening time … why? You've left them to that. You've abandoned them to that – and there's no alternative. They have no alternative … And that was sanctioned by blooming Jeremy Corbyn himself. Jeremy, the NEC, whatever. It was really public. They supported the efforts to quash the HDV. The HDV is symbolic, it's totemic of the political divide.'

The spectrum of what is acceptable for Labour councils to do has been substantially reduced, all because of Haringey and the poison that has flowed from it.

Nonetheless, speaking to anti-HDV/Momentum councillors they have plenty of ideas for what to do next. They want to abolish council tax for low-income residents, bring building and other council service contracts back in house, extend free school meals to every primary school, and municipalise failing care providers, to name just a few things they've discussed. With the new cabinet now in place after London's 2018 elections and a very different leadership in office, it will be a test case of Corbynism in action and will receive lots of attention. But, of course, it all costs money. And until the day comes when Corbyn enters government they will not be able to implement it without some pretty drastic cuts in other areas. As one councillor told me: 'They are extremely statist by instinct. It'll be a case study in what Corbyn would like to do nationally except they'll have no money. So then they'll probably all just start fighting each other.' There are some indications that this has already started to happen. Without a common enemy to unite them, the disparate threads of the left often begin to fall apart.

So, expect to hear a lot more about Haringey over the coming years. But whether or not Momentum and the Corbynistas have the numbers, whether or not they're right or wrong to slowly fill the party with their own people, the manner of conducting the contests is within their gift. And those contests did not show the party or the left in their best light. There have been accusations of sexism, bullying, intimidation and racism. Unfortunately, such happenings do not stop at Haringey's frontiers.

Chapter 8

FEAR AND LOATHING IN THE LABOUR PARTY

We can create a new kind of politics: kinder, more respectful, but courageous, too.

Jeremy Corbyn, 2015

Of all the bigotries that savage the human temper there is none as stupid as the anti-Semitic.

David Lloyd George, 1923

Kind hearts are more than coronets,
And simple faith than Norman blood.

Lord Alfred Tennyson, 'Lady Clara Vere de Vere', 1842

When I was a kid, there was no doubt in my mind who the nice guys in politics were. It was just, to my teenage mind, obvious. Labour seemed modern, tolerant, open. Comfortable with the nation that Britain was then. The Tories seemed permanently angry at the notion of the now. They wanted Britain to be something that it no longer was and wished the people in it would just change or go away. In 2002 the Conservative Party's chairman, one Theresa May, appeared to agree. Some people, she said, had started calling her party, for its stance on gays, ethnic minorities and other social issues, the 'nasty party'. It was a brave thing to say to a party that did not want to hear it and it damaged her with the grassroots. It was a plea for a more inclusive, open and tolerant party. Over fifteen years later, I was in the auditorium at Symphony Hall in Birmingham, to hear her finally put the issue to bed as prime minister:

'The main lesson I take from their conference last week is that the Labour Party is not just divided, but divisive. Determined to pit one against another. To pursue vendettas and settle scores. And to embrace the politics of pointless protest that simply pulls people further apart. That's what Labour stands for today. Fighting among themselves. Abusing their own MPs. Threatening to end their careers. Tolerating anti-Semitism and supporting voices of hate. You know what some people call them? The nasty party.'

It was a good line and she said it with relish. And the joke worked. It couldn't have worked at any other time in the Labour Party's history. Because although it was being delivered by a Conservative prime minister at a Conservative Party conference for obvious political reasons, the joke contained within it a pretty weighty kernel of truth. Because, if I'm honest, if I think about some of the things I've seen and heard over the last couple of years, I can't with certainty say who the nice guys in British politics are any more.

The influx of new members means that Labour politics is more exciting, more vital, more rambunctious than it used to be. It is more *political*, in every sense. I don't think many, speaking objectively, would think it kinder. Most new members are decent, just folk. They would be a credit to any party. However, there is also a significant minority that no party should want. Some are thugs.

Some local parties have remained relatively undisturbed. Some have been turned upside down. Wallasey Constituency Labour Party is in the latter camp.

Wallasey, on the northernmost tip of the Wirral on Merseyside, has previous. Many of the Liverpool and Wirral Labour parties were, as incubators of the Militant tendency, at the centre of Labour's internecine battles of the 1980s. Few thought that they would return.

But in early summer 2016 I'd heard whispers that the local party had been inundated with new members and were causing enormous trouble to the local MP, who just happened to be Angela Eagle, who just so happened to have resigned from the shadow cabinet in the wake of the referendum and who was now making a (short-lived) run for the leadership.

I went up to make a film for *Newsnight.* Rumours were swirling that Eagle might face a motion of no confidence from her own party. Labour would then face the unedifying spectacle, to add to what were then a thousand other unedifying spectacles, of a candidate for its own leadership being denounced or even deselected by her own local party.

Kathy Miller was the new chair of Wallasey CLP. As I sat in her kitchen sipping tea, she made no attempt to hide her fury at Eagle. The astonishing thing was that Kathy had joined the party only a year ago, with the Corbyn wave. She was already the chair and was presiding over a local party now over 1,200 strong.

I had no doubt that, in her contempt for Eagle, she was speaking for many of her fellow new recruits: 'She [Eagle] has been doing such strange things recently. For months, we've had her coming to the party and she has always shown support for Jeremy, saying he's been doing such a good job. When asked about the referendum: "Oh well, he's been running up and down the country like a 25-year-old." Less than a week later, apparently he hasn't shown any leadership qualities. Well that's a load of rubbish.'

The mood in the party was fraught. Just as I was finishing a couple of interviews, a newsflash appeared on my phone: a brick had been thrown into Angela Eagle's office window.

No one was hurt, but, frankly, that was just luck. The brick was lobbed right through the office window, on to the building's main busy staircase. As one of Eagle's assistants, Helen Osgood, a kindly, middle-aged lady, who'd only just started working for the MP, showed me around, looking at the shards of glass, scattered across the staircase, it was hard not to think of how easily those same shards might have been stained with blood.

Helen had been excited to work for her MP. Now she was just plain scared. This took place only weeks after the murder of Jo Cox. As I stood staring at the shards, I was transported back to that fetid early summer night in Birstall and to the sight of her shoes, still in the road, now police evidence for the first political assassination in Britain for thirty years. You couldn't help but wonder if that summer was yet done with us.

That was exactly what preoccupied Helen's family: 'We didn't expect anything like throwing something through the window, but we did know that the environment in which we were working was becoming increasingly hostile. I mean, my son has made me have a little alarm thing on my keys now because he's worried about me. Especially when we do the surgeries.'

This was a woman probably paid south of £30,000 a year. A part-time caseworker in one of the poorer constituencies of England, she was, more or less, a civil servant, certainly not a party warrior. Neither she nor her colleagues deserved this. While I was there several police officers were in the building, taking statements. A police cordon was around the window and blue lights flashed through what was left of the glass; this at the constituency office of a British Member of Parliament in 2016. As I stood outside, filming a piece to camera, a driver sped past and screamed, at the top of his lungs: 'JEREMY CORBYN!' and cackled. Politics felt dark.

That same day, the office received a death threat via voicemail. I also obtained a copy of an email threat it had received shortly afterwards.

> If! You become the leader of the Labour Party you will split it and make labour lose buy also you will too have time to enjoy it, you will die your Bitch.
>
> Leave the UK. Or Die.

I don't think spelling is scumbags' strong suit so, as you can see, I've reproduced it verbatim.

Rightly, there was much concern about these developments. MPs, especially those who had resigned from the front bench, felt less and less safe in their own constituencies. Worse, many Corbyn supporters in the country, overwhelmed by the bitter taste of betrayal, appeared to be indifferent. The day the brick was thrown through Eagle's window, her staff posted a message about the incident on her official MP's Facebook page. I couldn't quite believe my eyes. Thousands of messages from thousands of separate individuals, expressing neither concern, nor shock, nor good wishes, but each and every one saying simply #VoteCorbyn, again and again and again. It was a simple but complete act of defiance. Two fingers, in two words.

Many to whom I spoke were convinced that Eagle had done it herself, to engender sympathy and to derail the Corbyn project.

Worse still, although there was considerable concern across the country at these developments, many MPs felt there was indifference at the top of the party. Eagle called on Corbyn to 'rein in' his supporters, saying that actions like that were 'being done in his name, and he needs to get control of the people who are supporting him and make certain that this behaviour stops and stops now. It is bullying. It has absolutely no place in politics in the UK and it needs to end.' Corbyn replied condemning the action, but chose to engage in a bit of 'whataboutism',* to point out various equivalences, saying he too had received death threats.

The dark turn of Wallasey politics wasn't confined to a single brick. More concerning for Labour nationally was how quickly the party had descended into bitter civil war between competing factions. This wasn't surprising when you learned that many of the figures who had been involved with Militant and other far-left infiltration groups in the 1980s on Merseyside, had returned to the fold. Principal among them was Paul Davies, who had been central to the efforts to try and expel Frank Field in Birkenhead, just down the road, in the early eighties. After rejoining the party to vote for Corbyn, he had already climbed back to become vice-chair of Wallasey CLP. *Newsnight* had sent another reporter up in 1981 specifically to make a piece about

* This happens a lot.

his activities and wider far-left infiltration. Now I was there in 2016 on the same story. History was repeating itself.

I met Davies in a café, above a theatre overlooking New Brighton shipyard. He was charm personified. Knowledgeable, funny, curious. Unlike many higher up in politics he was unafraid to be interviewed and unafraid to answer questions about his actions.

I also don't have much doubt that, politically speaking at least, I wouldn't want to get on the wrong side of him.

Quietly but with force, he spoke to me of his anger at Eagle and her colleagues and what should happen next: 'There will be a move to punish Angela and MPs – I don't think we should punish people. But they should be prepared to take the same route as they thought fit for Jeremy Corbyn. He faced a vote of no confidence and then they thought he should resign. So, if they face a vote like that in their constituency, they should resign.'

As softly spoken and kindly as he seemed, I knew that many of his local party would not recognise this Davies. Talking to Councillor Moira McLoughlin (a veteran of the battles of the 1980s) and a new recruit to Wirral Young Labour, James Fields, their experience of recent meetings had been grim, as Fields recounted:

'Within Wallasey, the tone of the meetings has been appalling. We've had reports of violence, homophobia, appalling arguments between grown men and women. There have been homophobic comments aimed at Angela Eagle who wasn't present at the meeting, homophobic gestures made towards people at the mention of Angela's name. Someone even threatened to punch somebody. What angers me is this is a blatant contradiction of our own rules, our own values.'

When I put those accusations to Davies, his answer was revealing: 'We're being asked to believe that among the councillors who were there, the trade union officials who were there, the people who supported Angela, the people who don't support Angela, not one person stood up to object to intimidation, or, worse, to object to homophobia. Now I would criticise anyone – anyone – who heard a homophobic comment or saw a homophobic gesture at a meeting who didn't challenge it ...'

I put it to him that perhaps they felt they couldn't, perhaps they were intimidated.

'Well, that's a good excuse, you see, isn't it, to say: "I couldn't complain about the intimidation because I felt intimidated."'

I left Liverpool with little doubt that although no one could be certain about who said exactly what to whom, a culture of bullying and intimidation was gripping parts of the Labour Party. Labour HQ, unusually as I was to discover, agreed. It suspended Wallasey CLP (a move that was almost without precedent), and suspended Davies personally.

It is the complaint of many Labour MPs, councillors and members that HQ has not always acted so decisively. And perhaps it can't because inherent in some of the uglier edges of Corbynism is a political sectarianism: an unshakeable belief that the other side is not only wrong but immoral.

Over the past few years I have spoken to a great many Labour Party members and attended many meetings and campaign events. Generally they are comradely and genial.

I also don't doubt that there have been many incidents of intimidation and bullying. Politics, all round, has become coarser. Before 2015 factional fighting within the party was relatively minimal. Today it is all-consuming. Those who find themselves on the wrong side of that divide can often find life uncomfortable.

Moreover, there is something about the hard left that is totalising and sharp-edged. I have rarely felt more troubled than I did reporting on Jeremy Corbyn's speech for the Durham Miners' Gala. Corbyn was due to speak at about three o'clock. For our piece to make the seven o'clock news, I knew we had to be done and out of there by four. But we wanted a bit of excitement by filming a piece to camera of me talking in the crowd at the end of Corbyn speaking with the crowd roaring all around me. Standard TV news stuff.

However, bitter experience taught me that you can never be sure when Corbyn will start or finish. I didn't imagine I'd be out of there quickly, but made my way through the incredibly dense, sweaty crowd avoiding the outstretched hot dogs and tomato sauce, to make it to the media pen just in front of the stage.

I sat and waited. And waited. And waited. Thirty minutes went by. Then 45. Then 60. Still no sign we might reach the grand denouement. I knew, if this kept up our piece wouldn't make that night's news.

I decided I could wait no longer and opted for a change of tack: I thought I'd stand up and do a whispered, shorter turn and make a virtue of the fact we were in the crowd with the speech still going on. I whispered the new plan to the cameraman, Mike, and he, gratefully, gave me the thumbs up.

I stood up and started to speak. Almost no sooner had I done so but I received a wail of fury. Two elderly women at whom you wouldn't look twice at a bus stop shouted at me: 'Sit the fuck down!'

'Yeah, sit the fuck down, you fucking scum!'

I understood it must be a bit annoying to have your view temporarily blocked by a camera. But given it was for less than thirty seconds, I hadn't been expecting cold fury for it. And throughout the speech it kept happening to others, especially photographers from the papers. At one point, one of the people who had come to watch the speech ducked under the barrier tape separating us from the crowd, and said that if the snapper didn't stop, he would make him.

That wasn't all. At one point Corbyn mentioned an opponent or someone outside the party, and one of the old ladies not far from me screamed: 'Hang 'em! Hang 'em!' Somehow, Margaret Thatcher's dementia came up and someone else screamed: 'Bitch! Good! Let her rot!'

Eventually he finished and I got the piece to camera I needed. As we were about to leave, a man who had been standing in the front row approached me and came close to my face: 'You wanna be careful dressed like that, lad, dressed like a Tory round here.'

I replied that I was wearing a suit because I was working and that in any case I wasn't sure that only Tories wear suits.

He replied: 'You're a fucking Tory.' Another woman approached me at the same time. 'I've seen you on Sky. You're a Tory. You might think you're high and mighty now but when change comes you'll be on the floor and no one is going to give a shit about you.'

I was stunned. I'd never met this person. I suspect she knew almost nothing about me. But I was, in her own mind, the enemy. If you ever doubted why Laura Kuenssberg, a journalist with whom I've been lucky to work and from whom I've learned much, had to have security at the Labour Party conference in 2017 – then don't. This is why.

I've seen or experienced variants of this many times. At the Conservative Party conference in 2015 I emerged still wearing my official lanyard. A woman approached me, right up to my face, and whispered: 'Fucking Tory scum.' I replied instantly to say that I wasn't a Tory, I was a journalist. Almost at once she transformed, her complexion lightened and she smiled: 'Oh, I'm so sorry! I thought you were a Tory, have a lovely day!' With that, she scuttled off, back up the line, presumably in the hope of better hunting.

But journalists only get half of it. The real intimidation and acrimony is experienced all over the country by ordinary Labour Party members.

There is an obvious form of harassment: the abuse, the name calling, the bullying. This is what we hear about, what we read about, that which escapes the confines of the meeting room. The best way of getting some of that across is by a conversation I had with a source formerly of the London Labour Party. Even though they left the party in disgust and anger, they did not wish to be named, but it's worth reproducing part of our conversation at length:

> SOURCE: On the one side you've got the very well-documented, serious aggression: scum, swear words, accusing us of being social cleansers, ethnic cleansers, etc., so all that really nasty stuff. And then also, for example, in one of our local Labour Party Facebook groups, there was a discussion where people were wishing death on Hilary Benn and wishing death on Tony Blair etc. All the usual off-the-chart nastiness.

But then you've got the slightly cleverer ones who don't do it like that. And actually ... they're the ones who have created an almost even more pernicious atmosphere locally. And this is mirrored all over the country. Where, when you challenge them or when a councillor would disagree with them on something, they would immediately accuse them of something. So they would accuse them of abuse, they've accused them of harassment, intimidation and the rest.

So if you challenge someone in a meeting – happens in politics! is politics in fact! – suddenly there were lots of formal complaints going in to, say, the council, or the standards body. Similarly, complaints were being made to the local party, and when the selections battle started, complaints started to be made against non-Momentum councillors from Momentum activists – and Momentum councillors.

This created an environment where people who were not Momentum, they just started being really careful about what they said. They started shying away from having public debates or certainly private debates against people because they didn't want to be accused of various different things. I remember one councillor saying to me – and I agree with this completely, I wouldn't either – this councillor said to me that they would not be in a room on their own with certain other councillors, because they just couldn't without an independent witness, because they couldn't trust that they wouldn't end up being accused of something. And then it's your word against theirs –

ME: These are fellow Labour councillors?

SOURCE: Fellow Labour councillors. So that is the level of farce and stifling political environment that you're in, where people will literally not be in the room with their fellow Labour members because they don't trust them not to bring up some random allegation against them. And they will. They just lie. So that's something that hasn't fully come out properly yet.

This stuff about the aggression … Look at the slightly cleverer people. It's these people who are not getting expelled from the Labour Party, and actually a lot of these people I actually feel quite sorry for them. Not all of them – but there are a lot of people who just say really stupid things, but actually they … I don't know … sometimes I think, actually, some of these people have challenges and mental health issues. And in the days gone by, Labour was able to kind of, be OK – that was a safe environment for them to be kind of bonkers but it was OK. It was like a safe, it was like a family place –

ME: Because politics attracts eccentrics.

SOURCE: Yeah, exactly, and we can carry our eccentrics and oddballs, and that was OK. But now what's happening is the eccentrics and oddballs, spurred on by the slightly cleverer ones in the middle, and of course by Corbyn and whatever … they're the ones that go out there and say the completely mad things but they're encouraged and stoked by higher-ups. And it's those people who are playing a more dangerous game and getting away with it.

ME: If they lie as much as you say, how do you think they justify it to themselves then?

SOURCE: It's for the cause. They don't want people who don't support Corbyn.

ME: And anything else can be justified on that?

SOURCE: Absolutely.

The source went on to allege that, at one point, one of their colleagues spent a night in a police cell as a result of a totally false accusation by a Momentum member. They claim that it was only thanks to CCTV happening to be present on the site where the alleged incident took place that they were exonerated.

This is just one local Labour Party. There are many, many more stories to tell, all with their own variants and peculiarities and prejudices. But up and down the country, in branch after branch, you might well come across an infection that is new and yet the oldest prejudice of all: anti-Semitism.

JEREMY AND THE JEWS

It must be a novel and unsettling experience for Jeremy Corbyn to be the subject of a protest. However, in the first half of 2018 he unexpectedly found himself on the receiving end of quite a few. In early April, I was outside Labour's Victoria Street headquarters on a drizzly Sunday afternoon. In front of me were hundreds of angry Jewish protesters. Some of them were Labour Party members, some had been and were no longer, and some had never had any formal affiliation with the party at all.

A couple held aloft a flag of Israel. Many more brandished placards of: 'CORBYN OUT' or 'ZERO TOLERANCE ON ANTI-SEMITISM'. Every time Corbyn himself was mentioned, he was roundly booed. One speaker lamented the destruction 'of the once great Labour Party'. Several Jews there told me they were scared of Jeremy Corbyn and several more that should he become prime minister they would leave the country. 'Why take the risk?' one man said. For a people who for too long have had to live with a sense of unease and danger in their bones, it seemed incredible that those old instincts of persecution, flight and hazard, were being activated in modern Britain.

And by what? If I stepped back and really thought about it I could believe neither my eyes nor my ears. This a protest about anti-Semitism in a British political party – in the Labour Party – in 2018.

It was the culmination of weeks of ongoing tumult. By the time you read this, many of the events will have receded into the dim recesses of our brains. But, suffice to say, Jeremy Corbyn bungled it.

Again and again and again. What should have started as an incident that could have been shut down and isolated became bigger and bigger and bigger because of ham-fisted handling by the leadership and the wider reaction of its supporters. But all of it revealed something rotten deep within Corbynism and within the new Labour Party.

At the end of March 2018, it was revealed that Jeremy Corbyn had, in 2012, chosen to comment on this image on Facebook.

It was a mural painted by the Los Angeles-based artist Mear One. It had been on a wall in east London but was removed by Tower Hamlets Council in 2012 after complaints that it was anti-Semitic. Look at it closely and ask yourself, as you examine the obviously Jewish figures, with their stereotyped big hooked noses, playing Monopoly on the backs of the workers in front of Illuminati iconography, if you disagree with that conclusion.

Jeremy Corbyn saw this on Facebook and did not see much of a problem. Rather, he enquired as to why it was being taken down.

Corbyn later claimed not to have looked at the mural in any detail. Nonetheless, when the story broke, his response to the upset was widely condemned as feeble and begrudging. It took four iterations of a statement before he finally struck the right tone. Corbyn, who initially said that there were only 'pockets' of anti-Semitism in the party (and before that had refused to acknowledge its existence, or condemn it in its own right), was forced to retreat. In the end, he conceded: 'I recognise that anti-Semitism has surfaced within the Labour Party, and has too often been dismissed as simply a matter of a few bad apples,' he wrote (without mentioning that he had done exactly that just one day before). 'I acknowledge that anti-Semitic attitudes have surfaced more often in our ranks in recent years and that the Party has been too slow in processing some of the cases that have emerged.' It was too little, too late. The result was that the row spiralled out of control. In the meantime, his closest allies made it worse. Diane Abbott claimed that the whole thing was just a 'smear campaign against Jeremy'.

This didn't come out of nowhere. Only a year before, both the former London mayor, Ken Livingstone, and the Bradford MP, Naz Shah, were suspended from the party for making anti-Semitic comments. Corbyn responded by asking the human rights campaigner Shami Chakrabarti to head an inquiry into anti-Semitism. The report largely exonerated Labour and its leadership but made twenty recommendations. At the time of writing most of those had not been implemented.* Before any of this, many Jews had been very concerned at the prospect of a man becoming leader who had described Hamas as 'my friends' and defended a Palestinian politician who had been convicted of blood libel and Holocaust denial in Israel (among other rather choice associations). It was a powder keg waiting to blow. After the mural story emerged, many party members came forward saying they had either been victims of anti-Semitism in the party themselves or had seen it happen to others.

Leaving aside the particulars of the events themselves, anti-Semitism in the Labour Party teaches us much about its current

---

* The report's credibility was blighted by Chakrabarti's ennoblement as a Labour peer shortly after it was published (at the time of writing the only peer Jeremy Corbyn has appointed). She was given a seat at the shadow cabinet table not long afterwards.

politics and culture. Many people, however, doubt that the problem exists. They are wrong. Whether it's the Oxford University Labour Club mocking the Jewish victims of the Paris supermarket attack and calling Auschwitz a 'cash cow';* whether it's a Jewish Labour MP, Ruth Smeeth. receiving a 1,000-word death threat calling her a 'yid cunt', after walking out of a meeting outlining the Labour leader's response to anti-Semitism; whether it's Haringey councillors telling me about assertions made in meetings of 'Jews having big noses, controlling the media and being wealthy' (when they resigned, a Momentum activist tweeted: 'At least [you] will have more time to count your money'); I could go on. Even figures on the Corbynist left have accepted it is a problem, including Jon Lansman.

Where does it come from? Historically the Labour Party was pro-Israel and pro-Zionist, helping establish the Jewish state in 1948. Most British Jews were left wing and aligned themselves to the Labour Party. In the general election of 1945, 27 of the 29 Jewish MPs elected were Labour.†

But anti-Semitism springs eternal and has flowed anew under Corbyn's Labour. That is no coincidence. Corbynism's locus, as we have seen, is in foreign policy, and nothing could be more central to that view of the world than the Israeli-Palestinian conflict. His politics is a culmination of the political ideas of the New Left of the 1960s: that Israel was not an answer to a deep and just desire for national belonging but a colonialist and later apartheid-like enterprise. As the memories of the fires of the Holocaust faded, politicians like Jeremy Corbyn and Ken Livingstone became influenced by these ideas and made their way into national politics. Many like them, who share that analysis, have joined Corbyn's Labour under and because of his leadership.

Corbynism, as we've seen, with its views on Russia and the West and foreign regimes, is fundamentally about power, and it's worth

---

* After months of obfuscation and delay, including an NEC report that was never published, it was decided not to expel the perpetrators.

† One of the others was a Communist.

recapping: it is, in its essence, a rather crude power-ordering lens through which to see and order the world and guide your sympathies. Any one group or state that is perceived to be politically, economically and/or culturally dominant is instantly perceived as suspicious. Any group that is considered weaker or oppressed is inherently more virtuous. Israel and Jews suffer because they fall smack bang in the middle of the Venn diagram of power. They are militarily dominant in their region, they and their diaspora are wealthy and influential, they are closely allied with the West, and, worst of all, they have an oppressed and culturally and politically weak enemy in their midst: the Palestinians. Any one of these is usually enough to get Corbynistas rattled, but all of them come together to form a noxious political cocktail. Hence online the term 'Zio' is one of abuse, applied even to people with neither Jewish heritage nor especially strong views on Israel. It is a code, a code for someone who believes in oppression, someone stronger than the weak, someone who is an imperialist. For Corbyn and his fellow travellers, therefore, especially in the Stop the War Coalition and like-minded groups, Israel isn't always about the Israeli-Palestinian conflict itself, or, at least, it isn't exclusively. Israel instead becomes a symbol of Western imperialism and Palestinians the embodiment of its many victims. As Dave Rich argues:

'In 2010, Jeremy Corbyn led a rally outside the Israeli embassy in London with the slogan, "In our thousands, in our millions, we are all Palestinians." It doesn't matter how many people die in Syria, or even how many Palestinians die there, Corbyn will never lead a demonstration chanting "In our thousands, in our millions, we are all Syrians" unless he can blame the West for their deaths. This is about a political outlook that sees Israel, Zionism and those Jews who are not actively opposed to Israel – which, in reality, means most Jews in Britain – as part of a global network of power and racism, on the side of the oppressors against the oppressed. Campaigns against colonialism and apartheid, and the civil rights movement, are its formative political experiences, rather than anti-fascism and the Holocaust, and the old class politics has been replaced by identity politics.'

Jews' unusual position within society also confuses the Corbynist power prism and its understanding of racism. As a Jewish Labour source told me: 'I don't think he [Corbyn] personally is anti-Semitic exactly. I think it's because anti-Semitism is a form of racism outside his usual cultural understanding – it doesn't fit the anti-colonial, neo-imperial stuff which others do.' The Corbynist view of racism is a relatively rigid one. Racism is generally about imperialism and colonialism, about racially based inequality, and is about fighting the legacies of old empires and the exploitation of powerless races and people by more politically dominant whites. It is why Jeremy Corbyn and his colleagues performed so well and spoke with such passion about the plight of the Windrush Generation and their appalling treatment by the Home Office in spring 2018. It was a depressingly familiar tale of disrespectful and indifferent treatment towards black people by white people. Corbyn and others are less able to process the idea of a racism and systematic bullying towards a group of people they reflexively consider to be white and powerful – indeed, sometimes extremely powerful. They are therefore less careful and at times positively reckless in their language and actions. Jeremy Corbyn looked at that mural and blithely commented on it because fundamentally he doesn't consider Jews to be oppressed. He would never have done so if it had depicted Muslims for the opposite reason. One is about freedom of speech, the other would be an appalling culturally imperialist gesture that revealed awful attitudes about modern Britain. As one Labour moderate, Richard Angell, told me:

'For a group of people who claim to really care about injustice they have a bizarre notion of it. For them, what's happening to the Palestinians is so bad that a few Jews getting shouted at on the way to the synagogue is kind of neither here nor there in the scale of injustice happening. But the mindset that comes to that conclusion is a really pernicious one, because it does believe Jews should collectively be held responsible for various things that happen whether in their name or not, that they are somehow responsible for a state they may never have visited … and that therefore, by just being Jews and going to synagogue on a Friday night or engaging with the LP in some way, they're somehow reinforcing the power of the Israeli state to occupy the Palestinians' and there's something really pernicious about that.'

This is why removing anti-Semitism from the Labour Party under the Corbyn leadership will be so difficult. Most Corbynistas, from the man himself down, don't understand it as a form of prejudice. For Corbynistas there is a hierarchy of racism and anti-Semitism is at its bottom. It is entwined with their own thinking and mythos and way of ordering and viewing the world. As a former Labour activist, Nora Mulready, told me: 'There's no way that anti-Semitism will be put out the Labour Party while Corbyn is its leader. It's impossible. His politics have given it a petri dish in which to fester and grow.'

Is Jeremy Corbyn an anti-Semite himself? I've not met even his harshest critic who thinks he personally dislikes Jews. But he is presiding over a party in which anti-Semitism is increasingly common. Responding to the Windrush scandal, his own equalities secretary, Dawn Butler, appeared on Sky News and said that institutional racism was when an organisation 'fosters a [negative] environment which affects one particular race or group'. The profound irony did not seem to occur to her that for many British Jews that is precisely what the Labour Party has done. Or there's the man who wrote the book on institutional racism, Lord MacPherson, who chaired the inquiry into the investigation of Stephen Lawrence's death, and defined institutional racism as follows:

> The collective failure of an organisation to provide appropriate and professional service to people because of their colour, culture or ethnic origin.
>
> It can be seen or detected in processes, attitudes and behaviour which amount to discrimination through unwitting prejudice, ignorance, thoughtlessness and racist stereotyping which disadvantage ethnic minority people.

Read that and ask if the Labour Party does not emerge stained. Even if on balance you think Labour doesn't fit all the hallmarks of institutional racism, that it is even in doubt is staggering. That has happened on Jeremy Corbyn's watch.

The reaction to the allegations themselves reveals much about how elements of the hard left view the problem and compound it. It is laced with paranoia and suspicion. When they see hundreds of Jews appear outside the Labour Party HQ to protest against the party's behaviour and practices, the general response is not one of horror or self-reflection. They do not ask: 'How did it come to this?', but instead: 'Why are they trying to damage us?' The base reflex of some of the Corbynist left is one of accusation. Their politics is one born of it, their natural assumption is that everyone – the Tories, the media, the world – is out to destroy them. Some of that paranoia is justified, but sometimes it also blinds them to truth. They assume that every complaint, every attack against 'Jeremy', is part of a wider, orchestrated attack, either from within the Labour Party, or from without. In this respect, once again, the parallels to Donald Trump and his movement are obvious.

So when I said on air and online that many of the Jews who had attended were not members of the party, with no dog in the intra-Labour Party factional race, I received nothing but opprobrium. Hundreds of messages came from supporters of the Labour leader alleging that the protesters were plants. 'Tory stooges,' said one. 'In other words, they are Tory supporters,' said another, and 'Quite a few Tory Party activists there.' When I pointed out that some said they would leave if Corbyn became prime minister, another replied: 'You mean #Jews had a country to start with? … other than the land of #Palestine they stole, obviously. I'm having a wee gamble and saying they're probably no great loss.' And then, of course, the customary dose of 'whataboutism', the negation of inconvenient facts because journalists have supposedly failed to cover stories that you consider more important: 'Did you cover yesterday's march on Apartheid Israel's massacre against Palestinians? Thought not.' The lack of regard for truth, the relativism and peddling of personalised narratives can give the Russian ambassador a run for his money, or indeed (once again) President Trump.

That paranoia is mixed with another powerful ingredient: unshakeable self-belief.

It is striking that whenever Corbyn is challenged about anti-Semitism personally, or about his party, he replies with some variant of the idea that because he and Labour have always campaigned against racism, it is heresy to imagine they are even capable of such prejudice. As he told the BBC's Martha Kearney: 'The idea that I am some kind of racist or anti-Semitic person is beyond appalling, disgusting and deeply offensive. I have spent my life opposing racism.' It is a sentiment oft repeated by Labour Party members: that since theirs is a party designed to combat prejudice, it cannot therefore be guilty of it. But you can't refute accusations of racism by cachet. It is not enough to have an aura of saintliness. Corbyn and his supporters are sometimes guilty of being so convinced of their own virtue, of their own unimpeachable morality, that the idea that they could be guilty even of unthinking racism (as many of us are) is uncomputable. This notion is so powerful that one Labour figure compared it to me as being like the Catholic church: the idea was endemic in the ecclesiastical hierarchy that none of its priests could possibly do anything wrong because it is a holy institution.

There is a more powerful reason still why so much anti-Semitism has been tolerated, and that same reason underpins the toleration of other unsavoury types in the party too. In a micro-sense, it was summed up by the case of Alan Bull. Mr Bull by all accounts is a bit of an unpleasant individual. A member of Peterborough Labour Party, he had posted various nasty articles, including one claiming that the Holocaust was a hoax. Christine Shawcroft, the head of the party's dispute panel, a long-time Corbyn ally and a founder of Momentum, did all she could to dismiss any allegations of impropriety, including reinstating Mr Bull as a candidate. She said this ought to happen 'because there is a lot of local party politics' going on – effectively that Mr Bull was one of theirs, was on the left, and ought to be protected and not thrown to the wolves.

This is central to the hard left's thinking: that everything always is secondary to the wider fight, to the wider conflict, almost anything can be sacrificed on its altar. As one leading Labour centre-right figure put it to me, citing that same example of Mr Bull:

'He posts it in June in a group with 2,000 people in it, gets complained about in July and nothing happens. He's then a potential candidate for a council seat, gets selected in October – another complaint goes in, nothing happens. In November, the Local Campaigns Forum, which has the leader of the Labour group on it and many others who are senior in the local party, sees the evidence that he posted about Holocaust denial, and some really vile anti-S stuff about David Miliband and the Rothschilds. He then gets approved as a candidate; two Labour councillors then hear he's going to a full council meeting as an observer, wear Labour Against Anti-Semitism T-shirts as a protest – nothing happens. He then starts doing campaigning as a candidate and they basically go, we've had enough, we published the stuff he's already put on the internet saying, this person is campaigning as Labour and I can't go and campaign for them while they're doing that. That, because of the magnificence that sometimes comes out of Twitter, ends up in the *Jewish Chronicle*, and the next day he's finally suspended.

'Why does it take from June to March for a Holocaust denier to be kicked out? Because institutionally the people around Corbyn believe there's no limits to their left, somebody has joined because of this exciting call to get a socialist economy, you can almost justify anything in their name, and therefore it must just be the right of the Labour Party, having a go of them. They don't police the borders of the left. So Ken Loach can come out and champion the right of people to question the facts of the Holocaust, and yet still be the person who introduces John McDonnell on the conference floor. How is that consistent with our values as a party? Anyone is welcome so long as you agree with the cause. And anything you do is excusable in its name. That's why bullying and intimidation are systemic and holistic throughout the party.'

There has been a similar phenomenon with black, Asian and minority-ethnic (BAME) issues. Sam Jury-Dada, a councillor in a ward in Southwark, was deselected in mid-2017. She was on the right of the party. She told me how she was deselected and the subject of racist abuse within her local party. Her deselection meant a ward that is 60 per cent BAME will now have three white representatives. When she asked if her local party members thought this was a problem, they sneered: 'One of the councillors is Irish. Don't you consider that an ethnic minority?'

It's hard to be certain but generally most of those responsible are not racist or especially sexist. But I do think that the hyper-factionalism and ideological nature of the pro-Corbyn wing makes some of them if not indifferent towards questions of diversity, then at least a little sniffy. Ultimately, when winning control of the party is the prize, when you're engaged in a big internal struggle, then everything else becomes secondary to achieving that goal, including diversity. Some BAME councillors are especially vulnerable. A source near the top of the party who is not unsympathetic to Corbyn told me: 'I think some of it comes down to us being unaligned. You often have a lot of BAME Labour figures, especially older black and Asian women, community elders, who are not especially ideological. They're therefore vulnerable to being picked off.' I've heard a lot of stories like this over the last year.

In a way it hasn't been the case hitherto that the Labour Party has been dominated by a highly sectarian world view. For the true adherents of the hard left, if not Corbynism, then it is a totalising ideology. Because it is at root Marxist, its followers view the world through a prism of competing interests and suspect that every organ of the state and wider civil society are attempting to alienate and oppress them and those about whom they say they care. They think that all private enterprise and private-sector involvement is wrong, and therefore anyone even remotely involved in it is a cipher of the capitalist project. It is in no way pluralist. For its most stringent followers, opposition is illegitimate because it is helping prop up the overall capitalist and immoral political and social order. If you are not onside, you are not to be trusted and are occasionally despised. Any methods are also justified in the struggle. Worse, you're just immoral and to be judged. This is a view shared only by the harder edges of the Corbyn movement – but it is there.

That world view, that hierarchy of priorities, with maintaining dominance supplanting all else, helps also to explain why the culture of the party has become so much coarser in general. It extends beyond anti-Semitism and includes wider bullying and harassment, some of which I've already detailed, but also, troublingly, examples of misogyny and broader racism too. In fairness to the new regime, this is not all of Corbyn's making. The mechanisms and procedures of the Labour Party are slow and cumbersome and that pre-dates Corbyn's ascension to the leadership. Arguably, in a party like Labour, always made up of competing organisations and power bases, disciplinary matters have always been difficult because different bits of the party stick by and defend their person in any given circumstance. But there is also no doubt that this system is made worse by the presence of deep factional war, judged against which even severe complaints about misconduct are considered less important than the war itself. Moreover, Jeremy Corbyn has been in office for three years, but there has been no sign at all of streamlining or improving the procedures as yet.

Alongside general harassment, I've come across examples of sexism and sexual assault that have not been treated properly by party authorities. Rachel Saunders was deputy mayor of Tower Hamlets and a councillor there for a decade. In the late autumn of 2017 she decided to step down, partly out of frustration with the culture of intimidation within her local party, especially towards women, and the lack of means to do anything about it. She wrote on a little-noticed blog at the time:

> Still, though, Labour women from all backgrounds – different ethnicities and class backgrounds – tell a very similar story. We are undermined and our contributions trivialised. We are held

> to account for what our partners do. We are sexually harassed. Many of us have experienced smears based on a fabricated private life. There are routine attempts made to intimidate us, shut us down. This is often worse for BAME women, who have racism and cultural expectations to deal with too.

I met her to discuss what had happened to her and what she'd seen:

> ME: One line really leapt out at me – 'Some men in the Labour Party think that women's bodies are there for their use.' What did you mean by that?
>
> SAUNDERS: I think there are a number of different things. Partly just sexual harassment and most of my experience in Tower Hamlets is kind of low level, but for a period of time fairly constant – being pushed around, being groped, the feeling that wherever you were, what you wanted didn't matter. If someone wanted to feel you up, if someone wanted to move you to the other side of the room and someone wanted the space you were standing in. I've supported other women who have experienced things worse than me in terms of being groped. There's something about the belief that you can be told what to do because you're a woman, or you can be pushed around, or you're ripe for groping or poking and saying, *Are you pregnant?*, *Why aren't you pregnant?*, all very personal questions which are very routine …
>
> ME: Have you been groped in Tower Hamlets?
>
> SAUNDERS: Yes, in a room packed full of Labour Party members. Occasionally in a bar or a pub and everyone has had a few drinks and there are hands slithering around. All I would do is bash it away, but other people have had tougher experiences than me.

ME: Within Tower Hamlets?

SAUNDERS: Yeah, but not my stories to tell.

ME: Have you tried to get Labour to do something about it?

SAUNDERS: I haven't used the formal complaints procedure because I think it's pointless. My experience in supporting other people who have chosen to use it is that it goes on for months and months, it never goes anywhere. At the point at which it reaches a formal point in the process where people have to submit statements, there's enough intimidation and pressure that goes on that it very rarely goes any further, because in order to reach a formal point in the process you have to tell your whole story, give your name, the accuser has to know your name, it's very easy to bring pressure to bear to ensure it doesn't go any further.

ME: Do you think Tower Hamlets is an outlier?

SAUNDERS: When I wrote that blog I got lots of kind messages of support from women across the party and lots said that this is entirely familiar, we're dealing with this all the time.

ME: You're not just talking about sexual abuse but also more traditional intimidation – what happened?

SAUNDERS: There was a period of time when there was a lot of conflict in TH Labour group and I was one of the people challenging Lutfur Rahman and the people close to him. Some of it just constant phone calls, sometimes nonsense legal letters, you grow to ignore them but you get them. Sometimes people putting notes in my pocket saying: 'I KNOW WHERE YOU LIVE, I KNOW WHERE YOUR PARENTS LIVE, JUST

> BECAUSE YOUR SISTER DOESN'T LIVE HERE DOESN'T MEAN SHE'S SAFE.'
>
> ME: But people will think that's extraordinary to be happening in the Labour Party?
>
> SAUNDERS: I'm afraid it's not extraordinary, sadly.
>
> ME: Did Labour HQ know about this intimidation?
>
> SAUNDERS: Yes. There was a period of time when I was deputy leader when I was talking to Central Office about it but it didn't stop it.
>
> ME: Would other Labour women identify with your experiences?
>
> SAUNDERS: Yeah. This is not extraordinary. I'm not unusual at all.

Too many complaints have become bogged down in byzantine Labour Party procedures that are themselves waylaid by the party's byzantine internal politics. Many female MPs are extremely dissatisfied that the party is insufficiently robust to online abuse towards female party members and officials, and that allegations of sexual assault are never taken seriously enough. Jess Phillips has said: 'The system needs a very robust, independent specialist element to it. The first point of contact should be with an independent person who the victim can absolutely trust and [who] doesn't know anybody, [so that] there's no fear or favour that you're about to shop in the mate of the person who answers the telephone.' She has also called for an arbitration panel with access to specialist advice, so that crucially decisions are not being 'made by the friends of the people involved or somebody from that wing of the party or this wing of the party'.

Richard Angell, the director of Progress, goes further, telling me: 'I think that is one of the things that's changed with the new establishment that has come on to the NEC and had, seems to me, no governance training; certainly no diversity training; no unconscious-bias training, and is led by a sense of injustice that it was trapped out of power for a lot of time, has no regard for due process, no regard for the Nolan standards of public life, and I think is so committed to its outcomes that almost any means will justify it. And I think that has resulted in it having corrupt practices from time to time.'

How much responsibility should Jeremy Corbyn, John McDonnell and others take for these actions and pockets of culture that have emerged within the party?

On the one hand, neither Corbyn nor the rest of the Labour leadership can be held responsible for every action that an idiot takes. No one could also doubt Corbyn's personal kindness and commitment to a just politics. He has also routinely condemned acts of violence, intimidation or bullying within the party. As in the case in Wallasey, there has sometimes been swift action to deal with problems.

But why did we (rightly) routinely assail Nigel Farage with examples of unpleasant incidents and people within his party? Why did he resist it so fiercely? Because we were essentially saying that he, as party leader, was responsible for his party's culture and, howsoever much he might dislike it or abhor it, ultimately the buck stopped with him.

One MP who has had big problems with his local party was more blunt to me: 'He knows it's going on. He turns a blind eye. It's useful for him.'

Moreover, although Corbyn can rightly say Labour has never had the most straightforward of dispute procedures, he has now had three years to change things. Corbyn's allies say that only recently have they been in full control of party mechanisms now they control the general secretaryship, but this seems a little mealy-mouthed. The leader of the Labour Party can change the Labour Party if they so wish it. Even the most diehard Corbynista must accept that there were few allegations of bullying, anti-Semitism or intimidation before Corbyn. The party was more staid, less lively, but more civilised too. Whether he likes it or not, willing or not, many of the worst culprits came with him and because of him.

In April 2018, Len McCluskey, the general secretary of Unite, wrote an article slamming Labour MPs for helping 'smears' against Jeremy Corbyn. McCluskey, like many of Corbyn's allies and supporters, doesn't usually refer to Corbyn by his full name, preferring instead to use only his Christian name of 'Jeremy'. The use of 'Jeremy' is deliberate. It reminds the audience of the man's ordinariness and friendliness. The idea that a man like that could be capable of evil is absurd and ergo his followers couldn't either. It doesn't just imply a familiarity but also a vulnerability. Things happen to 'Jeremy', not because of him. Events flow around him, he is manipulated and twisted by malign forces around him. He is a leaf blowing in the wind. But he's not, any more. He is in control. It's Jeremy Corbyn. It's his party. And only he can change it.

POWER IN THE LABOUR PARTY

So just how powerful are they? How complete is the takeover?

This might age horribly, but, right now, it's a mixed bag. On the face of it that might sound ridiculous. The left has never been more powerful in the history of the Labour Party. They control everything. More party members pour into the party. MPs feel under siege.

But neither Momentum nor the left is an omnipotent force. They have not attempted to make moves against many councillors, because (as yet) they do not have the numbers. Nor do they have the inclination. They are not militant. They are not a secret sect within the Labour Party with secret handshakes and nods and winks and monastic devotion. Many members, and their pro-Corbyn activities, simply want to campaign and help the party succeed, and many thousands did exactly that in the general election campaign, helping ensure the re-election of many Blairite and centrist MPs whose internal politics they do not share.

Equally it cannot be denied that there is a battle for control raging – and there are casualties. Sometimes that battle has become very, very nasty. For a man who is gentility itself, sometimes Jeremy Corbyn seems indifferent to what is orchestrated in his name. As power beckons, the scrutiny of him and of those who claim to act for him will become greater.

But perhaps his foot soldiers move quickly because they know how quickly an empire can crumble. An impregnable fortress is impregnable right up to the point its walls are breached. And politics today moves quickly, too quickly to afford to stand still. Already there are warning signs. In the early days of 2018 Momentum lost several key selection contests for the general election. Of 29 winnable seats, only seven were won by leftist candidates. In Shrewsbury, in Morecambe, in Rossendale, in Corby, in Carlisle, Rochford and Southend, the Momentum candidates all lost out. Even in Watford, where the Momentum candidate was a close personal ally of Corbyn himself and was backed by the ever powerful Unite, they still lost to the candidate who had fought the seat in 2017. In some, like Norwich North, the Momentum-backed candidate didn't even make the shortlist. In the early days of the selection contests, Momentum seemed to have most success where they fielded the candidate who stood in the last election. It would imply that most MPs have little to fear from mandatory reselection.*

Even with the NEC elections, a set of elections for positions specifically created to (a) increase members' influence on the body and (b) increase the left's influence, the left won handily, but the members were hardly taking to the streets, not the 'landslide' of which newly minted NEC member Jon Lansman spoke. Turnout was only 11 per cent. As one source said at the time: 'It's almost hilarious. It was an

---

* Of course, just because MPs would stay in place doesn't mean the left wouldn't get more powerful. One of the points of mandatory reselection isn't merely to have a rotating change of personnel but to make MPs more 'accountable' to their local parties. Such an act would probably make MPs more aware of the views of their local parties (which is, after all, the intention of the reform) but also restrict their freedom of action.

election that they orchestrated, for positions they created, in an election they ran and that suits them entirely, one member, one vote, and they still could only get 60,000 people to vote for them and they say they have 200,000.'

Of course, that 'moderate' source could only muster 40,000 so they're not in much of a position to crow. But, all the same, it's instructive. It adverts to the fact that many of the hundreds of thousands of members who have joined the party for Corbyn, and who might normally be considered as being in the left's camp, are not fully signed-on ground troops. We know from surveys that many paid their £3 and voted for Jeremy (perhaps twice), they might even occasionally have wanted to do a bit of leafleting, but turning up to meetings in draughty leisure centres every Tuesday and Thursday night, that's not for most of them. They are the left's reservists, at best, only to be called upon in an emergency.

It's also worth bearing in mind that the potential for infighting, especially as Momentum groups begin to exercise power on councils and potentially even national government, is immense. The left, of all Labour traditions, has a rich history of splintering into ever smaller and more insignificant sub-factions, the People's Front of Judea, the Judean People's Front.* At the moment, their attachment to Jeremy Corbyn and sense of being under siege are enough to bind them together. That might not always be the case.

And that's the true bearded elephant in the room. What happens when Corbyn is no longer there? When he hangs up his cream jacket for the last time? There is no agreed-upon successor. Different heirs apparent have come and gone: Clive Lewis, Rebecca Long Bailey, Angela Rayner have at one time or another illuminated the Corbyn sky, shone and burnt up, no longer the preferred successor; discarded by the Corbyn team as not being quite right: too disloyal, too ambitious, too right wing, too slow (that's not in any particular order, by the way). I'm sure a few more will have come and gone by the time

* Though, given it's likely both these groups would be Zionist, I doubt either would be especially welcome.

you read this. But none, I suspect, will be able to hold a candle to the man himself.

And that, perhaps, gives us a clue to the biggest long-term weakness in the left's domination of Labour. How much of the Corbyn coalition is precisely that, Corbyn's? Is it transferable to another politician, even if they play the same tunes? Or will someone else, possibly from the soft left or Miliband wing of the party, do it? If they offered change, if they appeared authentic, if they had personality, I don't see why not.

Because, as we've seen, so much of the Corbyn revolution isn't solely ideological: it's personal; it's cultural. Not all of his acolytes are sad doctrinaire Trotskyites obsessed with the Velvet Revolution. They're normal young and old who have been dealt a bad hand and they wanted a politician to speak to their experience. If another candidate from another wing of the party did that, then the left's support might be more brittle than it seems.

Because ultimately Labour is more than just a party, it's a movement. It's the political equivalent of Birmingham in the Industrial Revolution: the city of a thousand trades and different monikers for each bit. You have Fabians, Christian socialists, Methodists, syndicalists, unionists, revisionists, Bevanites, Bennites, Brownites, Blairites, the right, the soft left, the left, the hard left – the Bieberites are probably in there somewhere. If the 120-year(ish) history of the party tells us anything, it's that no one tradition dominates in perpetuity, even if it looks like nothing will crack the deepest, coldest factional grip.

Even mechanisms and constitutional wheezes designed or thought to cement the control of one group can in ways no one can quite anticipate at the time come to buttress and aid the fortunes of another. The electoral college was heralded by the left in the 1980s, only to hold them back in the 2000s. One member, one vote was likewise heralded by the right as a means of keeping the left out and distilling the power of the trade unions. Other sections of the Labour Party have to sit and wait.

To my surprise, elements of the left recognise it too. I was at a drinks reception at the 2017 Labour Party conference with a senior

Corbynist member of the shadow cabinet and a young Blairite new-intake MP. I was shocked at the extent to which they would openly talk of 'your faction', the pretence of sharing the same makeup shorn, out of the glare of the public gaze. This senior Corbynista was clear: 'Your faction has to bide its time.' The Labour left waited for a long, long time to take its turn once again in the sun. In the late 1970s and the 1980s the Bennite left looked like they would sweep all before them. They failed. In the 1990s it looked as if Blair had destroyed the left for ever. He hadn't. Creeds can resurrect themselves. The political constellations can reform. Sometimes everything can be won and lost on a single night. Jeremy Corbyn could tell you all about that.

Chapter 9

THE NIGHT EVERYTHING CHANGED: THE 2017 GENERAL ELECTION

He may be a mutton-headed old mugwump,
but he is probably harmless.

Boris Johnson on Jeremy Corbyn, 26 April 2017

Nothing has changed! Nothing ... has ... changed!

Theresa May, 22 May 2017

I think Theresa May has won the own goal of the season.

Gary Lineker, Twitter, 9 June 2017

We clearly underestimated Jeremy Corbyn.

Nick Timothy, Theresa May's former joint chief-of-staff,
8 August 2017

It was five minutes to ten on Thursday, 8 June 2017, on the Sky News election night set in west London. I sat, feverishly, awkwardly, in my chair under the glare of the studio lights. The truth is, it was a stretch to say that I was sitting in it at all. I'm a fidgeter at the best of times, and my legs and arms were essentially doing the mambo as my torso tried to remain still. I hadn't expected, only a month or two before, to be covering another general election and I certainly hadn't expected to be doing the on-air analysis and presenting for Sky on election night itself from the studio. I'm not often nervous, but this was more than enough to send me over the edge. As sad as it might sound, this was a childhood dream.* My then boss – the redoubtable head of politics at Sky News, Esme Wren, approached me and perhaps sensing my apprehension said: 'You know, Lewis, I actually think it will be quite a dull night.'

Over the preceding weeks I'd travelled over a thousand miles on the road across Britain, north, east, south and west and wherever I could, stealing an afternoon here and there and scuttling back to Osterley in west London for election night rehearsals. In those endless run-throughs, we'd each time practise a different outcome. It's fair to say we hadn't prepared for the one the real thing was to deal us. Different scenarios had been programmed by the software developers to which all of us on set had to react in real time, some hilariously outlandish. The first week was a Tory landslide, indeed a landslide so enormous that the Tories even won Hackney North off Diane Abbott† and the Lib Dems won in uber-Leave Boston and Skegness. In another, the Greens seemed to overcome seven centuries' worth of sectarianism in Northern Ireland by winning both Unionist Belfast East and Nationalist Belfast West. At the start of the campaign, this absurdity seemed only marginally less likely than the prospect of Labour picking up seats. Although we rehearsed a scenario in which the Tories won a much smaller majority than forecast, of around 20, at no point did we rehearse a hung Parliament, much less a Labour victory. At one point, on the final rehearsal, almost as an afterthought, someone piped up: 'Stupid question, I know, but do we have a coalition builder still? Just in case?'

The idea that the Tories were cruising to their biggest election win since the 1980s followed a remorseless, grim logic that persevered right up until the last possible moment. An hour or so before our

---

* Yes, I'm afraid to say that you read that correctly. At least I put the wasted years to good use.

† Actual majority (despite her well-publicised campaign problems): 35,159.

election night programme went on air, in a pep talk for the hundreds of people who would bring the evening to life for the varied array of politicos, obsessives and insomniacs watching from home, the head of Sky News, John Ryley, told us all he thought the night would be 'historic'. Adam Boulton, the elder statesman of Sky, sitting – unlike me – entirely confidently and securely in his presenter's chair, then told the room that he'd been talking with Downing Street throughout the afternoon and that they and Lynton Crosby, the Tory generalissimo, were confident of a majority of between 40 and 60 seats. Nowhere near the titanic win they'd hoped for at the start of the campaign but a comfortable one all the same. Earlier in the day a Labour source had texted me to say exactly the same thing. The night's rhythms, we thought, were already familiar.

At five minutes to ten, the first glimmer came that those rhythms would, in fact, be rather more discordant. John Ryley gingerly walked on set and asked my colleague Ed Conway, economics editor at Sky who oversaw our on-screen graphics for the night, to take off his microphone and go backstage. Ed returned, a few moments later, ashen-faced. He turned to me and said: 'Lewis ... how many seats do the DUP have?'

The 2017 election is one over which historians will linger long and one that I will never forget. It is an event that has fundamentally transformed our politics. At around 11 a.m. the next morning, after a 13-hour session of excited hand-waving, St Ives, the final constituency, was declared (a surprisingly narrow Tory hold), and I reflected on air that, in a neat piece of historic symmetry, it was the second time in half a century that a Conservative prime minister had gone to the country on a 'Who governs?' prospectus only to be told by the electorate that, whoever it was, it might not be them. And the parallels did not cease there – just as the election of 1974 was a pivotal and important one, eventually paving the way for the Winter of Discontent, the ejection of old Labour, the rise of Thatcherism, so 2017 might reshape our politics for a generation in ways which for the moment we can't fully see. Its shockwaves, its effects on the Brexit process and on the permanent balance of forces within both the Labour and Conservative parties, will continue to be felt in British and European politics for a long time to come. If anyone in your life ever says that voting doesn't change anything, then you need only reply with one date: 2017.

That's why we have to understand what those 32,203,481 meant when they cast their votes on that early summer's day in 2017. Crucially we mustn't delude ourselves about it, hoping to divine an intent that wasn't in fact there. L. P. Hartley once famously said that 'The past is a foreign country. They do things differently there.' He meant that the distant past is very different to our own age and that consequently it can be hard to understand. But in one respect I think that he was wrong. In many ways days long ago lost to us can appear clearer in the mirror of history than those that have just passed. Events of centuries gone by have clear narratives and progressions: event A led to political force B which led to revolution C. By contrast, if you find yourself in the immediate wake of a storm, you're far less able to see its effects properly. You're disoriented, unable to see the new lie of the land. So it is with 2017.

It seems almost unimaginable now that we thought Liz Kendall might become Labour leader, that Britain would reject Brexit, that Hillary Clinton would defeat Donald Trump and that Theresa May would win a landslide. And yet, at the time, each seemed not only a plausible outcome but an inevitable one. We're much worse at seeing the recent past for what it was and what it means for our immediate future than we are at getting to grips with the fall of Rome or the rise of Charlemagne. And because of that occlusion it's natural that we more easily succumb to false narratives, the wrong lens or, indeed, fake news. There is much of all those surrounding what happened on 8 June 2017. What follows is an attempt to put on the right lens. To understand – to use Hillary Clinton's phrase – what happened. Because if we continue to misunderstand it, then the consequences for the Labour Party and for British politics threaten to eclipse even the extraordinary events of the year when – this time to misuse a Theresa May phrase – everything changed.

WHAT HAPPENED?

Let's take a moment to recap what exactly happened on that fateful night, the easy bit. The Conservatives gained 20 seats but lost 33 and so ended the night with 318 seats, 12 fewer than they had won in 2015. Jeremy Corbyn's Labour, meanwhile, having trailed the Conservatives for months in the polls, gained 36 seats and lost 6, giving them a net gain of 30. Conservative losses were mainly in London and the south-east of England – with a handful of pickups in the Midlands and the north off Labour and, indeed, in Scotland, where they won 12 new seats and scored their best night north of the border since 1987. This was crucial. Had May not won these she would have had only 306 seats in the Commons and even with DUP support would have been unable to muster a parliamentary majority, would most likely have lost a Queen's speech, and therefore it's entirely possible we'd have had a second general election or that Jeremy Corbyn would be prime minister today.* How ironic that after years of Scots bitterly complaining that they must endure Tory governments for which they did not vote, forced upon them by the English, today we have a Tory government only because of Scottish votes, one of a constellation of ironies thrown up by the election.

Labour meanwhile picked up right across England, both north and south, and began to recover in Scotland too, picking up six new seats.

---

* I don't propose to say much more about Scotland in the context of the general election in this chapter. This is not because it isn't interesting – it most certainly is – but the reason will become obvious. My analysis that so much of the general election result is rooted in the Brexit divide does not apply to Scotland, because it was an overwhelmingly Remain country in the referendum and so the same dynamics did not apply. Indeed, the political culture in Scotland is so different to England and Wales that it makes it difficult to address the same issues in one book. Suffice to say, the realignment of politics there after the independence referendum, rather than the Brexit one, saved Theresa May's neck. There were plenty of people who – though not natural Tories – saw Ruth Davidson's Conservatives as the unalloyed party of the Union and voted accordingly to shut down the prospect of a second independence referendum that Nicola Sturgeon had courted.

The party had an exceptionally strong result in London. I remember after the 2015 election many greybeards ruminating that the party had reached its zenith in the capital. Not so. Under the leadership of the MP for Islington North the party gained seats across the city, including in Kensington and Battersea, Conservative strongholds.

Labour got 40 per cent of the vote. That's 10 per cent better than Ed Miliband achieved only two years before. It was the biggest increase in the percentage of the popular vote recorded by any party since Clement Attlee led Labour to its most famous victory, in 1945. It was the first time the Labour Party had made a net gain of seats since 1997 and the party's best performance in terms of percentage of the vote since 2001 – and was considerably better than Tony Blair's last election victory in 2005. Overall, the famous first-past-the-post British system, which is supposed to deliver us stable, one-party majoritarian governments, worked perfectly once again, giving us our second hung Parliament in seven years and first minority government since 1974. UKIP collapsed and the Lib Dems essentially stood still, while the SNP didn't look nearly as fearsome as it had only two years before, losing over 20 seats. Two-party politics had picked up more or less where it had left off in the early 1970s.

You know the rest. May stitched together a pretty tawdry deal with the Democratic Unionist Party. She remained in Number 10 – against my initial expectation on election night, when I publicly speculated she might become our shortest-serving premier since Andrew Bonar Law. At the time of writing, she's still there. But as soon as Big Ben struck ten that night, she transformed instantly from Boudicca to Mrs Brown – and her boys have (rightly) never forgiven her. Corbyn became similarly transfigured, from the worst Labour leader in the party's history to its saviour – and his critics were neutered. Only a year before, 172 of his own MPs had resigned in disgust at the quality of his leadership. Now they cannot deny they partly owe their often substantially swelled constituency majorities to their leader.

And yet, and yet, and yet … Contrary to the giddy pronouncements that would follow from senior Corbynistas, it is always worth remembering something else: Labour came nowhere close to winning the election. Although their seat performance was anaemic, the Conservatives achieved a bigger percentage of the vote than at any time since Margaret Thatcher's best landslide in 1983, with 43.3 per cent. Though the result was better than expected, Jeremy Corbyn still led the Labour Party to its third election defeat in a decade. Indeed, the result, in terms of raw scores on the doors, mirrored that first defeat of the 2010s: Corbyn did about as well – in terms of seats – as Gordon Brown did in 2010. The party still needs over 60 seats to win an overall majority of one. Although the Labour corpse is flickering in Scotland, it is far from standing upright or even getting to its knees. The party also lost a handful of seats in former working-class fortresses.

Still, no one could deny the party its achievement. It had started the campaign 25 points behind the Conservatives, riven by internal disputes. Personally, Corbyn appeared to be pitied by many middle-class liberal voters who despaired of his sclerotic leadership and loathed his ambivalence towards their beloved European Union, while also being disliked by the party's more culturally conservative working-class base. Corbyn began the campaign with a catastrophic personal approval rating of –58. Because of this – and because of May's apparent popularity – the Conservatives doubled down on the leadership question. Every Tory poster was emblazoned with the candidate's name followed by 'Standing with Theresa May'. Yet on election night it became clear that the country had decided that it barely wanted to be in the same room with her, let alone stand close. And Jeremy Corbyn, for one, was certain he understood why.

WAS IT AUSTERITY WOT WON IT?

At 4.55 a.m. in Islington Town Hall, Jeremy Corbyn, the leader of the opposition and Labour candidate in Islington North, was re-elected for the ninth time. He surveyed the room but remained dazed. The scale of what had happened had not yet hit home. He had sat down at 10 p.m. to watch the election results with his family and closest comrades as the undertaker of the Labour Party. As soon as Big Ben struck ten, he emerged, almost instantly, as its messiah. And as he made his victory speech at his count, he shared his thoughts with a nation looking, for the first time, at Corbyn as a man who might be prime minister by mid-afternoon:

'I've travelled the whole country; I've spoken at events and rallies all over the country. And you know what? Politics has changed, and politics isn't going back into the box that it was before. What's happened is people have said they've had quite enough of austerity politics; they've had quite enough of cuts to public expenditure, underfunding our health service, underfunding our schools and our education service, and not giving our young people the chance they deserve in our society, and I'm very, very proud of the campaign that my party has run – our manifesto for the many, not the few.'

This is a refrain repeated by Corbyn and his coterie again and again, a din that has only got louder as time has elapsed. The election was about austerity, the idea that in the years since 2015, with the easy cuts made, the public had had enough of the Tories wielding the axe. The austerity debate is also code for a wider, longer-standing argument within the Labour Party, namely that the public has shifted to the left as a result of the financial crisis. My problem with this analysis is a fundamental one. It's wrong. It's just wrong. The 2017 election simply wasn't about austerity.

Let's start off with the obvious. David Cameron and George Osborne won in 2015 pretty handily in a general election where austerity and public spending were pretty much the only issue that featured. Their majority was small, but in an election in which everyone had expected a close result and after the government had hacked at public spending more than any administration for decades, they received a measured thumbs-up from the electorate. They were rewarded with 2 million more votes than the Labour Party, Cameron's government became the first since 1983 to increase its majority from one term to the next, and he became the first prime minister since Harold Macmillan to increase their vote share while in office. Oh, and by the way, it fought that election with an explicit promise to shave further billions off public spending. Labour went down to its worst defeat since 1983.*

The 2015–17 Parliament was the shortest since 1974, and so the gap between these two elections was extremely brief. A lot happened in those two years – but at no point, in that time, was there any great indication that the Conservatives were paying an economic or political penalty for their continued embrace of the Osborne austerity agenda. On the contrary, at every electoral test in those two years the Conservatives performed well. The Tories did very well in both the 2016 and 2017 local elections, with the Labour Party – then led by Jeremy Corbyn and avowing an unashamedly left-wing and anti-austerity policy – doing badly. Even in the Greater London Assembly elections of 2016, the Tories lost only two seats and 1 per cent of the vote. The Tories won the Copeland by-election in the spring of 2017, the first time a governing party had won a by-election off an opposition party since 1982. It also performed well in the austerity-hit Stoke-on-Trent Central by-election, held on the same day. Moreover, at no point after the Corbyn leadership began in 2015 did the Conservatives fall behind Labour in the opinion polls. Look at the graph opposite. It shows the aggregate of opinion polls from 2015 onwards. As you'll see, the Conservatives were consistently ahead right up to the general election. If there had been any great swing to Labour when it started to make profoundly anti-austerity noises or if there had been any great indication that the public had become weary of the Tories' economic policies, then presumably May would not have called the 2017 election at all.

And that extends to the 2017 election campaign too. Before the election was called the Tories were on course for a majority of over 100. Are we to believe that after six years and eleven months of the Tories in control of the Treasury levers the public had a sudden change of heart on austerity?

---

* Of course, the reduction in the number of seats was especially due to the losses in Scotland, but Labour lost seats to the Tories in England and Wales too.

The aggregate of UK opinion polls from 2015 onwards

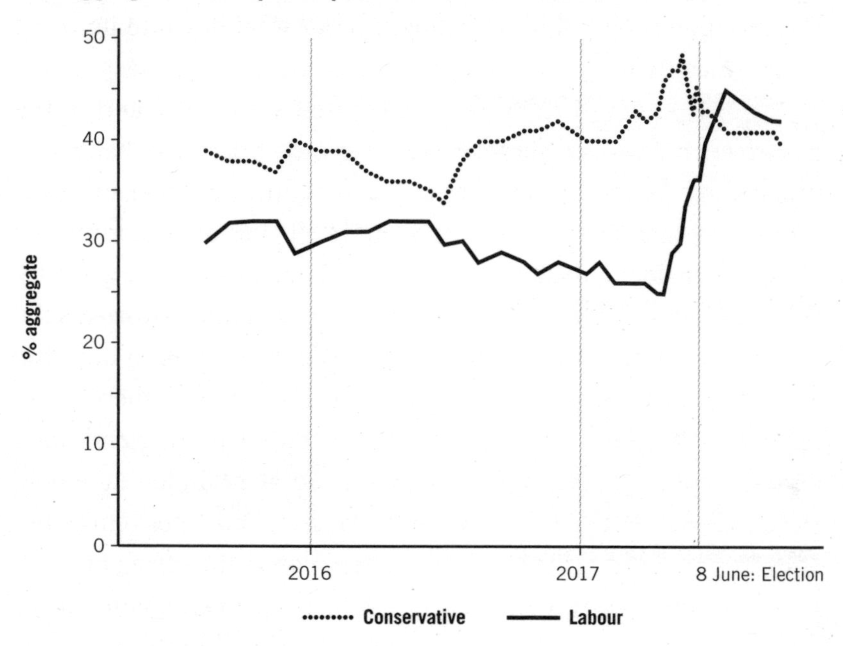

Source: UK Polling Report

There's some evidence that public opinion has shifted a little bit since 2015, and a little bit more since 2010. Austerity attrition is perfectly logical: with every year of wage stagnation, spending cuts and price rises that goes by the public appetite for more must wane. But the surprising thing is that it hasn't that much. If we take the November 2017 budget, Philip Hammond's second and the twelfth budget or autumn statement since the Conservatives came to power, YouGov asked the questions as set out overleaf.

This is complicated but worth going through the numbers in detail. Note the two columns: the first is when the questions were asked after Hammond's first budget, in March 2017, and the second after his pre-election November budget. The results make interesting reading for anyone thinking that the election changed public opinion on this question: 46 per cent of people still think that public-spending cuts are necessary versus only 25 per cent who say

	8–9 March	22–23 Nov.
Thinking about the way the government is cutting spending to reduce the government's deficit, do you think this is... Good or bad for the economy?		
Good for the economy	34	34
Bad for the economy	32	35
Don't know	34	31
Being done fairly or unfairly?		
Fairly	22	24
Unfairly	44	41
Don't know	34	36
Necessary or unnecessary?		
Necessary	47	46
Unecessary	24	25
Don't know	29	28
Too deep, too shallow or at about the right level?		
Too deep	24	22
Too shallow	11	14
About the right level	27	26
Don't know	38	38
Being done too quickly, too slowly or at about the right pace?		
Too quickly	25	22
Too slowly	13	18
About the right pace	27	26
Don't know	34	35
Having an impact on your own life, or not having an impact on your own life?		
Having an impact on my life	34	29
Not having an impact on my life	39	42
Don't know	27	28

Source: YouGov, 2017

they're not. That figure has ticked up by only 1 per cent since March. That's not exactly a convincing basis to conclude that Jeremy Corbyn and John McDonnell's anti-austerity crusade to persuade the public that the cuts are 'economic vandalism' has made much impact. Indeed, even if you go back to 2015 the numbers haven't changed that much. At the time of the 2015 election 55 per cent of people said that austerity was necessary. As of the end of 2017 that's down to 46 per cent – a change but still vastly outnumbering those who think they're unnecessary.

After all the heat of the campaign and the most anti-austerity candidate possible, virtually the same number of people think the cuts are good for the economy as bad, just like before the election. And the number of people who think the cuts are too deep has actually gone down, while the number of people who think they're too shallow has gone up! Likewise, compared with 2015 the number of people who think the cuts are too deep has gone down by 20 percentage points. Today, all told, 44 per cent of people think the cuts are going either too slowly or at about the right pace versus only 22 per cent who believe they are going too quickly. And maybe that's not surprising, because more people think that the cuts aren't having an impact on their lives at the end of 2017 than they did in 2010 and 2015. According to all the data, the British population as a whole were feeling the effects of austerity less than they were in 2015 and much less than in 2010, when the cuts first began.

Everyone knows, you might be spluttering into your Ovaltine, that Jeremy Corbyn boosted turnout among young people substantially because they are anti-austerity. You've been to the rallies, you've seen the placards, you've heard the roar of the crowds. It was the quality of campaign – it inspired everyone. Or if not everyone then at least those under 55. And, after all, even if the oldies may be urging the government on to wield the axe, hey ho, they're dying, and the reaper's scythe is coming for them pretty soon anyway.

But the young are no more spendthrift than the old. When you look at the age breakdown of YouGov's data, this is what you find:

	18–24	**25–49**	**50–64**	**65+**
Necessary	46	41	46	57
Unnecessary	21	25	29	23
Don't know	34	34	24	20

So Corbyn's foot soldiers, the 18–24 group that voted for Labour in 2017 by a forty-point margin over the Conservatives, are as likely to think that cuts are necessary as the 50–64s (a majority of whom, by contrast, voted for the Tories). Whatever was motivating all those inspired youngsters to the polls for the Labour Party, there isn't much evidence to suggest – beyond a committed core – that it was austerity. Jeremy Corbyn's unequivocal stance on the subject certainly helped boost turnout and bring together disaffected left-wing voters who had drifted off to the Greens. But that was it. At most the party maximised the country's anti-austerity coalition, stemming the bleeding from the 2015 result, for sure, but not coming close to surpassing the plurality of voters who still backed the pro-cuts Tories.

There is therefore little evidence that in the election of June 2017 austerity fatigue was the driving issue, as much as the top tier of the Labour leadership would like there to be. Rather it was the Conservatives' decision to vacate this spectacularly successful fortification atop the political terrain that contributed to Labour's unexpected advance. It wasn't so much that the voters changed their minds on austerity in 2017 by comparison to 2015, or that Labour came up with a better answer, but rather that the principal political question posed by politics – and its leading right-of-centre politicians – changed.

In 2015 that question was simple: who do you trust with the nation's money? And the answer wasn't Labour. As Jon Cruddas said at the time: 'The Tories didn't win in spite of austerity. They won because of it.' Cameron and Osborne's great strategic political achievement was to reduce all of politics down to those narrow parameters. 'How will you raise the money?' Tory ministers would bellow it with imperious glee as they shot down even the nimblest Labour media performers with a single bullet day after day after day on every radio and TV station for five long, gruelling years. Had Miliband suggested shelling out fifty quid for a new pair of net curtains for Downing Street, the Conservative spin machine would have translated it into a Facebook ad saying it proved that Britain was going to lose its credit rating and become a neo-Soviet state in about thirty minutes flat. Labour found it impossible to escape that rhetorical quicksand. Whether or not it was good for the democratic process it was very good for the Conservative Party, not least because it appealed to voters' fundamental instincts about money, waste and their own sense of personal finance, which in turn reinforced a very Conservative view of political economy. As the Tories constantly reminded us, you can't spend more than you've got in perpetuity. This central plank – however wise the actual policy of austerity itself was – looked like it was to form the basis of a lasting Tory hegemony.

But then the essay question changed. And it wasn't changed by Labour, or the media, or the voters, but stupidly, absurdly, by the Tories themselves. Instead of the economy and spending, they decided they wanted to talk about Brexit. Finally blessed with a majority that had taken ten years of modernisation and graft to build, they used it not to hammer home their advantage and build on their success but instead chose to hold a referendum on EU membership. Whatever the rights and wrongs of it, all that came at a cost. It removed the solid, sturdy oak plank of austerity and replaced it with a much flimsier one. For years, the Tories had destroyed Labour by saying that their opponents were dangerous fantasists. Miliband and his band of merry men were radicals, intent on engaging in a utopian experiment that could destroy Britain. The message was simple: don't take the risk. As David Cameron was to tweet in the days leading up to the 2015 election:

@David_Cameron
Britain faces a simple and inescapable choice – stability and strong Government with me, or chaos with Ed Miliband
11:26 PM – 3 May 2015

It never gets old. Whatever your political views, I think we can all agree that the three years of Conservative government that followed from Cameron's 2015 win haven't been characterised by much stability. Nonetheless that tweet says a lot about the politics of the time. 'Inescapable' is, I think, the key word. Cameron, like Blair before him, had managed to make it appear as if no political choices were possible – or at the very least, that they were highly circumscribed. His politics was sensible and straightforward. Miliband's was dangerous and impossible. Brexit shattered that cosy vision of politics. Suddenly the Tories were the ones who looked risky, the ones indulging in their own scary ideological crusade, their own utopian fantasy. Their competence card – always the most potent weapon for a Conservative government – was shredded. No longer could they argue that they alone could guarantee stability; rather they appeared to be the ones injecting the instability into the system. The reason why John McDonnell can now stand up and say that Labour plans on nationalisation, when Ed Balls would have struggled to pledge to buy a postage stamp, is because the Tories have shown that the menu of options available to order in politics is much bigger than they had convinced everyone it was.

And it was about more than just competence. In introducing the Brexit infection into the British political bloodstream, the Tories had taken a leap into the dark. As a consequence, they couldn't see the Remainer antibodies, which would destroy them and boost Labour. It was this – not austerity – which proved their undoing. The Conservatives had chosen to fight in a twenty-first-century Brexit-fuelled culture war rather than a traditional twentieth-century political battle about the size of the state and public spending. And in a culture war, freed of the endless austerity artillery crashing down on them week in, week out, Labour could finally raise an army hitherto unavailable to them and advance.

REVENGE OF THE REMAINERS

Look at the wordcloud below. What would you say are the main themes?

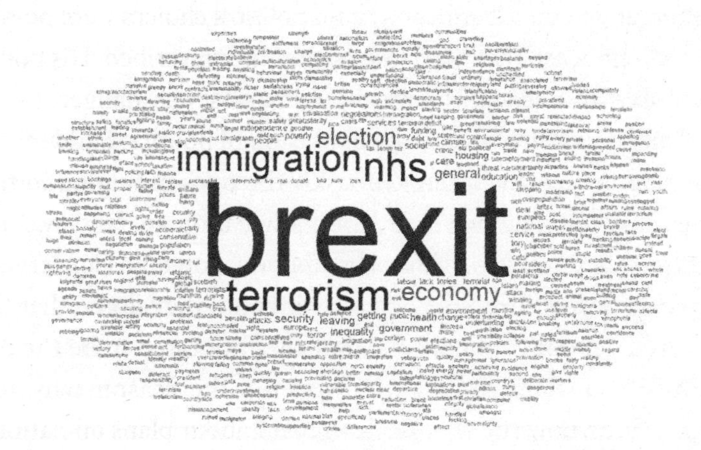

This is the British Election Study (BES) survey where they ask (as they always do) 30,000 voters during an election: 'As far as you're concerned, what is the single most important issue facing the country at the present time?' More than one in three said Brexit or the European Union, compared to only one in ten who said the NHS and one in twenty who said the economy. Austerity is there somewhere. Probably.

Save for a handful of days, Brexit remained the single most common answer given by their thousands of (different) respondents every single day. The only time it was displaced was for terrorism on a few occasions, for obvious reasons, after both the Manchester and London Bridge attacks which occurred – almost without precedent – during the campaign. For anyone who lived the election, day in, day out, Brexit's dominance might seem peculiar. Although Theresa May called the election on a Brexit prospectus, in the day-to-day of the campaign Brexit was a shadow – and not a long one. It looked to us at the time as though bread-and-butter issues had come to dominate. As David Runciman, Professor of History at Cambridge University, remarked to me just before polling day: 'The extraordinary success for Jeremy Corbyn and Labour has been to turn this into a traditional bread-and-butter election campaign and I'm amazed.'

But, it seems, not for the first time in twenty-first-century Britain, the media and political elites were having one conversation while the public was having another.

Indeed, it was on the same day I talked with Runciman that I realised just how wrong we were all getting it. On the Saturday before election day I'd made a film from Cambridge, the Remainer fortress in the Fens. The initial idea was to find out whether the Lib Dems had any hope of a comeback there. The former MP Julian Huppert was popular and he'd only narrowly lost his seat by a few hundred votes to Labour back in 2015. What else do you do when in Oxford or Cambridge and making a piece for the news? You either get on your bike or you get out your oars and craft a belaboured metaphor. I did both. And after nearly drowning on the Cam as one of the oars disappeared over my head (I was very much a theatre man at university), I spoke to my squad. With the camera rolling, the captain, Rob, a graduate student a little younger than me, said something that at the time seemed as likely as my becoming a rowing blue but in retrospect was more prescient and on the money than I realised. He said that 'as a Remainer, the ideal outcome of this election for me would be a hung Parliament. I've convinced myself that we're not going to leave and I think a hung Parliament would make that much more likely.' Rob wasn't keen on Corbyn's Labour but like his teammates had warmed to him: 'I could see him as a potential prime minister – much more so than say six months ago,' another said. 'He speaks well – he comes across well. Much more so than Theresa May.'

At the time, I took this to be interesting but not especially revelatory. I should have paid more attention. I had thought that Corbyn's success in keeping some of his Remainer voters on board had been a coup – that his 'constructive ambiguity' on the subject had worked. At the start of the campaign I had assumed that the general election of 2017 would be a realigning election. I know that because I had the misfortune to conduct an interview with the Royal Television Society about my travels. If it isn't too gauche to quote myself and, if nothing else, in the interest of full disclosure that I was just as wrong as everyone else, this is what I had to say:

'This is what psephologists call a realigning election, i.e. an election, the significance of which stretches far beyond the next Parliament and realigns the voter bases of each of the parties, for potentially a generation to come.'

I wasn't wrong – it was realigning and it has reconfigured the voter bases of the parties. But it did so in a way that neither I nor, more importantly, Theresa May had imagined. The Remainer coalition, like Rob and his rowing team, correctly intuited that the best way of preventing Brexit, or at the very least of slowing its pace, was to vote Labour. Even though Labour was committed to Brexit, had whipped its MPs to vote for Article 50 and was being led by a leadership who in the past had been vociferous in their opposition to the European Union, those voters felt (correctly) that the only way to glaciate Brexit was to deprive Theresa May of her majority, or at the very least deprive her of a large one. The only way to do that was to vote Labour. And once you understand that, you understand nearly everything about the 2017 election.

You don't have to take my experience for it. All you have to do is dig into the data and the sorts of seats Labour won to see just how reliant the election result was on Brexit. In those seats in England and Wales that Labour won in 2017 the average vote to remain was 52.5 per cent.* Labour led the Conservatives by 54 to 26 per cent among Remainers; the Conservatives beat Labour by 65 to 24 per cent among Leavers. Perhaps no surprise then that many MPs – unhappy with their party leadership – majored on the EU issue: Darren Jones, the newly elected MP for Bristol North West, who defeated a Tory incumbent, whose election material featured the blue-and-yellow flag of the EU, says: 'To be honest, in my election campaign I just didn't use the Labour manifesto or refer to it at all.' He says 10,000 people switched their votes towards him in June: 'Lots of people voted for me

---

* That's not to say they all voted to remain – some were Leaver seats, but more of that in a moment.

because of my pro-European stance; I won over a lot of Remain Tories in affluent areas.'

Nearly 1.1 million Conservative voters switched to Labour compared with 2015. A quarter of the Lib Dem vote went to Labour too. Having had their vote go up fourfold in 2015, 650,000 pro-EU Green voters switched to Labour, or around an enormous two-thirds of its 2015 vote. Overall more than 50 per cent of all Remain voters voted for Labour, compared to just a quarter for the Conservatives and 15 per cent for the Lib Dems.

And if you think about it – it makes perfect sense. How else would Labour have won Kensington? Or Battersea? Look at the table below: it shows the half-dozen or so seats that saw the Tories' biggest decreases in vote share.

Richmond Park	–13.1%
Battersea	–10.8%
Chelsea and Fulham	–10.3%
Kensington	–10%
Hampstead and Kilburn	–10%
Putney	–9.7%
Tooting	–8.8%
Vauxhall	–8.6%

These are some of the most Remainer seats in the country. Consequently, the Tories lost their rock-solid seat of Kensington, lost Battersea, which no one had thought was ever coming back to Labour, and even in Chelsea and Fulham, one of the closest things the Tories have to an inner-city London seat these days and a seat the party has held since 1910, the majority was slashed from 16,000 to around 8,000 with a 10 per cent increase in the Labour vote. A pretty good indication of the sorts of people who were exercised by the election can be gained by judging which seats sported the greatest increases in turnout: of the twenty seats with the best turnout in the country, all but one were Remainer seats. Or, to put it another way, of the constituencies that posted the highest Remain votes, their turnouts increased by 5.5 per cent. If you compare that with the top 20 Leaver seats their turnouts increased by a much more modest 1.6 per cent.[1] Where turnout was up most, the Labour vote was up most. Conversely, the Tories only did better than Labour in seats where turnout declined.

Bluntly, if anyone tries to tell you this wasn't the Brexit election and you need even more psephological snippets to throw at them, just remind them of this. In the most strongly Remain seats in the country, Labour's average vote share went up by 13 points and the Conservatives' went down by three. That's an eight-point swing from Tory to Labour. In the top 20 Leave seats, by contrast, the Tory vote share went up by 15 points, mainly because of UKIP's collapse (plummeting by 20 points even in these Brexit bastions).

I could have eaten my already much gnawed hat on election night when Canterbury went for Labour and I spluttered out that it was the first time since the Great Reform Act in 1832 that the Conservatives hadn't held the seat. We spent much of the rest of the evening talking about the student surge. But, in a way, we should have been paying even more attention to those London seats in that box above. Because they were a kind of control. Many of them don't have big student populations (if students can afford to be spending their money on Hampstead rents then they've got their priorities all wrong). What they represented was the undoing of the Cameron coalition: the sort of comfortably off, socially liberal, bourgeois seats that Cameron in his modernisation project had courted so assiduously. While he did not exactly make it cool to be a Conservative, he was a sufficiently reassuring and 'modern' presence to make sufficient numbers of middle-class urbanites either vote Conservative or at the very least feel that they did not have to vote Labour. Over the panzanella and the prosecco at the weekend dinner parties, it was finally OK to say you were a Tory.

Brexit changed all of that. The modernisation was undone, almost at a stroke. It laid bare the Conservative Party, perhaps as it always was, some of its most prominent members dabbling with forces that many liberals felt were dark if not outright dangerous. No one could epitomise that better than Boris Johnson, during the 2012 Olympics a near London folk hero, now *persona non grata* in the city he twice led.

May's fate was probably sealed in the days following her ascension to the premiership. She wasn't able to articulate at that time precisely what Brexit meant in policy terms but she was able to in rhetoric ('Brexit means Brexit'). She and Nick Timothy saw the 52 per cent as one glittering enormous prize, ripe for the picking. They divined (correctly) that the referendum result articulated a deep unease about the speed and form of cultural liberalism and globalisation. May put it best in her now infamous 2016 conference speech line: 'But if you believe you're a citizen of the world, you're a citizen of nowhere. You don't understand what the very word "citizenship" means.'

If Cameron sought to 'bring the Conservative party up to date', May seemed to wish to roll back the clock. She appeared to embody a more patrician past. If Cameron was an ideological and political product of the 1980s, May – although not all that much older – seemed the epitome of a child of the 1950s, the sort of woman who might have preferred a repeat of *Heartbeat* compared to a Cameroon evening of Scandi noir. Television and popular culture habits aside, her style has had much to recommend it. She is nothing if not morally upright. No one could accuse her of the casual insouciance and sometimes breezy arrogance of her predecessor. It is difficult to accuse the ever assiduously prepared May of doing too much 'chillaxing'. But there was a cost. At times she seemed to embrace a positively retro Conservative vibe. She toyed with the reintroduction of fox hunting. She wanted to reintroduce grammar schools. She eschewed social media. The Tory Party had regressed.

But it was more than that. May and her coterie of advisers decided that they had to pursue what appeared to be the hardest of hard Brexits. That meant leaving the customs union, it meant leaving the single market, it meant leaving the jurisdiction of the European Court of Justice at all costs, and ending freedom of movement. It meant – whatever its rights and wrongs – the biggest forced removal of political rights (the right to live, work and study across an entire continent) from British citizens in the era of universal suffrage. Governments are usually in the business of giving people rights, not taking them away. And it did so on the basis of a decisive but slender majority of 52 to 48 per cent in a highly divisive referendum.

Imagine if David Cameron had won that referendum and then said, right, we have 52 per cent of the country and now we have a mandate and on that basis join the Euro, join Schengen and give up the rebate on budget contributions? Even assuming the Remain majority had supported it (they wouldn't), consider the political backlash from the Leaver minority. It would have been truly virulent. It was an extraordinary folly not to believe that Mrs May would experience vituperation in reverse in 2017.

The biggest mark against her card is that she didn't need to do it. She, perhaps uniquely in British politics, had the credentials to chart a middle course. After all, though she was nominally a Remainer, she had kept her counsel to an extraordinary extent. Much to the consternation of David Cameron and the Stronger In campaign, she refused to be drawn into its activities. Will Straw, the director of Stronger In, told me that despite repeated entreaties from the campaign she refused: 'She polled well. People respected her. But she just wouldn't do it. She was clearly thinking about the future.' And that political foresight helped her become Conservative leader and prime minister in the first place in that she was acceptable to both Leaver and Remainer Tory MPs.

So it could have been for the country. She was in a unique position in that she was not beholden to the promises of the Leave campaign. In the chaos of post-referendum British politics, she could interpret the referendum result as she saw fit. With no leadership contest to fight, she did not need to tack to her Brexiteer right. She could have said that the result was close, that although we would be leaving the EU the relationship would remain close. That Britain would stay in the customs union and have a longish stay in the single market before leaving (but that after leaving there would be no going back). That is the approach endorsed on the night after the referendum by Dan

Hannan, one of the architects of the Leave campaign and longstanding anti-EU Tory MP. He told Evan Davis on *Newsnight* that as a compromise, given the vote was so close, we should agree to stay in the single market but leave the EU.

If a leading light of the Leave campaign could embrace such a position, May surely could have done the same. Instead she chose the opposite. In tracing the political dividing lines around the unyielding words of 'Brexit means Brexit', setting up a Department of International Trade and appointing the leading Brexiteer and former defence secretary Liam Fox to it, she boxed herself in to leaving both the customs union and the single market. She also seemed to become a leading Leaver overnight, with apparent disdain for the views of the 48 per cent,* many of whom were Tory voters. In other words, she became a partisan, her hands soaked in Brexit blood, happy to live with headlines imploring: 'Crush the saboteurs!' And, indeed, the manner of the election itself was what brought this into view. She called an election specifically so she could exercise her will without impediment. As she said on the steps of Downing Street when she stunned the country:

'Every vote for the Conservatives will make it harder for opposition politicians who want to stop me from getting the job done.

'Every vote for the Conservatives will make me stronger when I negotiate for Britain with the prime ministers, presidents and chancellors of the European Union.

---

* The not inconsiderable irony, of course, is that one of the objectives of the election was in fact to secure a sizeable majority not to 'crush the [Remainer] saboteurs' but, as a Number 10 source told me later, to 'buy her the space she needed' from the hardcore Brexiteers in her own party, to pave the way for the compromises with the European Union she knew must surely come. The torrid summer of 2018, trying to pass Brexit-related legislation through the House of Commons with no majority, dependent on a zealous group of Brexiteer backbenchers, illustrated the heavy price she paid for not having that space. Nonetheless that is not the message with which she went to the country; indeed it was precisely the opposite. By July 2018 this had given her a credibility problem on both sides.

'Every vote for the Conservatives means we can stick to our plan for a stronger Britain and take the right long-term decisions for a more secure future.'

But that's the point. There were plenty of people who didn't want to make her stronger. Didn't want her to get the job done. Instead of draping herself in the cloak of the nation, she came late to wearing the crimson red of the Vote Leave banner. She paid a price.

What else do we seriously think motivated the mass Conservative exodus in Battersea or Kensington? Or, indeed, the millions and millions of direct Conservative to Labour switchers who characterised this election? Despite spanning only a two-year period, 2015–17 saw the highest recorded level of combined Labour–Conservative switching as a percentage of Labour and Conservative voters at the previous election (in either direction) in modern history – do we credit that these Tory voters had just been waiting for a true socialist alternative all this time and had simply been voting Tory until the right one came along? That they found the prospect of extra taxation on their wealth or their income so appealing they just couldn't resist? That their views on austerity had altered that quickly in only two years? That they found Miliband's prospectus that bit too centrist or mushy but Corbyn's radicalism made them drop their glasses of Barolo and jump into their Jags to cross their boxes as part of the forward march to socialism? Hardly.

No, there were just thousands of Conservatives, dotted in key seats, who felt that Brexit was an issue so profound as to betray their party and vote for a septuagenarian socialist who on the face of it at least was committed to Brexit too. And it didn't matter. Because they'd worked out, just like my rowing friends on the Cam, that, somehow, doing so would throw a Remain-shaped spanner in the Brexit works. It was perhaps their last chance to change, ameliorate or even stop the process altogether. They were right. The politicians didn't see it. The public, as ever, were much smarter than them. Consequently, eyeing up a new hegemony, Mrs May thought she could snap Labour's hold on socially conservative Midlands and northern voters. She got some, but not enough. She therefore swapped a lot of very useful, well-distributed liberal votes in Remainer urban and semi-urban seats for a few useless votes in Labour industrial seats with big majorities. Unfortunately, piling on 3,000 votes in Gateshead doesn't get you anything in our system. Ultimately, May's gamble did not pay off because she did not anticipate that, politics imitating Newtonian physics, such an action would prompt an equal and opposite reaction; that she could gain those votes but they would come at a cost. Her gamble was that Remainers would have nowhere else to go. She was wrong.*

I've spoken about the Conservatives here a lot, probably more than anywhere else in this book. Maybe as a person who has purchased a book about the recent past and future of the left you're feeling a little short-changed or annoyed. Maybe you're the bibliophile equivalent of one of those people who wear T-shirts saying 'Never Kissed a Tory'. But I do so deliberately here for one central reason: I think it illustrates how contingent so much of Labour's performance was and could be again. A political contest is never just about one side: your opponents matter just as much, and the left is often guilty of endless, sustained self-examination without ever paying much scrutiny to what the Conservatives are doing right (or wrong). And in this case it's crucial. It's my firm belief that had Theresa May charted a softer course, not just on Brexit but on a swathe of other domestic policy issues that undid some of the detoxifying work of the Cameron era, she would not have lost her majority. Jeremy Corbyn's Labour didn't have to do much to make sure that happened. Those circumstances may not exist at the next election. Rather, those seats gained were

---

* One interesting contrast with the May strategy is that of Tony Blair in the election two decades before. In 1997 Blair moved the party to the economic liberal centre. He bet that his blue-collar base had nowhere else to go and would stick with him while he courted middle-class centrist voters. At first, at least, that gamble worked for Blair. In effect, May was playing the same game but in reverse. She calculated that in advocating a hard Brexit she could unlock the UKIP treasure chest. In it would lie four million votes of 2015. And she could do it while keeping her liberal, well-off, educated voters who had been a key component of the Cameron coalition. It worked for Blair. It backfired spectacularly for May.

very much rooted in the exigencies and particular and peculiar circumstances of June 2017. It would be a big mistake to believe that they are bound to be replicated next time.

A HALF-FINISHED REVOLUTION

Theresa May might have weathered all of this. Indeed, in conversations I've had with members of her team they told me they had anticipated a little bit of erosion of their Remainer vote.* But, the reasoning went, they would be more than adequately compensated for by the slew of Leave Labour seats that would replace them. Who needs Bath or even Battersea when you have Scunthorpe and Stoke? And they'd be swapping a string of Jacks for a flush of Kings. Because in winning Scunthorpe and Stoke you'd be achieving realignment; a permanent change to the way working-class people vote. A decimation of the Labour base. We should be in no doubt that Theresa May aimed to destroy the Labour Party. And she was using Brexit as her weapon of choice.

That didn't happen. Or, at least, it didn't happen to the extent Theresa May anticipated. She should have spent more time talking to actual voters because it didn't take long being out and about in the country to feel it going wrong. As I travelled, I expected to find legions of Labour voters fleeing the party, taking their orders from the PM, the *Sun*, the *Mail*, the *Express* and the myriad of invidious Facebook ads that journalists like me never see, being told that the only way they could get Brexit was to vote Tory. I travelled a thousand miles in 30 days and I found fewer and fewer of them as the weeks went on.

Instead, in town after town the Labour vote seemed relatively solid, especially as the campaign wore on. I had started the campaign telling my bosses that my films would tell the story of the emergence of the new Conservative hegemony, a new Tory England. I went to Hartlepool on Teesside thinking that nowhere could show that better.

---

* They just assumed it would peel off to the politically harmless Lib Dems.

A Labour majority had been dwindling down to just over 3,000, caught in a vice between UKIP (2nd) and the Tories (3rd). The Tories had against the odds won the Tees Valley mayoral election only a few weeks before, and if their plan to capture the UKIP vote would work anywhere, it had to be here, a Labour seat since Harold Wilson's party had won it in the 1964 election. It was ground zero of the campaign.

And it was in the still near alabaster-white grandeur of the Imperial Bingo Hall in Hartlepool, not far from where my dad hails, that I had the twin realisation that the Tories had lost their own gamble and I had lost touch with the people I thought I understood.

I love filming in the north. As a man who very frequently finds myself having to stand in shopping precincts bothering people as they go about their business, asking them to talk about obscure political issues to which they have hitherto mostly given very little thought, my heart sinks if I have to do it in London or what you might loosely call the greater south-east. People are too used to seeing camera crews and TV reporters and ignore them accordingly. But in places like the Imperial and Hartlepool, just the camera generates ripples of interest. So it was that night. Walking in, seeing its enormous ceiling, grand palisades and faded leather banquettes, I couldn't help but think of my own childhood – night after night in the cabaret clubs of my early summers with my grandparents, the familiar, endless, near-hypnotising rhythm of the numbers: 'Blue seven-ty-six – red for-ty-two – wh-i-te six-teen – gre-een fif-ty th-ree.' Game after game, after game.

The bingo caller wasn't the only person to have a hold on the room. To my surprise everyone we spoke to in that room was voting Labour. Every. Single. One. And yet they were all Brexiteers too. It broke the election algorithm that had rooted in my brain. This did not compute. Though the bingo banquettes weren't totally full, there were dozens of families and friends out for the night, enjoying a pint or three, hoping that their lucky numbers would come up. What quickly became clear was that Theresa May's definitely weren't. In between games, mother and daughter Pat and Louise summed all of it up. Labour voters all their lives and, like the rest of the room, Brexiteers too. When I asked how they intended to vote, there was almost no hesitation: 'Labour,' Louise said, choosing a red bingo dabber from the assorted multicoloured collection that we'd laid out for her (my production values are at times truly unparalleled).

Her mum, Pat, virtually barked at me: 'Hartlepool's always been a Labour town. Always. And Labour have always been a working-class government [sic].'

I toured the hall. On table after table, whispering to family after family amid the endless din of quick-fire numbers (seriously, you want to see athleticism, go to any town in the north of England and see elderly women dabbing about twenty tickets at a time), nearly everyone said the same thing. They were sticking with Labour. Brexit wasn't enough to push them over to the Tory column. When I put to Louise and Pat the idea that they might have to vote Conservative to get the Brexit they had voted for, they looked at me as if I'd just started reading the numbers in Greek. It wasn't that they didn't understand the principle – they just hadn't even heard it or thought about it that way. When I put to Louise the piece of Westminster logic that she voted Brexit, therefore she must vote Tory, she simply replied: 'I know what you're saying but I don't want to see any more zero-hours contracts either.' Labour went on to win with 52 per cent of the vote and a swelled majority of 7,650.

And it wasn't just Hartlepool. Heading back home to Birmingham, it was the same story. And, in some ways, this was even more damning of Tory strategy. Birmingham isn't congenitally Labour like other cities north of the M25. There wouldn't have been the prospect of a Jarrow march from Birmingham – we couldn't be bothered: 'Long way to London, 'innit, bab.' It's a city that instead votes Labour with a shrug rather than a cheer.* It's one of the few cities outside the capital to retain a strong Tory presence on its council (indeed, it was controlled by the Conservatives until quite recently) and in which in

* Some of that comes from the history of its industry. Famously 'the city of a thousand trades', unlike other cities or industrial towns which came to be dominated by large trade unions, Labour's disparate and diffused industrial base made the spread of labourism slower.

2017 the Tories thought they were seriously competitive in a number of seats, not least Birmingham Erdington and Birmingham Northfield.

Obviously, these are two seats I know well. The first is where I was born, in the north of the city, and the latter at the other end, the home as we've seen of the old Longbridge Rover plant. Nick Timothy, Theresa May's co-chief of staff and right-hand man at the time, also grew up in Erdington, and I'd followed his career a bit since he ascended with his master to Downing Street. His political hero was Joseph Chamberlain, father of Neville and mayor of Birmingham in the late-Victorian period before ascending to the cabinet. And it's little wonder Timothy admired the man of whom Churchill said: '"Joe" was the one who made the weather.'

You can make a strong case that it's because of Chamberlain – 'our Joe', as he came to be called – that the Conservatives are still competitive in Birmingham. His was a very different type of Toryism from the laissez-faire Thatcherism to which we've been accustomed in Britain since the mid-1970s. Chamberlain was an interventionist, statist even. He had no compunction in using the power of the council to intervene in markets he considered broken. He municipalised (effectively local nationalisation) the gas, water and electric companies and used the profits to build the city – the sewage system, the university (the clock tower at the centre of its glorious muscovite architecture is still known as the 'Old Joe'), the Town Hall. He also had no compunction about channelling the spirit of Queen (later King) and country. He draped himself in the cloth of nationhood, arguing for a system of imperial preference: free trade for the English-speaking Empire trading zone, tariffs on the rest. It is not so difficult to imagine him squinting through his trademark monocle, speaking in the Brexiteer language of 'global Britain'. It was his intellectual inspiration that Timothy funnelled into Theresa May's speeches when she began talking during the abortive leadership contest (in Birmingham) of 'a new Conservatism': relentlessly focusing on working-class interests, intervening in free markets, patriotism and Brexit.

I think it's fair to say that 'Chamberlain Conservatism' would have been a little too recherché a name for this new project, so Timothy coined another, which was a bit earthier: 'Erdington Conservatism'. Our home seat has been Labour since 1945 and the Tories had it firmly in their sights, alongside three or four others in the city. As I walked past St Barnabas church on the high street, where I remember my mum and dad getting married on a crisp October day nearly a quarter of a century before, I couldn't quite believe it. There's no reason why you'd have been to Erdington. It's just north of Spaghetti Junction and most people are keen to get out of it (if they can) and then explore the salubrious bits around it.

But take it from me, if you went, you wouldn't be expecting to see the blue rinse brigade to be holding a bring-and-buy sale there any time soon. It's poor. It's almost unchanged from when my family used to live there. There's been some immigration since, Polish and Romanian shops where the Blockbusters and the Woolworth's used to be. But the big factories that my grandad, nan, great-uncles and great-aunts had worked in for decades have long gone and with them the bonds between Labour and voters weakened. And the area voted to leave the EU in a big way. Timothy thought that, with a Tory leadership less rarefied than in the Cameron and Osborne years, a reworked blue-collar agenda, strong UKIP votes in constituencies across the city and the political quicksilver of Brexit, it was a once-in-a-lifetime elixir of Tory success. Now, in this new Britain, it wasn't despite Erdington being deprived and culturally dislocated that Timothy and the Tories were targeting the place, it was because of it.

So it was in Northfield, too. To make a film I needed a visual metaphor and quick, so called upon some local knowledge: the snooker hall where – can you believe? – my school sent us one term for our PE lessons.* Enjoying a game of snooker and a pint or two, there was almost no one who had been lured by the new conservatism. Again, aside from the hall owner, Barry, no one was switching to the Tories.

* I'm reasonably certain this actually made me less healthy. I was pretty fat as a teenager and always walked via the Moby Dick fish and chip shop with my mates for lunch. And as this was before the indoor smoking ban the air, as you might imagine, was thick with a near viscous smoke. You could almost write your name in it.

One man, Richard, who had started the campaign being uncertain about Corbyn but had warmed to him, summed up the mood, looking at me incredulously: 'I'm going to vote Labour, like I usually do, because they represent me and my interests best as a working-class person.'

And there were plenty of ex-Ukippers too, defying the neat lines drawn for them by Number 10 by returning home to Labour. Again, I put it to them that Theresa May said that, as Leave voters, they had to vote for her. I've seen sheets of A4 printing paper look less blank. *Why?*, Roy, a now unemployed ex-Rover factory worker, asked me. 'You can vote for anybody as long as we're leaving.' He had drifted away from Labour, had voted UKIP for a few elections and now was returning to his old party. Roy wasn't alone. Labour's performance with UKIP voters vastly exceeded expectations, not least those of anyone in Downing Street. Indeed, across the country more of UKIP's 4 million supporters in 2015 switched to Labour than stayed loyal to the party.

Corbyn's ambiguity had worked. Middle-class Remainers had voted for him hoping to stop Brexit. Working-class Leavers, whose Labour bloodlines ran deeper and redder than Number 10 had realised, had stuck with the party more than the Tories ever thought they could. On election night Labour held all of its Birmingham seats, including Erdington and Northfield. In many ways, the election came too early; it was too close to the referendum result. Many Leavers, like Roy, assumed that Brexit was a done deal, that it was beyond democratic adjustment. Remainers, in desperation, did not. Had the election taken place later, after the parliamentary process with all its inevitable compromises and 'treachery' had begun, then the Leaver outlook might have been different. As so often, May got the timing wrong.

Moreover, May thought Leave voters were a bloc. They weren't. They were an amalgam of people who, yes, were conservative and always voted Conservative; some Labour and others who would never vote Conservative; some UKIP who would never vote Conservative; and some who never voted and would never be convinced to vote Conservative or for any party or for anything else again. I had an early glimpse of this in Blackpool towards the start of the campaign. A young man, certainly no older than 25 and probably a fair bit younger, said he had voted for the first time for Brexit: 'I like the pound,' he told me on the pier as the late-spring sun shone – 'I never want to give up the pound. I wanted to … make Britain great again, so to speak.'

I smiled and searched for the mutual recognition, the thrill almost, on the man's face of his channelling a Trump slogan. Yet immediately I saw, with his seriousness, that his intent was something else. He didn't know he was using a Trump line. It was a feeling, something deep within him, a young man who could have no knowledge of the time he longed for,* but that something, as we sat among the deckchairs, chipped paint and flickering amusement lights, had been irredeemably lost.

I said to him, you must be voting Conservative to guarantee the Brexit you voted for. He looked utterly nonplussed: 'Why would I do that?' These people were never a coalition that could be neatly transported from the uniqueness of a referendum campaign to a general election.

May's team made a profound misjudgement, in their idea that you can treat voters as neat items on a ledger that can be moved from column to column for this reason or that. The tyranny of big data in politics again and again leads us to expect that people will behave with the tidy, predictable outcomes that our algorithms tell us they will.

But people are emotional and complex and never more so than when it comes to politics and questions of identity. I can't tell you how bewildering some of my conversations with voters can be, totally upending any expectation we might have or forecast we might make in Westminster. I've had people tell me they won't vote for Jeremy

* When I asked when he thought Britain had been at its best, he replied the 1600s, a time when Britain didn't even exist yet and is most commonly remembered for a massive fire, a huge plague and a devastating civil war.

Corbyn because 'he's unprincipled', 'doesn't believe in anything' or 'lacks ideals' – despite the fact that it's nearly universally agreed that whatever we think about Corbyn, a lack of principles or idealism probably isn't one of his faults. I've had people tell me they can't vote for Labour because Gordon Brown sold all the gold – when I ask what that has to do with Brexit or 2017 at all, reply there is none. I've had a man tell me with all the certainty in the world that he couldn't vote Conservative because his history teacher was a Tory and he couldn't stand him because he gave him the cane. I've heard a young woman in Newcastle inform me she was going to vote Labour because 'my mam does', and when asked if Theresa May in any way tickled her fancy, she replied, no, because 'I don't know who she is.' A woman in Merthyr Tydfil told me she couldn't vote for Jeremy Corbyn because he had a beard.

The idea that voters will listen to politicians' songs and then dance predictably to their tune is madness. Voters are emotive jivers, not restrained, predictable ballroomers. The dance did have clear patterns, though. May did gain Leaver Labour votes. She gained hundreds of thousands, mostly from working-class communities. Brexit was a huge issue on both sides of the column – it was the Brexit election. But partly because of timing, partly because of circumstances one side cared about it more than the other. It was not enough – this time – to transform Labour's working-class base in her favour. It was, however, an echo, a shining glimmer of things to come.

DID CORBYN MAKE THE DIFFERENCE?

There was much debate in the aftermath of the vote as to whether another leader could have done better or would have done worse than Jeremy Corbyn. Had history followed the path straight ahead of it in 2015 and Andy Burnham had become leader, some wondered privately, might he have done more to convince even greater numbers of pro-Europeans to come over to the cause and further traditional Conservatives too?

We'll never know. I suspect that Burnham's path – or indeed the path of any Labour leader in the aftermath of the Brexit vote – would have been similarly ambiguous to Corbyn's. All putative leaders would have faced the same structural constraints as he did. Indeed, it is entirely possible a leader like Owen Smith would have had a worse result than Corbyn. His pledge to reverse the referendum would have probably given May and her team precisely what she wanted, an excuse to rerun the referendum. That might have increased non-voting Leaver turnout and prompted a greater exodus of Leaver traditional Labour voters.

There is no doubt that at the start of the campaign Corbyn's Labour was heading for defeat. It probably wouldn't have been such a profound defeat as the early polls predicted because of the hidden Brexit basis, but reasonable defeat it would have been. But if it was a Brexit election it was most definitely also a Corbyn vs May campaign and Corbyn came out of it far better.

Corbyn can also boast a distinctive coalition. We know all about the young – a group that probably would have been less galvanised under a different leader – but there was also what the Labour whips in the 1970s used to call 'the odds and sods': the smaller parties who while usually almost entirely absent from the House of Commons have, since 1974 in particular, managed to claw away the raw numbers of votes of the two main parties. This has been an especial problem for the Labour Party. For a start, ever since the creation of the Labour Party in 1900, the centre-left or progressive vote has been split, to a greater or a lesser extent, between the Labour and Liberal parties. That split went on steroids in the 1980s with the breakaway SDP. Many a Labour leader, including both Tony Blair and Gordon Brown, has at one time or another eyed up their place in the progressive pantheon and dreamed of bringing the split to an end. But that's not all – the Greens and others have all nibbled at Labour's slice of the political pie. Corbyn had a real appeal to many of these voters. The none-of-the-above types, the outside-the-system people who felt isolated from two-party politics and who had in the past felt that voting Labour didn't say as much about themselves as they would like and certainly less than voting Green or nationalist or Lib Dem would have done. In 2017 Labour gained more than 2 million votes from smaller parties, not least some 42 per cent of 2015's Green voters. In a 2017 BBC interview Caroline Lucas was asked whether she could think of a single thing about which she disagreed with Jeremy Corbyn. She replied that off the top of her head she 'couldn't think of anything'. Tens of thousands of her voters apparently shared that sentiment.

There is also no doubt that Corbyn's performance was much stronger than many assumed. I am sure that there was genuine antipathy towards Corbyn from lots of Labour voters at the start of the campaign. Before I started my general election tour I was doing a weekend shift at Sky's Millbank offices on Saturday night (life at Sky is just insanely glamorous sometimes). On the Sunday after May had called the election virtually every paper's front pages carried the astounding news that May was at 50 per cent in the polls. She was riding higher than even Tony Blair had been. I said that if these polls were correct then May would be looking at a majority of over 200. Leaving aside this sky-high performance, in the run-up to the election, all but one of Britain's forecasters had predicted a majority for the Conservatives, with the predicted size of this majority ranging from a low of 48 to a high of 124, with a mean majority of 70.2.[2]

Should I and the rest of us have been more circumspect? Well, a bit, but I don't think those polls were entirely wrong. As we've established, there was probably always going to be a Remainer reckoning. One of the reasons May did well in the local elections in May, only a month before the general election, is because the electorates were different. High-information Remainer voters decided not to vote in local elections because they knew it wouldn't make much difference to the issue they really cared about. But the other reason is that at that point Corbyn had not got anywhere close to sealing the deal with his own supporters. We know now that many Labour voters made their minds up much later in the campaign than those who backed the Tories. More than half (57 per cent) of those who voted Labour made their decision in the last month, and more than a quarter (26 per cent) in 'the last few days'. Conservatives were more likely to have known how they would vote before the campaign started.* There were all sorts of reasons for that, some of them policy, which we'll come on to in a moment, but it was partly because Corbyn himself impressed, especially by comparison with an increasingly wooden May. After that weekend, I spent a few days in the south Wales Labour heartlands, including Merthyr Tydfil, the constituency of the very first Labour MP and Labour Party leader, Keir Hardie. Reaction was genuinely hostile. One lady, Karen, a lifelong Labour voter, was typical: 'I've never voted Conservative before, but I'd genuinely have to consider it. I've never seen such disarray in a party.' Another lady, in her eighties, was more succinct: 'James Keir Hardie would be ashamed of Corbyn.'

Tellingly the reception was a bit better just down the road in Gower, in the Mumbles. Wealthier and more Remainery, it was one of the party's 27 gains. When I was there, checking in a local bookie's, Ladbrokes was offering 1/14 odds for the Tories to keep it, despite its being, at the time, the most marginal seat in the country. In the end, because of Europe, Gower might have always come back home for Corbyn. His achievement was to make sure Merthyr and Bridgend and the other clutch of south Wales and north Wales seats May was eyeing enviously stayed true. And from all the data we have now we know that was no foregone conclusion.

Political scientists and pundits are fond of stroking their chins and sagely ruminating that political campaigns don't matter, that elections are deterministically shaped and destined by events years in the making. 2017 put paid to that theory. Look at the table below. It gives some indication of just how important the campaign was in delivering the shock outcome. At the start of the campaign only 50 per cent of Labour's 2015 voters said they were going to vote for the party again, a shocking rate of attrition considering it had only been two years since the previous poll. That compares to 68 per cent of the

* Ashcroft polling.

Tories.* Labour managed to win new voters to its cause – people who had not voted for them last time (20 per cent of its total vote). But as important were the 19 per cent of its 2015 voters it managed to win back who were not planning to vote for the party at the start of the campaign. Thus the story of the 2017 election is as much as anything one of Labour managing to get its 2015 coalition back together, which at the start of the campaign was far from assured.

2017 vote	Loyal	Returners	Pre-campaign recruits	Campaign recruits	Total
Conservative	68	5	18	9	100
Labour	50	19	11	20	20

Timing and loyalty of each party's vote (%)

Source: British Election Study, 2017

The Tories by contrast only got 5 per cent of its 2015 vote back† and won over a small number of voters by comparison to Labour during the campaign. This speaks to the abysmal quality, organisation and policy on offer and May's declining stature and cack-handed performances.

The graph opposite, which shows the British Election Study's daily tracker of the perceptions of the party leaders, shows that Corbyn did indeed prove much more acceptable to the British public than his detractors had imagined. As the campaign progressed, his favourability went up and up and Theresa May's went down and down.

And he partly did that with a policy offer that was winning. But it's not the one he thinks.

---

* Having said that, both of those figures are quite low by historical standards. The Remain/Leave cleavage was already taking effect. It was just that at the start of the campaign Labour was especially hard hit because it was bleeding support from both directions, from both Remainers and Leavers. The campaign changed that.

† Given that much of the 2015 vote it lost were the young and Remainers, given how the Tories continued to major on the themes of a hard Brexit, this is not surprising.

British Election Study's daily tracker

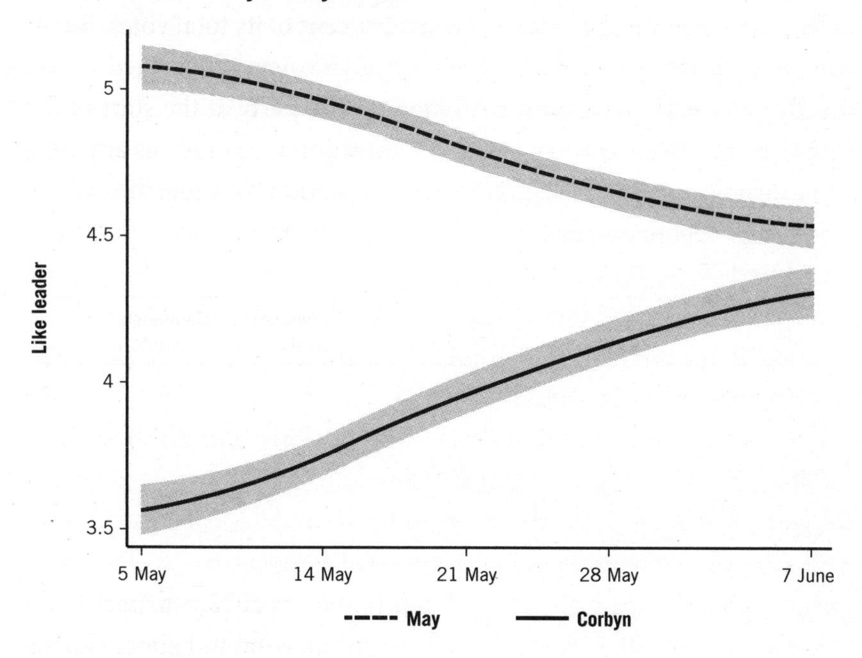

Source: British Election Study, 2017

JEREMY CORBYN DID NOT WIN THE 2017 ELECTION BECAUSE HE WAS A RADICAL

The 2017 Labour manifesto is one of which Jeremy Corbyn and his supporters are inordinately proud. It is also a document that hasn't exactly been underexposed. In the wake of the election barely a senior Corbynista has completed a speech without extolling its virtues. Corbyn himself has called it a 'programme of hope'. Emily Thornberry, the shadow foreign secretary, called it 'the real star of the campaign'. Even Polly Toynbee – no fan of Corbyn or his project – called it a 'cornucopia of delights'. The right were conversely excoriating. The *Telegraph* screamed that the document represented 'a fantasy land blueprint for a socialist Britain'. It is widely credited with being the saving grace of the campaign, especially by comparison with the Conservatives' rather dismal policy offering. And, indeed, with being largely responsible for the turnaround, in terms of how the campaign was received and perceived both by the media and by the public.

But there is yet another fundamental misunderstanding: that people liked the manifesto because it was radical – because it lived up to Corbyn's reputation. The truth is, as we've touched upon, one of the best-kept secrets about Corbyn and the 2017 manifesto is just how traditional and middle of the road it was. When it was leaked, to much fanfare a few days early, were there legions of Blairite MPs taking to the airways to denounce it? No. Because nearly all of the Labour Party agreed with it.

We've encountered some of this but it's worth recapping: Jeremy Corbyn's and John McDonnell's policy on austerity, despite the fanfare, was much the same as Ed Miliband's and Ed Balls'. McDonnell pledged that Labour would run a current-budget surplus if elected, reduce debt as a share of GDP and only borrow to invest – a near-identical stance to that adopted by Balls in 2015 (and the same as that of Gordon Brown). Most astoundingly, the Labour leadership quietly accepted the government's changes to welfare benefits. The Labour manifesto didn't even mention the government's welfare benefits freeze up to 2020 and the party seemed unclear as to whether to change it. The 2017 manifesto, the first one written in decades with the left of the party at the helm, pledged not to increase income taxes on anyone but the absolute richest. So much for income redistribution! Even tuition fees, the policy most commonly touted as the proof of Corbyn's progressive pudding, was undoubtedly popular, but it finished a journey that Mr Miliband had begun. We forget now that one of Miliband's first major policy initiatives was to pledge to reduce fees to £5,000 a year from £9,000. Some might say (and Corbyn's acolytes certainly would) that that summed up the Miliband years, neither quite here nor there, but nonetheless what it does show is that the pledge to abolish was hardly something out of Mao's Little Red Book, nor out of the political ether. Such ideas had been circulating in the political atmosphere (as far back as 2007 Gordon Brown had considered their abolition too). Indeed, far from being a policy designed to scare the horses, it was a good old-fashioned, middle-class bung.

The word 'socialism' didn't appear once. What it did contain was the phrase: 'We still need to be tough on crime and tough on the causes of crime, too.'

Indeed, you could make a strong argument that the 2015 manifesto was a more radical document. It contained a key pledge that was one of the more radical we've seen from the Labour Party in recent years and more radical than anything in 2017: the mansion tax. The first major new tax on wealth proposed by a British political party in decades – and certainly enough to cost the party a few seats in London in 2015. There was neither hide nor hair of it in 2017. And perhaps that isn't so surprising when you consider how London-centric the Labour leadership has now become.

Miliband cuts an odd figure these days. I saw him speak most recently at the Labour Party conference in Brighton. He was speaking at a fringe event in a large hall but unfortunately happened to be doing so at the same time as Jeremy Corbyn at another venue. Consequently, the venue could have been quite a bit fuller. He again speculated as to whether, had he been more radical, he might have been more successful himself. He's said that his own instincts lay in that direction but he was repeatedly advised to rein it in and now regrets it. Perhaps that's not especially surprising given, as we've seen, just how close the Corbyn prospectus in fact lay to the Miliband one. But the truth is for the reasons I've already outlined – of Corbyn's 'radical authenticity', of his place in the zeitgeist – that Corbyn got away with it. Miliband could have stood, word for word, on the 2017 manifesto in 2015 and he would have performed much the same as he did.

And here's the thing. You couldn't have had one without the other. Corbyn unbound and unrestrained would probably have been anathema to the electorate and a traditional stack of Labour bread-and-butter, middle-of-the-road policies presented by a traditional middle-of-the-road Labour politician like Owen Smith wouldn't have worked either without Corbyn's personal zeal. The mistake now being made by those at the top of the Labour Party is to believe that the election was half won by the radicalism of the manifesto; that it was – as we've heard a million times – an endorsement of a more left-wing Britain. I've spoken to several people at the top of the party's leadership who believe that it was the first step – the next must be to go bigger. That could be a great mistake.

SO ... HOW GOOD WAS IT?

A popular meme doing the rounds on Twitter after the election was 'Jeremy Corbyn is the Prime Minister.' This was clearly a rather optimistic take, but it would be churlish not to forgive the left their exuberance and joy. The 2017 campaign came as a near total surprise and they began it in circumstances that could not be more inauspicious, at a time of the prime minister's choosing, heavily outspent, when the social basis of the party itself appeared to be torn asunder. Many – this author included – had been talking not only of a new Conservative hegemony but of the potential for Labour destruction: the strange death of Labour England, mirroring what had happened in Scotland, which was no small part of the prime minister's motivation.

That this did not occur was in no small part thanks to the constructive ambiguity of Corbyn and McDonnell; whether by accident or design, for at that moment they managed to apply a tourniquet to the Labour Party's Brexit bleeding. Corbyn also deserves enormous credit for his personal resilience during the campaign. As May shrank, so Corbyn grew. He seemed to warm to the country and the country warmed to him. He learned from his earlier mistakes with the media, when he seemed irascible and curmudgeonly, and far from some Marxist hardliner instead appeared a quintessentially English figure, grandfatherly, giving gifts of homemade allotment-grown bramble jam on *The One Show*. His manoeuvring around appearing in the TV debates (which inflicted a great deal of damage on Theresa May) was conducted with élan. He was also smart and played the political game much better than he would like any of us to realise, producing a manifesto that was sensible on policy, had clever retail offers, was not a product of the 1970s ideological dogmatism for which he has so often been accused. And because of all of that he translated a 20-point deficit into a three-point one on polling day.

If that is the music to Corbynistas' ears, let this be the scratching of long nails on the blackboard. I don't believe that the Corbyn surge, the glorious defeat of 2017, would have happened without Brexit. Of course, there would almost certainly not have been an election without the referendum result – but that is only a tiny part of what I mean. Without the Remainer realignment, there is no way that Corbyn would have won the seats he did. Every bit of data we know about the election shows this. It is the irony among ironies (and there are lots of them around in post-Brexit Britain) that it is the European Union and its biggest supporters which should have saved the career and political fortunes of a man and political tribe that had spent decades opposing that same institution without hesitation.

WHAT DOES THIS MEAN FOR LABOUR?

The 2017 general election and its aftermath aren't just important because of the Jupiter-sized spanner it has thrown into the bowels of the Brexit process. For long after we have (or have not) left the bloc, the narrative of the 2017 election will be fought over by the various wings of the Labour Party. Likewise, far beyond Britain's shores, it is being cited as proof of what the left can do if only it is true to itself. Because the left in Britain are now psychologically bullet proof, they finally can say that the left can win. At the Durham Miners' Gala, a few months later, Len McCluskey appeared to have allowed the warm beer and decent weather to go to his head a little when he said: 'And let me say this to those merchants of doom, the whingers and the whiners, who say we should have done better, we didn't win. I say we did win!' He was roundly mocked, but he was misunderstood – I suspect he didn't mean Labour but his wing of the party, the left. For if they didn't take the country with them, the election set the seal on a leftist dominance within Labour the like of which we have never seen.

The great glorious defeat of 2017 has provided the left with cover. Ever since the late 1970s the left both in the UK and around the world has been dealt defeat after defeat. The response was that Labour should move to the right. And with each defeat that came the call became louder: 'We haven't changed enough.' Perhaps the best elucidation of this argument was given by Tony Benn. Speaking as part of a BBC documentary in 1995 he gave an almost chilling exposition of the left's view about the necessity of compromise and what had happened to the party over the past two decades:

'I've seen so many failures based on the idea of give up everything you believe and you'll win. You give it up and you don't win. And then people say we didn't give up enough and you have to give up even more. And I think that is the tragedy since, well, since I suppose you'd say since 1974. It hasn't appeared to stand for anything, people aren't fools, they see that, so they say better the devil you know.'[3]

This was the primary argument put forward by the Labour left throughout the 1980s and 1990s. Even the 1983 Labour manifesto, rightly regarded as the most left wing since the war, was for the Bennites a starting point, not a destination.

For the Blairite right of the Labour Party, the lessons of the defeats of the 1980s and early 1990s were precisely the opposite. Before 1997 these competing narratives were locked in competition. It's easy to forget now that such a contest even existed, that it was obvious that the Labour Party after the disaster of 1983 and the subsequent defeats had to move to the right to win. But there were many who cited the fact that Labour, despite becoming ever more centrist in the 1987 and 1992 elections, had failed to break through into government and it had yielded little. Indeed, the fact that they had moved was offered as an explanation for their defeat. After the shock defeat of 1992, when Neil Kinnock's Labour had widely been predicted to triumph against John Major's Tories, Ken Livingstone, then an MP, was uncharacteristically quick off the mark to offer his twopenn'orth. Sitting next to his best political friend, one Jeremy Corbyn, in a BBC election studio on the day after the shock defeat, he said:

'The party and the trade unions will want to digest this. We were told if we got rid of our unilateralism, if we drop our commitment to public ownership, we've done all these things on the promise that it would win us a victory. This is a worse defeat than we've had in the previous two elections, this is a defeat fought after the worst year for the British economy since 1931, we should have had a majority of a hundred. This is much worse than last time.'

It was an analysis with which the man on his literal if not figurative left agreed. Jeremy Corbyn, when asked by an interviewer whether he thought Kinnock should resign, had this to say: 'He is the one who has put forward the policy changes in the party which have moved us in a more right-wing direction. He's the one who has not put forward a programme of arms cuts and abolishing nuclear weapons.'

It wasn't obvious in the mid-1990s what should be done, or, at least, if it was obvious to some it was still competing territory. While some, like Blair and Brown, believed the party should win different voters, win Tories who had never even considered voting Labour, many on the left advanced the argument that essentially the party didn't need those people. That there were plenty of Labour voters out there, but until they were given something to vote for they could never be motivated to turn out. Labour seem destined to repeat those arguments. But this time, for the first time, it will be the left in the driving seat, driving them forth to the next election. Dennis Skinner put the case in his usual bellicose fashion in the days after 1992:

'Let's get back to basics, let's represent our class. Let's talk about building houses, taking down the dole queues, let's talk about taking on the bosses. The trouble is in the course of the past several years we've had our people wining and dining with the City of London and what happened in the election campaign? The City of London criticised the Labour Party. It's time we represented our class. There are plenty of underprivileged people out there, there are more than 3 million on the dole according to the real figures. There's now 20 per cent of our population who are pensioners who need help, people who haven't two halfpennies to rub together, there's 160,000 people who are homeless, some of them living in cardboard boxes. It's time we were building houses again, we don't need liberals and PR to that. What we need is a bit of class politics.'

Skinner, that scion of traditional Labour politics, might think that all of this means a new beginning for the sort of class politics on which he was raised – but if I'm convinced of one thing about the future of Labour and the left around the world, it is that class politics will no longer be at its centre. Those people who haven't two half-pennies to rub together will be less and less likely to vote for the left – and many of the voters who remain in the Labour tent, whether conscious of it or not, might find themselves less and less likely to want them.

Chapter 10

WHAT COMES AFTER: THE NEXT ELECTION AND THE FUTURE OF THE LEFT

Revolutions can no longer be achieved by minorities.
No matter how energetic and intelligent a minority may be,
it is not enough, in modern times at least, to make
a revolution. The co-operation of a majority,
and a large majority too, is needed.
Jean Jaurès, French socialist, 1914

I've got lots of stamina; don't worry about that.
I cycle every day – it's OK.
Jeremy Corbyn, 2017

The date is Friday, 5 May 2022. Sajid Javid, the prime minister, is preparing to go to Buckingham Palace to see the Queen. He has been up all night and has recently returned from his constituency in Bromsgrove. The world's journalists are crowded into the poky stretch of road that is Downing Street. It is unseasonably warm and they're all keen for the pictures of the smiling prime minister, after an extraordinary night.

Meanwhile, the Labour leader, Jeremy Corbyn, is in the car, on the way from his constituency home in Islington, where by now he has reached his thirty-ninth year as its MP, to his count at the Sobell

Leisure Centre. He and his most senior advisers are locked in hushed but urgent conversation. Corbyn's phone flashes, it's John McDonnell. Corbyn answers and they too have a solemn but determined exchange. His advisers can barely look at each other.

Corbyn arrives at his much-delayed count. He is smiling, shaking hands, walking a little more slowly, not bounding quite as tiggerishly as he did the last time he performed this ritual, an age ago, in 2017. The last five years, under attack from party, bits of the media and the wider establishment, reaching a near unbearable crescendo during this election campaign, have taken their toll.

Half an hour later, he's led by Islington's local election officials to the stage to hear his count. In television news galleries across the networks, there's a scramble to take the live pictures. 'Go to Corbyn. No – CORBYN!' screams a studio director in the Osterley Sky News Gallery. Adam Boulton interrupts his guest: 'Sorry to cut across you, Diane, but we're going to go live to Islington for the count of your leader, just down the road from you in Hackney, Jeremy Corbyn. No question of course of his not retaining this rock-solid Labour seat in north London, but obviously the party and the country are going to want to hear what he's got to say now we've got some idea of the overall result.'

Corbyn stands, faintly smiling, appearing slightly dazed, staring at the returning officer as she reads out the names of the candidates and their vote tallies, Corbyn is among the first: 'Corbyn, Jeremy Bernard, the Labour Party candidate, thirty-nine thousand, one hundred and twenty-six.' She hasn't finished even her penultimate syllable before a ringing cheer goes up around the room. Corbyn remains impassive, but his modest smile sticks. His majority is enormous, improving even on his 2017 performance. The din finally drains away, so the returning officer resumes her familiar verbal rhythms: 'Richards, Gloria Patricia, the Liberal Democrat candidate, five thousand, one hundred and –'

She finally finishes her register of names, making her way through the various joke candidates, protest parties and oddballs attracted by the star power of standing in the seat of the leader of the opposition.

She rounds off, as everyone knows she will: 'So I do hereby declare that the said Jeremy Bernard Corbyn is duly elected to serve as the Member of Parliament for the Islington North constituency.' Cheers again, louder this time, for longer.

Corbyn steps forward to the microphone. He waits a moment, surveys the room, takes a breath and begins:

'Madam Returning Officer, can I just start by thanking you for all the fantastic work that you and all of the council staff do, in running such a smooth and efficient count here tonight. I'd like to thank the police for all the work they've done and of course my fellow candidates. I'm only sorry I didn't get to spend as much time as I might have liked with them, at the hustings, here in our wonderful community.

'It's been five years since the last election and much has happened in the interim. We haven't had all of the results in yet and we must wait for those. But if, as looks likely, we've come up slightly short of where we were hoping ...'

A trace of anger now rises in his voice.

'It is clear to me that the British people were not allowed to fully appreciate our message at this election. This was not their fault, and it wasn't yours, colleagues, either. And although I, of course, take full responsibility for the faults of the campaign, I was and remain bitterly disappointed that once again we were the victims of scaremongering, a wholly negative type of campaigning and outright war from the Tories' friends in the media. Our message was not and could not be heard. [Applause.] And yet, despite that ... my friends, despite that tonight we can say with certainty that millions of our fellow citizens voted yesterday for a better future, a future with equality for all, investment in our public services, a future where we move away from continued austerity and embrace hope. That gives us, in turn, hope for our own future and our own journey working together as one movement as a party. Thank you.'

In an anteroom of the centre, Laura, who had been due to accompany her husband on to the stage, is quietly weeping. Seumas Milne, Corbyn's head of strategy, who is, like the entire political world, watching his boss on the television, at the party's Southside headquarters, receives a text message. It's a message from James Schneider, Corbyn's former political adviser but latterly parliamentary candidate in Kensington, hoping to keep the seat after it was unexpectedly won by the party last time. 'I've lost, six hundred Tory majority.' Milne looks at the message but does not reply. Instead, he begins to make some calls.

In the background, the news of Kensington's loss is matched by the news that Bishop Auckland, Labour since 1931, has been lost to the Tories by a narrow majority, and Labour has failed, despite a guerrilla campaign by Momentum and the Labour Party machine, to take Swindon North, one of its top targets.

The pundits can barely contain themselves at this latest shock election night. David Dimbleby, the *éminence grise* of BBC election coverage, has somehow managed to engineer 'one more go' despite having promised to leave fifteen years before. He scratches his head and turns to Sir John Curtice, the psephologist, who himself has become an unlikely star of recent election campaigns: 'Quite extraordinary set of results this, John – generally Labour is doing very well in London – but they are doing better in urban seats overall. They've taken Altrincham and Sale West, Wimbledon and Iain Duncan Smith's seat of Chingford but lost Newcastle-under-Lyme and now Bishop Auckland ... What's going on? What happened to that Labour majority the polls told us we were promised?'

'In many ways, David, we're seeing a continuation of the trends we saw at the last general election and in intervening local elections too. The Brexit realignment the prime minister had hoped to see in 2017 does seem to be reaching something of an apotheosis now. We've seen that in elections since too: older, whiter places, traditional working-class vote drifting to the Conservatives in greater numbers. Younger people and more liberal voters turning out for Labour, but we seem to be seeing a bit of an enthusiasm gulf between this time and last. The numbers aren't appearing quite as much as in 2017 and certainly not in the right places. Labour are gaining thousands of votes in places they already have seats, but it's not yielding them much benefit in terms of new MPs in the House of Commons.'

'And what does this mean for the overall figures – is the exit poll still looking to be broadly correct?'

'Yes, David, it's well within the margin of error. So we're now looking at the Conservatives on around 314 seats, that's around three fewer than last time. Of course, that's taking into account the thirty or so "Conservative Nationals", Jacob Rees-Mogg's hard-Brexiteer splinter group – but given the main Conservative Party did not oppose them in those seats, and Mr Rees-Mogg has made it clear he will caucus with the main Conservative Party and vote for Mr Javid's Queen's Speech, then we're counting them as part of the Tory tally. Consequently it's tantalisingly close to an overall majority, and in practice the prime minister should be able to govern, again possibly with the DUP or, if a few more seats go their way, on their own. Labour are on 263 or 264, that's only a couple more than in 2017. Especially when we consider how favourable some of the polls have been, going into this election, that is a staggeringly disappointing result. As for the Liberal Democrats, a modest revival ...'

Across the country, hundreds of Corbyn activists wept with Laura. How after all the graft, all the heartache, was this possible? This government was now twelve years old. Brexit had been bungled and fudged. It was led by two tortured prime ministers and had clung on by the tips of its fingers. The Conservative Party and its unbridgeable divisions had been laid bare. Yet it had been returned. Labour was stuck in the mud. As someone once said, 'Nothing has changed.'

It had once felt like it was destined, written in the stars. Yet the forward march of Corbynism had been halted. His advisers spent the rest of the morning exchanging furious messages. On one thing, they could all agree, Jeremy mustn't be allowed to resign.

Meanwhile at Number 10 Downing Street, the prime minister, who against all the odds had survived, poured his team (though not himself) glasses of champagne. He had succeeded in becoming Britain's first elected ethnic minority prime minister. He was going to enjoy himself today.

* * *

What you've just read are clearly works of my imagination – in particular, whether Sajid Javid becomes prime minister or not is pure fancy. That, however, is one of the least interesting and least important details. For although the events I've described and the manner of their happening are fictitious, the scenario, whensoever it comes, is eminently plausible: the fact that, contrary to all of the hype and the hope, politics is in stasis. The political predestination in which so many on the left of politics believe is folly. Jeremy Corbyn might become prime minister, but the next leap is the highest and hardest. The following pages outline why that is so.

THE TASK AHEAD

As we've seen, the 2017 election left the Labour Party with 262 seats. If boundary reforms do not go ahead,* that means Labour will need a net gain of 62 seats on the 2017 result to win a majority in the next House of Commons.

Thanks to Corbyn's unexpectedly strong showing in 2017, there exists a far rosier electoral map than the one Miliband bequeathed him. After 2015's drubbing Labour would have required a swing of 8.75 per cent across the UK to get a majority of one. After 2017 they now only need 3.5 per cent. To become the biggest party Labour barely needs to draw breath.

To give some context to those figures, in 2015 there were only 93 seats where the majority was under 3,500 votes, i.e. what you might say were marginal seats. Of these, there were only 30 where the

---

* Boundary reform is a holdover from David Cameron's time in office. He had proposed to cut the number of MPs from 650 to 600 so as to 'cut the cost of politics' and equalise parliamentary constituency size. Whatever his real motivations, the effect would be to disadvantage the Labour Party. If the changes go through (and at the time of the writing, as a result of the hung Parliament and the DUP's dislike of the proposals, it is uncertain whether they will), then Labour's task will be a bit harder. Conservative high command will doubtless do all it can to get the necessary legislation through Parliament.

majority was under 1,000. Given Labour had to win roughly 100 seats to win a majority, that was an almost impossible task for Corbyn. After 2017 the picture is, by contrast, serene: there are 135 marginals and 51 have majorities of less than 1,000.

It is a task made easier again because of Labour's modest Scottish revival. In the aftermath of the 2015 election, when Labour lost 40 of its 41 seats in Scotland, many had spoken of the party's permanent demise north of the border. Although Ruth Davidson's Tories (rightly) demanded attention on election night for their best Scottish performance since 1987, becoming the second party of Scotland in the Commons, Labour won six new seats back from the nationalists. More importantly, Labour slashed into what had been previously unassailable majorities – most are now south of 5,000. This is important because of Labour's 64 target seats, 18 are currently occupied by the SNP, so a strong showing next time will be crucial. Either way, with Scotland back in play Labour is fishing with a larger net and it makes the task of catching a majority much easier.

For all of these reasons, the feeling in the Labour Party is that it is heading for government. As I dashed in and around the drinks events, receptions and parties of Labour's 2017 conference, the mood could be summed up in three words: 'One more heave.' At the Sky annual conference party, on the eve of Corbyn's 'victory' speech, with the champagne flowing and the mood merry, I spoke to a senior shadow cabinet minister. When I posited the thesis that the next election might not be in the bag as everyone assumed it would be, they gave me a dementor-like death stare: 'What did you study at university?' they spluttered.

'History and politics.'

'Then you will have heard of the Corn Laws?'

Vaguely irritated at the dripping condescension, I persevered: 'Yes – I have.'

'Then you'll appreciate that Brexit is the Tory Party's Corn Laws.'

I was not especially impressed by this. 'Well, even if you accept that's the case, what if the Parliament runs long? They'll probably have a new leader, the next campaign from them won't be as poor ...'

They rolled their eyes: 'Who? Just who? None of them could hold a candle to Jeremy.'

I reflected later that there was a lot in that exchange. The complacency was the obvious thing, but the reference to Brexit was also telling. On the one hand it ignored the deep problems that Labour itself has with the issue but it also spoke to a wider problem: determinism. As we've seen, the Labour left has a strong impulse, so unlike the rest of the Labour Party and probably a hangover from a Marxist analysis, that capitalism is eating itself, that the public are at some point fated to revolt and turn to Labour. It is a belief that was put on steroids by the 2017 result. A caustic pessimism has thus given way to an unshakeable sense of self-belief.

There are many reasons why Labour should be wary of this view. If the 2017 result was based on underlying trends that made it easier for the party to do better than it appeared, the next election, whenever it comes, may well operate in the other direction.

AN EXPECTATION PROBLEM

First, the expectations will be wildly different. In the 2017 campaign many assumed Labour was battling only for survival; anything other than being swept out to sea would do. The next election will be very different. Both the media and party members will assume the party is gunning for victory, not merely stasis or managed retreat. That will transform the narrative and contours of the election. Labour's policies will be scrutinised far more and the voters will probably give the prospect of a Corbyn-led government its full attention. They will look at Corbyn personally in a very different light, not this time as the plucky underdog with a Werther's Original in his pocket, but as a man likely to become prime minister with all the duties and responsibilities that entails.

Clearly, the voters and media were not really treating him in that way last time. Indeed, there is a case to be made that people thought his chances of becoming prime minister were so slender that it actually helped Labour. Labour MPs were able to say to voters on the doorstep: 'Look, you know Corbyn isn't going to get in – why not vote with your heart? And vote for me and the party?' They also appealed to a sense that an overwhelming majority for May would not have been a desirable outcome for either their local area or the country overall. There is debate as to whether or not that phenomenon was a real one; Tory and moderate Labour MPs say it was commonplace. In fairness, in my travels during the election I didn't hear much of it. I wonder if people really engage with politics like that. Either way, there is no doubt that the public and media will be taking a Corbyn premiership much more seriously whenever the next election comes, with all the inevitable consequences therein.

Secondly, the Conservatives won't make the same mistakes. Granted they will make other ones. But they had their fingers badly burned in 2017, and if history teaches us anything about the Conservative Party, it is that it is both adaptable and power hungry. They will (probably) do whatever it takes to win, especially now that they really fear a Corbyn government. Run into any Conservative MP in the Commons and it won't take long before the conversation turns to Corbyn and you can see the whites of their eyes. Fear has replaced the laughter and complacent derision; one of the only things binding the Tory Party together right now is a mutual revulsion at the prospect of a Corbyn government. They don't believe it would be just another Labour prime minister, but a Marxist Trojan horse. Moreover, and perhaps more importantly, they will probably not be led by Theresa May and in my view will probably (assuming they emerge from the Brexit morass in one piece) have opted for a fresh face, someone from the 2010, 2015 or even 2017 intakes. They will attempt to draw a line under the Cameron and May eras.

Perhaps this is why, since the 2017 election, Jeremy Corbyn has consistently talked up the prospect of an election and says that he is itching for it. He wants, understandably, to finish off his opponents while they're still struggling to get off the ropes. But I fear that he may be itching for a while.

A BREXIT PROBLEM

There are two broad scenarios for the timing of the next election. The first category of outcomes is highly speculative; but you might broadly file them under 'Brexitocalypse', i.e. the government falls because of Brexit because it can't get a deal through the House of Commons. There might be an election then as a means for the government to bypass Parliament on a sack-or-back-the-deal proposition.

Labour would then have to decide what to do – it would almost certainly be obliged to oppose the deal, but it would face an invidious position – on what grounds would it be opposed? What would it argue for instead? Would it argue for a deal that was more Remainery, conscious of how much of its 2017 performance was based on Remainer votes and hope that once again historic ties would keep the working-class Leaver voters with the party? We saw in the last chapter how many Labour voters did not connect the two issues – but would they stay indifferent in an election explicitly called because of the failure of a Brexit deal to pass the Commons?

Labour would have to show a lot more leg; by comparison to June 2017 it already has done so, in saying that it would support Britain remaining in a new customs union, thus explicitly backing a softer form of Brexit than the Conservatives. That was done for very sound strategic reasons: it had to give something to its new Remainer coalition and it was not convinced (as I am not) that many Labour voters could give a damn about the customs union. However, it's easy to forget now how little we knew about Brexit in June 2017. When the election was called it came only a few weeks after Theresa May had triggered Article 50 and only nine months after the referendum result itself. The Brexit negotiations themselves had not even formally begun. The positions of the parties, the policies they would pursue, were still nebulous, especially for Labour. If another election were called at the end of the process, on a Brexit prospectus, that would by definition not be the case. It is not therefore guaranteed that the way the public would view the situation would be comparable to June 2017, and Labour's ability to coat itself in a layer of 'constructive ambiguity' would be much diminished.

In this scenario, they won't just have a timing problem but a Brexit problem too, and it might not just come from the party's Leave constituencies. In summer 2018 it was becoming clearer that Remainers within the Corbyn coalition were becoming more and more restless and frustrated with the party's position on Brexit. In June that year hundreds of thousands of protesters marched through the streets of London demanding a second referendum in the form of a 'People's Vote' on the final deal. By coincidence I was with Corbyn and his team. But they weren't manning the barricades – they were in Jordan, visiting a series of refugee camps for World Refugee Day. I have never seen Corbyn more energised or in better cheer. He was sober about the work and talks he received from the UN but there was almost a holiday atmosphere among the top members of his team. They seemed happy and relaxed and excited by the work they were doing. Their minds were certainly not on the march in London. Just as I finished my interview with the Labour leader, in the car park of the Al-Baaqr Palestinian refugee camp in Amman, I received a message on my phone from my editor that the crowd was chanting Jeremy Corbyn's name – to his own White Stripes theme tune. But this time, it wasn't in acclaim – they were screaming: 'Where's Jer-e-my Cor-b-yn?!', angry that he wasn't there with them. As I received the news I asked his team if I could ask one more question. Corbyn refused. That was annoying – but more telling was their general reaction. It was clear to me that members of his top team, including Corbyn himself, did not know the march was even taking place. One of his senior aides even asked me where it was. Given so many on the march, younger, liberal Labour voters, formed the bulk of those attending, I found this indifference astonishing. It was just something they didn't want to think about. But in the medium term, Brexit is easily – if not the only – substantial threat to Corbyn's leadership. As the clock has ticked and the profound consequences of the act have become clearer, opposition to Brexit and the party's position has become stronger, even from Corbyn's friends. At the time of writing Momentum is planning a poll of its members on the prospect of a second referendum. Unite, under Corbyn stalwart Len McCluskey, is also changing its position. Corbyn's biggest problem would be, fairly or unfairly, being seen to have facilitated a hard Brexit. This would alienate him from his base both within the party and within the country, and severely undermine his position.

There are voices within the leader's office who get that but there are plenty who don't. They do not share the analysis of the Remainer surge helping Labour in 2017 and believe that whatever the outcome, they will fall into line with the party post-Brexit. As one senior Labour strategist put it to me: 'I think a lot of it is presentation, when a lot of people talk about it was the Remainers that voted for Labour last year. Look, if you think they voted because they are fucked off with the Tories, I agree with that, if you think it's because they think that Labour is going to reverse Brexit and by that we are going to stay in the single market and the customs union then you lose me there, because I have never met that many people whose grasp of it is that complicated.' Instead, this aide said, Labour must offer a different type of Brexit, which as the clock ticks down in the autumn of 2018, they will do: 'It's about managing expectation and it's about presentation. If we presented the position that what we are going to do is have the free trade agreement with the EU, but what we are going to do is have much more stronger union rights, state aid and corporate taxation and avoidance, no more EU corporate cosiness, then that's something we can win our people round with.'

It is, in effect, the idea of a left-wing Brexit (so-called 'Lexit'). The problem is, for many of the party's supporters, that might not be enough. It is ironic that Corbynism, a project of the heart, born of cultural values, should show such a tin ear to another cut from the same cloth, that of Remainerdom. There is no bargaining with it. Another source said of the leadership's approach: 'I think John [McDonnell's] and Jeremy's approach is, that he just wants a happy life. They are kind of like, the domestic policy is much more of an issue. Jeremy and John just want an outcome that is successful.' That head in the sand approach, the misunderstanding of their own base, so evident in the sands of Jordan, could yet cost the party.

They might be able to find a sticking plaster, once again, but the shadows in which to hide would be neither as dark nor as comfortable as they were in 2017. Ergo the blithe assumption that Brexit is destined to bring down the Tories to Labour's benefit, as that Corbyn ally said that night, is a little silly – it ignores the risks for Labour too. There are even more dramatic possibilities. By the summer of 2018, the extent of the lack of parliamentary majority for any Brexit solution at all had become all too clear. Theresa May, forced finally to show her hand in the form of the Chequers agreement, lost two cabinet ministers and laid bare Conservative division. The fissures within the Tory Party, obvious but just about obscured for so long, were to some extent formalised. Her government became more Remainery at the cost of sixty or so Eurosceptic (European Research Group) MPs operating separately from within. It finally became obvious that in the end the Tory Party is highly unlikely to vote as one when and if a deal comes before the House of Commons. It also became clear to me that May, if she has any hope at all of getting a deal through, will rely on Labour votes. She is likely to leave the vote to the last possible moment and – with the Fixed Term Parliaments Act on her side – argue that if the deal is defeated there will be no time for an election, all that would result is the hardest of hard Brexits. This would place pro-EU Labour MPs in the tightest of binds. Vote with their party to bring down a government – or risk national economic ruin? And worse – the possibility of being blamed for that ruin. May will make a pitch to those MPs: country, before party. She would be the Tory Ramsay MacDonald – but would at least, she would reckon, secure her place in the history books as the woman who made Brexit work.

For Labour such a scenario would be high risk–high reward. The task before Jeremy Corbyn is immense. Brexit remains the best chance of dislodging a Conservative government but at the same time is (as Bevin almost warned) a Pandora's Box. They risk a split themselves, with scores of Labour MPs walking into a division lobby to back the PM's deal. Or the government might fall – Labour gets their election and Corbyn himself has to assume the reins over the negotiations. The political jewel, the prize on offer, is glittering but sharp-edged.

In some ways, though, the bigger imponderables come if the Tories can survive the Brexit vote (an enormous if). In that scenario I suspect it is likely that this Parliament is played long and runs to 2022. By that time Corbyn will be 72 and will have been leader of the opposition for eight years (the longest period since Neil Kinnock held the post). For a candidacy anchored in zeitgeist and the youthful enthusiasm of its strongest adherents, that poses some difficulty. Will he continue to appear equally of the moment in 2022? Can that élan be maintained over such a long period? Will Corbyn, frankly, appear not only a bit passé but also past it? Especially if the Tories do nominate a younger leader. The problems the party experienced with Labour Live – the party's first music festival – illustrated the dangers of mixing politics and pop culture. The party, expecting thousands of young eager beavers, could barely shift the tickets. You can ride waves but sooner or later they will crash. If this Parliament is played long, that could prove a real issue. Conservatives I speak to want the next election in 2021 or 2022 and every Labour MP thinks it will come earlier. And, at the time of writing, the parties' preparations for the election would speak to that. By spring 2018 the Labour Party had chosen over 60 candidates in key marginal seats. The Conservatives hadn't chosen a single candidate across the whole country.

It may in the end not be in their gift to decide, but the Conservatives will do as much as they can to avoid another general election. They have the Fixed Term Parliaments Act to help them in that endeavour.* But whenever the next election comes and in whatever circumstances it is called, there are bigger structural problems for Labour at play too.

THE BISHOP AUCKLAND PROBLEM

There's a tendency in campaigning and political journalism to assume the next campaign will be just like the last. But it won't be, not just for the reasons I've already described: the circumstances, the topics, the Conservative leader and the tactics they employ – these are all known unknowns, as Donald Rumsfeld famously put it. We can anticipate them but we can't know exactly what form they will take. There are the 'unknown unknowns', events and forces we just can't anticipate. We can also divine a few 'known knowns', things we know and which will not change. Yet the most important of these seems to be largely

* There is much misunderstanding about the auspices of the Fixed Term Parliaments Act. Before the 2017 general election it was fashionable to say that Theresa May couldn't engineer a general election even if she wished it because of the terms of the relatively new Act, which requires a two-thirds majority of MPs to dissolve Parliament early and vote for a general election. It was said that it would look odd for Tory MPs to vote to end their own government and that Labour – languishing in the polls – would never vote for it. Both of these contentions proved to be nonsense. However, commentators who rather overestimated its importance then are proceeding to underestimate it in 2018. The truth about the FTPA is that it is easy to get an early general election if the government wants one. An opposition will always vote for it however unpopular it is; not to do so would appear frit and squander a rare opportunity to fulfil its sole purpose – to dislodge the government of the day. If a government doesn't want it, however, the FTPA assists its survival by firmly specifying what can count as a confidence vote. There is the added complication that the Act specifies that, although a government can lose a confidence vote by a simple majority of one, it then says that, unlike under the old system, which would mandate an automatic dissolution and general election, there will be a 14-day period during which another government could be formed. That government potentially could be another Tory one led by a different prime minister; or the Queen could send for Corbyn. It is a murky picture, but, generally speaking, I think the FTPA has the effect of buttressing a weak government and making it harder for the opposition to force an election, which would probably help the government play this Parliament long.

missed by party thinkers: the sorts of seats Labour will be seeking to gain will not be the same as in 2017.* The sorts of voters it will have to win and appeal to will be very different from those that brought it its unexpected surge last time.

The electoral coalition that Labour assembled in 2017 – assuming it holds together – is largely maxed out, i.e. of the sorts of people who switched to Labour, there aren't that many of them left to pick off. And even if the party can rally a few more, the problem is that it already holds most of the seats where those sorts of people live. Thanks to the well-documented phenomenon of voter sorting, i.e. the same sorts of people marrying each other and living close to each other, gaining new liberal metropolitan voters is increasingly useless for Labour. In the British system it doesn't matter how big a set of scales you need to weigh the size of Diane Abbott's majority in Hackney or Jeremy Corbyn's in Islington; every vote above a simple majority there is a vote wasted. This is already a problem. One of the reasons why Labour enjoyed such a mammoth increase in vote share in 2017 but not a corresponding slew of new seats is that its vote is inefficiently allocated across the country, just as Hillary Clinton found to her cost in 2016. When asked what young voters could do to help the Democratic Party in future elections, Barack Obama, only half jokingly, replied: 'Move to Nebraska.' Short of thousands of north London voters packing their bags and moving to Nuneaton,† Labour needs to simply do much better with voters who sit outside the cosmopolitan, liberal space, especially in the Midlands and the north.

---

* It will, however, have to hold on to some of the seats it unexpectedly gained then, these including surprising and disparate results like Canterbury and Kensington (majority: 20). Many of these are university seats. I suspect the next Conservative leader will not be so foolish as to engineer an election during university term time, hoping to disperse the student vote wherever possible.

† There is some evidence that as a result of high house prices this is happening in the south-east, with old Tory fortresses in the shires becoming more mixed as a result of migration from priced-out younger Londoners. Still, this will almost certainly yield only a limited dividend for Labour by the time of the next election.

That's a problem because it was precisely with those sorts of voters that Labour did quite badly in 2017. Take a look down the list of Labour's target seats for the next election.

Name	Majority	Swing to/away from Labour in 2017, %	Leave vote (2016), %
Southampton Itchen	31	2.6	60.3
Pudsey	331	8.0	49.0
Hastings and Rye	346	4.0	55.0
Chipping Barnet	353	7.0	41.0
Thurrock	345	0.2	70.0
Preseli Pembrokeshire	314	5.7	55.0
Calder Valley	609	3.6	53.0
Norwich North	507	4.6	57.0
Broxtowe	507	3.2	52.5
Stoke-on-Trent South	663	–4.1	71.0
Telford	720	0.1	66.0
Bolton West	936	–0.1	56.0
Aberconwy	635	5.7	52.0
Northampton North	807	3.1	60.0
Hendon	1,072	2.7	42.0
Mansfield	1,057	–6.7	71.0
Middlesbrough South	1,020	3.6	65.3
Milton Keynes South	1,725	–6.0	53.0
Northampton South	1,159	3.5	59.0
Pendle	1,279	4.8	63.2
Morecambe and Lunesdale	1,399	3.8	58.0
Milton Keynes North	1,975	7.0	49.7

What do you notice about this top 25? For a start, they're all Tory seats; they are nearly all outside London and, apart from Hendon, Chipping Barnet and Milton Keynes, are all only semi-urban. Some are seats that Labour lost to the Tories in 2017, like Mansfield and Middlesbrough and Stoke South, none of which had had a Tory MP before for decades. Many of the others should also have been lost to Labour on a uniform swing, but the Tories piled on votes that meant they didn't. Also, they nearly all voted to leave the EU.

The fact that they are Leaver seats might not in itself be relevant in the Brexit sense; it is entirely possible that if the next election comes in 2022 and we have left the EU in some form, the issue might not be as germane. But as a signifier of the sorts of seats they are, it will still be tremendously significant. And it is the characteristics of the voters in Leaver areas with which the Labour Party has been having more and more trouble: less formal education; whiter; older; less diverse; post-industrial; culturally hostile to immigration. These trends have been growing over quite a long time, they precede Brexit and will probably be there after it. Let's take a look at two seats that illustrate what I'm talking about, the first Bishop Auckland, for years a rock-solid Labour seat, in County Durham.

Bishop Auckland has been Labour almost without interruption since 1918. It is a semi-rural, sprawling north-east seat in former mining country. It's remote, isolated and poor. Its nearest train station is Darlington, a half-hour drive away. You look around its collection of smallish towns, old collieries, working men's clubs, and your every instinct tells you that this is a Labour stronghold. Yet it is now an ultra-marginal with a majority of 512.

At the zenith of Labour Party support, it boasted a towering majority of over 20,000. That figure has been declining gradually with every single election over the past two decades. There are dozens of seats like it across the north and Midlands. People in the north-east Labour Party, with whom I've spoken on many occasions, can't credit the idea that it might go Tory. But that's what they said in Mansfield and Middlesbrough South and Stoke South, with which Bishop Auckland has, demographically, culturally and politically, much in common – while it has much less solidarity in the party's new heartlands, like just down the road from me, in Streatham in south London.

Streatham used to be a Conservative seat. It was a sleepy south London suburb with good Victorian housing stock, full of middle-income businessmen and moderately off middle-aged folk. It was

Labour majority in Bishop Auckland

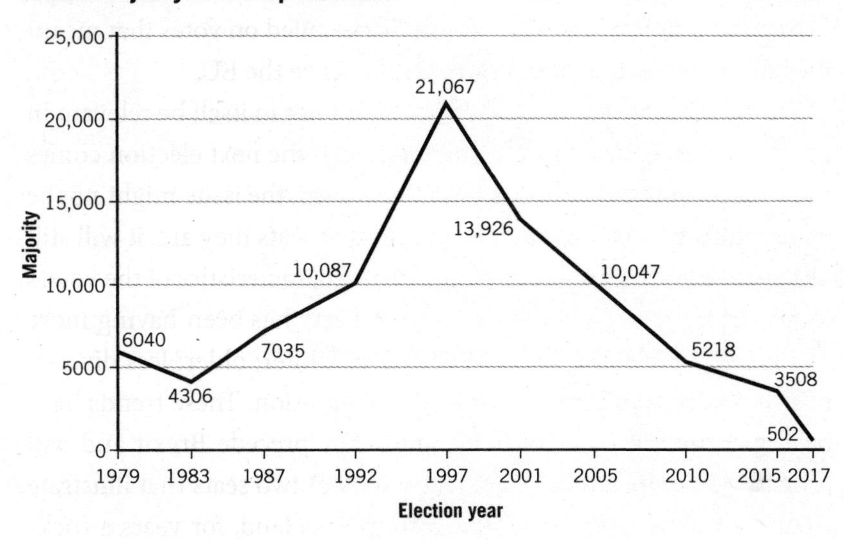

Source: Author's own graph

reliably Conservative until 1992, as gradually young professionals and ethnic minorities began to move in and came to outnumber its older residents. Nonetheless, outside landslide years, it remained relatively marginal and the party bled support to the Lib Dems in the New Labour years. Their collapse and Brexit, however, have made it overwhelmingly, astoundingly, tub-thumpingly safe for Labour, with a majority for the MP Chuka Umunna of 26,285. In the old days, you'd have assumed there must have been a coal mine next to the South Circular for a Labour MP to have a majority like that. Streatham and seats like it are becoming more Labour every year.

This twin process of the urbanisation/graduatisation of the Labour vote will almost certainly continue; we are seeing it all over the West in the voting patterns of social democratic parties. Seats like Streatham then will continue to weigh Labour votes, but what will happen to the Bishop Aucklands? It was a top Conservative target in 2017, and Labour were very relieved to cling on to it. But that doesn't mean it (and other seats like it) won't continue to trend the Tories' way. We thought – perhaps naively – that the 2017 election would produce a realignment in one fell swoop. The truth was more

Labour majority in Streatham

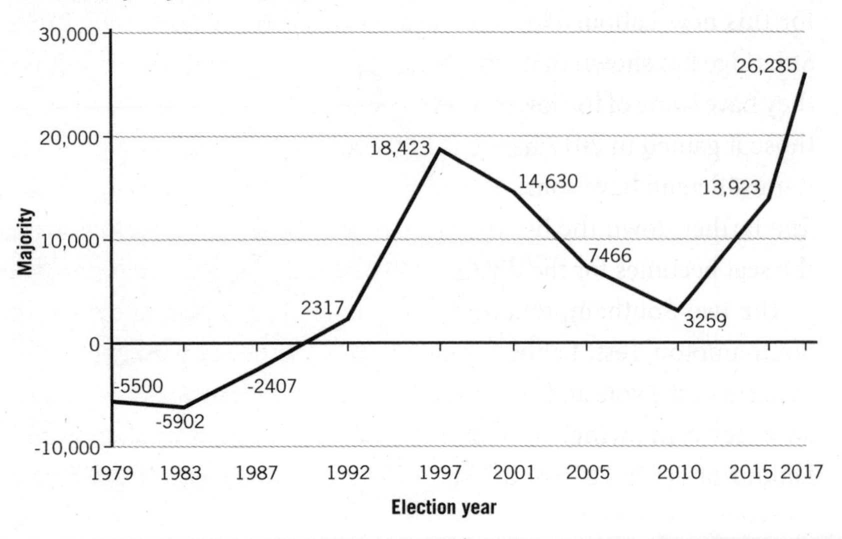

Source: Author's own graph

complicated than that; a realignment around the quadruple axes of culture and class and geography and education had been happening anyway – Brexit turbocharged it and it continues. But it's gradual; Corbyn's Labour held some of the negative elements (losing working-class support) at bay in difficult circumstances. But Labour must not believe that because it just about resisted those waves in 2017 in seats like Bishop Auckland it will continue to do so. The Labour tide in those places might still be going out and there's a fair few of them; you'd only need a small swing to the Tories in these places, and every one lost means a new gain is needed elsewhere – a few include Dudley North (maj. 22), Newcastle-under-Lyme (maj. 48); Barrow and Furness (maj. 209); Ashfield (maj. 441), Wakefield (2,176), Wolverhampton South West (2,185) and maybe even my own Birmingham Northfield.

And those same problems exist in seats it has to win off the Tories, not just retain. To win a majority, Labour must gain Morley and Outwood (swing to the Tories in 2017), Corby, Crawley, Southport, Scarborough and Whitby, Loughborough, Shipley, Worthing East and Shoreham, Rossendale and Darwen, Blackpool North, even

Truro and Falmouth. This is small-town Britain and an uphill battle for this new Labour Party. It's also old Britain: analysis from Paula Sturridge has shown that of Labour's target seats for the next election they have some of the lowest proportions of 18- to 24-year-olds, while those it gained in 2017 have the highest. Likewise the marginal seats it must defend have some of the lowest proportions of young people. The farther down the list you go, the less demographically desirous the seat becomes for the direction the Labour Party is heading.

The two Southampton seats encapsulate the party's dilemma: in Southampton Test, Labour romped home, adding on an extra 17.3 per cent of the vote and swelling Alan Whitehead's majority to 11,503, an 8 per cent swing. In neighbouring Southampton Itchen, a top Labour target in 2015 and 2017, Labour did less well, with only a 3 per cent swing, and the Tories clung on with a majority of 31. The difference? Test is wealthier and is where the city's universities are located. It voted Remain narrowly with 51 per cent. Itchen, by contrast, is much poorer, with lots of council estates and with nearly a quarter of residents living in social housing, and voted Leave by a 60 per cent margin. Labour, slowly but surely, in Southampton and elsewhere, is becoming the party of the educated rich and culturally connected, just as Piketty found. Labour and Jeremy Corbyn must find a way of building a viable electoral path connecting the two seats.

If you'd shown someone these lists from even 2005 and said that the Conservatives would be threatening Bishop Auckland (Labour maj. in 2005, 10,047) and Ashfield (Labour maj. in 2005, 10,213), and that Labour would be defending Canterbury (Tory maj. in 2005, 7,471), people would have thought you needed your head examining. But British politics has changed and is changing. Realignments do happen; places change and their culture and politics do too. It wasn't so long ago that London was the city of high Toryism, when Anglicanism vs Nonconformity was the dividing issue of the day for the voters. Not so long ago that every seat in Wales and Scotland returned Liberal MPs because they wanted to protect themselves against the established church. Not so long ago that Brighton was a staid seaside town full of retirees which like all the other seaside towns full of retirees sent a Conservative MP to Westminster at each and every election. Not so long ago when Glasgow and Liverpool elected Tories with eye-watering majorities because they were afraid of Catholicism and Irish immigration. The issues change, the dividing lines do too. Just ask the old Liberal Party.

Now it seems unlikely that Labour is going anywhere – the 2017 election proved the doom-mongers wrong on that score. But it doesn't mean that its voters and its makeup and the seats it can fight and win easily aren't changing. The politics of the Labour Party and the politics of the country are transforming, just out of view, with a series of whimpers peppered with an occasional bang, but it is happening all the same. And if it is realignment territory, that poses enormous questions. Increases in turnout won't be enough and Corbyn has already sucked the 'alternative left' (Green, Lib Dem, etc.) coalition dry. In 2022 (or whenever it is) Labour will have to win over some of the people the most ardent Corbynistas claim to despise above all others: Tories. Tories in places and types of people with whom Labour struggled most in 2017. As Peter Kellner has argued:

'Few political sentiments are so seductive as "one more heave". Labour's 41 per cent was the highest share received by an opposition party since 1970. It would take only a modest further shift for the party to win next time. The question is: where will those votes come from? There seem to be few Lib Dem, Green or Ukip voters left to squeeze. Labour would do well to hold on to all the younger voters and the older better-educated voters, whose choice this year was largely driven by opposition to Brexit. The one significant opportunity for Labour is the group with whom it most underperformed this year: working-class voters, especially in the Midlands and the north of England. These are constituencies Labour must win back if it is to enter Downing Street.'

The most recent electoral test we have bears this out. The local elections of 2018 were, whatever the spin placed upon them the next day, very disappointing for Labour. There had been much (ridiculous) speculation that the party might take Westminster borough; this was never a possibility. Wandsworth was more winnable but still tough. Nonetheless, despite their failure to win more councils (especially in north London, where the anti-Semitism row cost the party Barnet), Labour performed exceptionally well in London. Defending what had been a high base from the party's excellent 2014 performance (which shows how the Londonification of the party had roots that preceded Corbyn), Labour won more seats in the capital than at any election since 1971, winning roughly two-thirds of all council seats.

Outside the M25 it was another matter entirely. Labour failed to make any significant advances against the Conservatives, taking only Plymouth and Kirklees councils. As I prepared for another election night I was told by Sky's in-house psephologist and election supremo, Michael Thrasher, that 200 net gains would be a good night for Labour, anything south of 150 would be a disappointment. In the end, the party managed a net gain of only 77 seats. Many of the party's solid London and urban gains were offset by losses in the Midlands and the north. So while Labour became the largest party in Tory Trafford in Greater Manchester for the first time, it struggled in the same smaller towns, the same Brexit-voting bits of England that it struggled with in the general election. In Walsall, the Tories gained five seats, Labour lost two. In Amber Valley, the Tories gained two, Labour lost two. In Swindon, Labour made only one solitary gain. In Leeds, Labour remained dominant overall, but in the hyper-marginal suburb of Pudsey, which has a parliamentary majority of only just over 300, Labour lost two seats and the Tories gained two. In Hillingdon, a part of suburban London that is more representative of the rest of the country and which was controlled by Labour as recently as the late 2000s, the Tories gained two seats and Labour lost – you guessed it – two. This pattern was repeated in an awful lot of places, too many for comfort. In all of the sorts of places where Labour needs to do well at the next election, the party either did badly or was treading water.

Some people have said that Labour should just bide its time; that for every year that goes by, the country becomes a little more tolerant, more liberal, more culturally cosmopolitan. In that case it can wait for the majority to come to it. But that seems hardly likely to happen by 2022.* Therefore, for Labour and Corbynism to be truly successful and to craft a truly successful governing project, it must recognise those forces and find a way to ameliorate them for its own benefit. Otherwise on election morning in 2022 or whenever it is, Labour may find itself with a very unpleasant surprise.

A SCOTTISH PROBLEM

In Scotland, too, there are difficulties ahead. Although, as I've noted, Jeremy Corbyn successfully revived Labour north of the border, it is still limping.

Although we can't know how popular the SNP will be in 2022 (when it will have been in government in Scotland for 15 years), there is no doubt that it has effected a significant realignment in Scotland. Although it suffered in its old rural Aberdeenshire and Perthshire heartlands in 2017, it retained many Old Labour seats. Its grip on those seats – and their working-class voters – is weaker than it was, but it will still be hard to dislodge. For all the talk of its decline, especially since Theresa May refused its request for a second independence referendum in the wake of Brexit, the SNP is still polling first in every single poll, usually in the region of around 40 per cent. Indeed, it has scored a modest recovery in Scotland since the election as the lustre dimmed on Ruth Davidson's Conservatives. Support for independence meanwhile, while no longer on the boil, is still simmering. Some polls have, as of the spring of 2018, placed support at around 48 per cent. Brexit is still an unknown quantity and we have no idea how it will play in Scotland. But the SNP will not rest until it can drain every drop of political advantage from it. And even if the ques-

* And even if it does – what about those working-class white voters? They are the people whom Labour was founded to represent. It hardly does much good to write them off as a 'basket of deplorables' and wait for new voters to replace them.

tion is never again put, Labour is still struggling. Its new leader, Richard Leonard, an Englishman, is at the time of writing struggling to make much of an impact – as indeed did his six predecessors in the job.

Moreover, renewed Labour strength elsewhere in the UK might paradoxically serve the Labour Party poorly in Scotland. One of its problems in 2015 was that everyone assumed that there would be a hung Parliament. The SNP (fresh from its narrow defeat in the independence referendum nine months earlier) made the case to left-of-centre, naturally Labour-inclined Scottish voters that they could have their cake and eat it too: 'Yes, of course, you want a Labour government, and we would support them in the House of Commons – but you can get them while also getting an extra Scottish slice of the pie.' For Scottish voters it was a perfectly rational utility-maximising proposition – get a Labour government but one which almost certainly would give Scotland extra resources and money because that would be the SNP's price for a deal giving parliamentary support.* Of course, ironically, that very assumption and discourse partly led to its own nullification by an unexpected Conservative majority, in part delivered by English voters afraid of that outcome.

In 2017 that dynamic was not at play for the very simple reason that Labour appeared to be so far behind that it was impossible for the SNP to make the argument with any credibility. Scottish Labour voters could therefore feel that in those circumstances they might as well vote the way they would like, rather than what they felt would line their pocket: with their hearts rather than their heads.

It seems likely that, whatever happens between now and then, the next election will be fought under dynamics much more akin to 2015's than those of 2017. There will be much discussion of hung parliaments, probably with the view once again that Labour will be the biggest party. The SNP will therefore rightly be able to say once again that a vote for the SNP is tantamount to one for Labour but

---

* They weren't wrong to assume this, as we saw in an equivalent situation with the DUP and the Conservatives in 2017.

with a tartan twist. That might once again prove to be a difficult narrative to dislodge. It may also, this time, add in an argument that given Jeremy Corbyn has little experience of government, the SNP would moderate him and his excesses. Likewise the Tories will once more try to make the case to English voters that they risk being ripped off by a Labour/SNP 'coalition of chaos', though that argument will presumably be much less forceful after their own experience with the DUP and their own 13 Scottish MPs to protect. Nonetheless, they will find a way to press that button.

A YOUTH PROBLEM

There was much talk in the wake of the 2017 election result that British politics was being reformed along generational lines. Indeed it is; alongside education it is now one of the best predictors for voting behaviour. British politics has never been more polarised by age and the gap between old and young was never greater than in 2017.

Yet the picture is more complicated than it might appear. One of the ideas of the 2017 election that quickly took hold among the commentariat was that young people had been attracted to Jeremy Corbyn, inspired by his message and voted with their feet. As we've seen, there is some truth to this and, in particular, many of Corbyn's attributes make him a fantastic vehicle in the social media age. Labour did increase its share of the youth vote considerably – but it did not succeed in sending huge numbers of young people to the polls. Or rather, it depends on what you mean by young. In fact, there was almost no increase in turnout among the properly young – the 18–24s. Where there were considerably increased numbers was among people of my sort of age, the 24–35s and slightly older. As the British election study said: 'We can be confident, though, that there was no dramatic surge in youth turnout of the sort suggested by some other surveys. In short, there was no "youthquake".'

What there was was a revanchist move among older millennials. Why? Almost certainly a combination of the rise of identity politics,

Brexit and, yes, a slow recognition that the economic system as it is currently constructed isn't working for us, especially with housing. Jeremy Corbyn's unalloyed message on this score doubtless helped increase turnout in people of my sort of age a bit.

But there are several questions here. First, can the party sustain that turnout over time, especially over Brexit? If so, are there opportunity costs? That is, can it do so without alienating more traditional supporters? And, in the slightly longer term, is it sustainable? In other words, is the attachment of the politics of my generation contingent or permanent? The answer to that question is found in the answer to another: are millennials really left wing at all?

MARGARET THATCHER WOULD BE PROUD OF US

I glimpsed some truth about the politics of my generation at a pretty dingy basement flat party in Peckham. The location was an appropriate one. Most of the country knows the south London district as home to Nelson Mandela House and *Only Fools and Horses*' lovable rogue, Del Boy. Del is a buccaneering market trader who, charitably speaking, has a rather libertarian attitude towards government and the law. In one scene, he explains to his younger brother, Rodney, why his 'firm', Trotter's Independent Traders, doesn't pay any of its taxes: 'We don't pay VAT, we don't pay income tax or national insurance. On the other hand, we don't claim dole money, social security, supplementary benefit ... The government don't give us nothing, so we don't give the government nothing.'

Del is the ultimate embodiment of the principle, you get out what you put in – and doesn't believe anyone, least of all the state in the form of a copper patrolling the market, should get in the way of his own enterprise. He is, without processing it in this way, a liberal. As long as no one gets in his way and the way of his business, he won't get in anyone else's. He is an embodiment of the prevailing spirit of his age, Thatcherism. His is a politics which mirrors that of many millennials too. There is a line that runs from Margaret Thatcher, to Del Boy, to us.

The uncomfortable truth for Labour is that young people are more a product of Margaret Thatcher than of Clement Attlee. We were born in the 1980s and grew up in an intellectual and political climate she bequeathed, not the collectivist environment of the 1940s and 1950s. We are her political grandchildren.

I was there with a schoolfriend from back home, Richard, who, not untypically for people of my generation, had set up his own property business, and had a long conversation about that ostensibly innocuous thing: Sunday trading (it wasn't the best party). He seemed utterly baffled by the idea that the government should establish limits on what days of the week shops could open. When I countered by saying that it was important to protect the rights of shop workers to their Sundays or for family time, or still more that maybe we should be trying to encourage people not to spend every single day of the week shopping, he looked at me as if I was utterly thick: 'What's it got to do with them as to when I want to do *my* shopping? If I'm free on Sunday and I want to go and buy stuff that's *my* choice. And also if people are free to work on a Sunday and want to then that's *their* choice. What's the problem?'

As I walked home I pondered what I'd heard. It was a theme I returned to through conversations with friends and people of my age again and again as the years went on. It seemed clearer to me that people of my age didn't really conceive of society as many of the post-war generations had done: we weren't collectivist, we weren't social democrats – we were liberals. What had taken centre stage in our way of seeing the world was the primacy of the individual and of individual choice. Collectivist thinking, to the extent even of the state establishing certain basic shared norms, requirements and standards, seemed increasingly alien. My memories were stoked: I was taken back to an A-level history lesson, years ago. Our history teacher told us that before 1979 and before the abolition of capital controls it wasn't possible to take more than £35 out of the country without special permission from the government. For a classroom who were well used to spending more than that at the Bullring every weekend, this was a shock. That the government could exercise such control over our lives seemed as anachronistic and quaint as the window tax or rotten boroughs, learned about in another class on another day. Yet its abolition came only ten years before most of us were born.

This shift towards liberalism is unsurprising. It's a theme that Bobby Page, from IPSOS Mori's Generations project, told me has been little appreciated:

'In terms of Gen Ys, the things which define them are very different contexts they've grown up in – in terms of technology and culture. A much more individualised outlook – the big theme for them is a sense of personal responsibility which seems more in tune with Conservative positions, so it's that sense that people should take personal responsibility for things ... They are the least likely generation to think we should be redistributing money to the unemployed. That connection to the welfare state is much much weaker.'

This is borne out by Page's own data. So, for example, when asked whether the welfare state is one of Britain's proudest achievements the results are stark.

How much do you agree or disagree that ...
the creation of the welfare state is one of Britain's proudest achievements

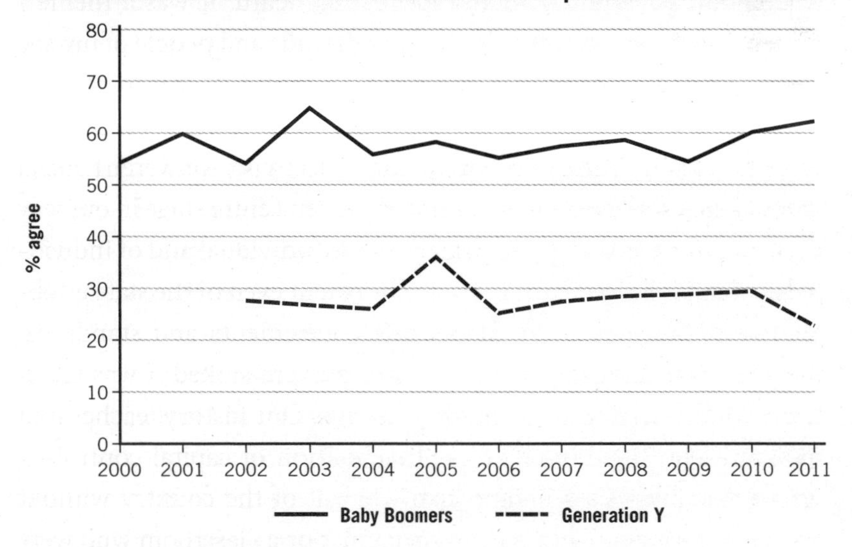

Source: Ipsos MORI Generations Project, 2013

Gen Ys (millennials) score right at the bottom of the generational league table here, with fewer than one in four young people agreeing that the welfare state is one of Britain's proudest achievements. Contrast that with the prewar cohort, where seven in ten said the opposite.

This generational hierarchy can be partly explained by the fact that voters of the prewar years are those who will remember the 'hungry thirties' and the hardships of pre-welfare state Britain. As the years have gone by, the collective memory of why the welfare state was introduced have receded, and each younger generation feels more distant from the reasons for its genesis. Likewise the term 'welfare state' itself might be considered somewhat arcane or confusing – and has become increasingly associated with welfare fraud. All of that said, it does raise real questions about the sustainability of operating something with which what is soon to be the largest demographic group has so little emotional connection and sits oddly with the idea that they are inherently left wing.

But even if we leave aside the term 'welfare state', with its modern connotations of fecklessness and idleness, and drill into the specifics, there are plenty of other warning signs for socialists. When asked whether the government should spend more money on welfare benefits for the poor, even if it leads to higher taxes, we find a similar generational hierarchy.

This isn't about semantics, this is bread-and-butter social democracy; taking from the rich and giving to the poor, and millennials aren't keen. Moreover, the best thing about this data is that it stretches back so far, nearly 25 years, which means we can compare the attitudes of different generations over time. What we see then is that Gen Yers have least support for higher taxes, even if it means supporting the poor, than any other age group. But, more than that, Gen Y are to the right of where other generations were even when that group were the same age. Therefore it's more than just an age effect, as sociologists would say, it's a generational or cohort effect. Just as millennials are instinctively more liberal on social matters, they are instinctively more conservative (or liberal) on economic matters than their elders.

How much do you agree or disagree that ...
the government should spend more money on welfare benefits for the poor, even if it leads to higher taxes

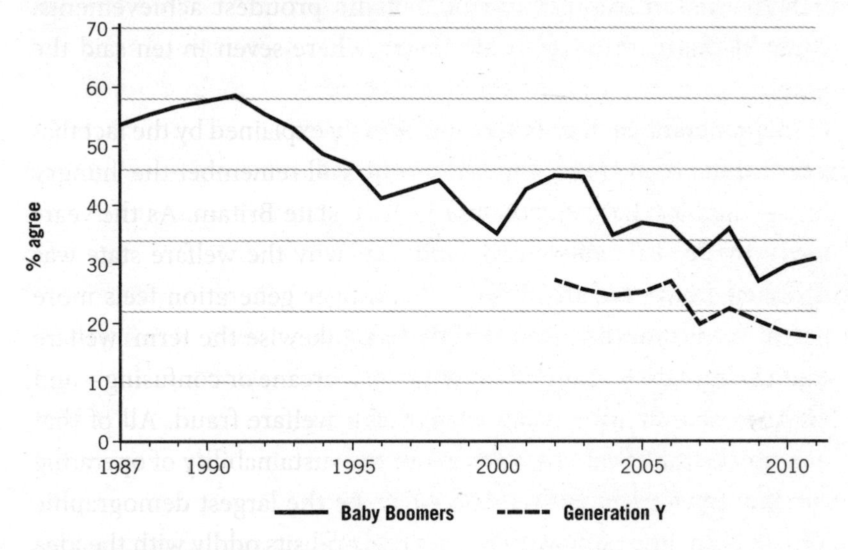

Source: Ipsos MORI Generations Project, 2013

They are starting from a different place – one where lower taxes and less social support is the norm, according to their more individualistic, less socialised world view.

This data is supported by other sources. The Centre for Policy Studies conducted polling at the beginning of 2018. From this we see that the youngest are more likely to believe that the government spends too much and raises too much in tax. It is the 'right-wing'

	18–24	25–39	40–49	50–64	65+
The government taxes too much and spends too much on services	26	27	28	27	23
The government taxes too little and spends too little on services	22	24	23	34	32
The government gets the balance about right	16	16	18	19	23
Don't know	36	33	31	20	22

Source: Centre for Policy Studies, *New Blue: Ideas for a New Generation*, 2018

over-fifties who are more likely to believe that the government doesn't tax enough.

When asked whether unemployment benefits are too low and cause hardship, millennials are the least likely to agree. As the next graph shows, every generation is less credulous about the idea that unemployment benefit is too low and causes poverty, but what is interesting is that Gen Y should be at the bottom at this stage of their lives. Consider that the young are by far and away the age group most likely to be unemployed; indeed, when much of this data was collected, youth unemployment was hovering at an eye-watering 20 per cent, and yet they counter-intuitively don't seem to believe they or their unemployed friends ought to receive more to tide them over. That's especially interesting when you consider the views of their parents (Gen X) when they were the same age that Gen Yers are now – at that time, in the early 1980s, when we were experiencing a similar youth unemployment problem, nearly 70 per cent of young people agreed that the dole was at too low a level.

Some of that might be attributed to media coverage or changing values, but the point is, millennials are starting the process so much further to the right than any other group at that age. This is more than just media, it's psyche, as Bobby Duffy explained to me:

'It's related to that sense of personal responsibility. I think it's probably because that generation hasn't had much help themselves – you think of student loans, nature of the housing market, etc., it has conditioned them to think, well, you have to look after yourself. And you can't particularly see that changing because if at any point in their lives they were going to think we need more redistribution then it would be now.'

After thinking about this for a while I wanted to test the theme, so I went to Bramcote College in Beeston, on the outskirts of Nottingham. It's a fairly typical place in a completely typical part of the country, with some absolutely typical young people. The conversations we had were revealing and worth reproducing, in abridged form, here, as an illustration of some of themes. Every answer was provided by a member of the dozen or so strong group of sixth formers.

Which of these two statements comes closest to your own view ... benefits for unemployed people are too low and cause hardship, OR benefits for unemployed people are too high and discourage them from finding jobs?

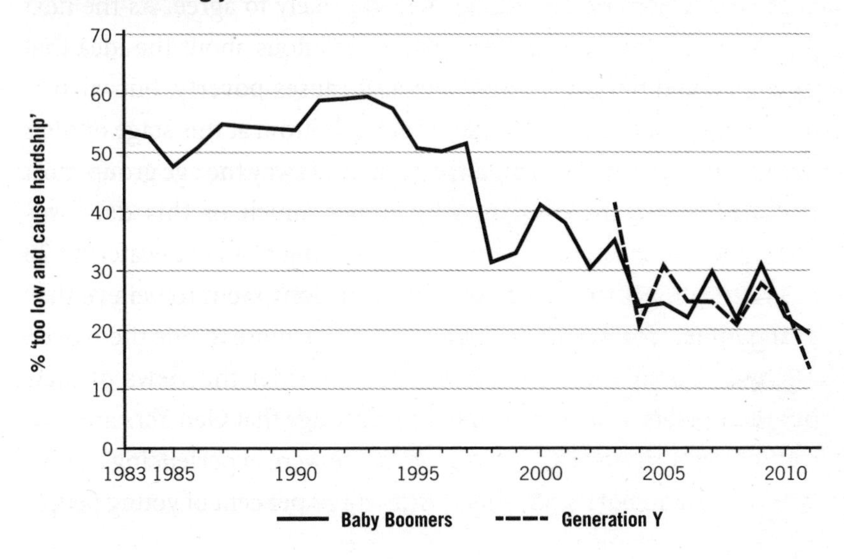

Source: Ipsos MORI Generations Project, 2013

ME: Do you think unemployment allowance should be time limited?

STUDENT 1: I think it gives people an incentive, if they have a time limit they know they have to work especially hard to get a job – we need that incentive with the society we've got now because too many people are relying on the benefits system. It's the tough-love way.

STUDENT 2: It would encourage people to not spend essentially their entire lives, perhaps, not contributing to society. The ticking time bomb situation might motivate them.

ME: Should the government have an inheritance tax?

STUDENT 3: No way. It's legalised grave robbing.

STUDENT 2: If a person had worked their entire lives and tried to create something and they want to pass it on to the next generation then I don't think the government should stop them.

ME: Should the government abolish tuition fees?

STUDENT 4: If you wanted the taxpayers to pay for you – they don't get anything from it – why should they pay it?

STUDENT 5: It's your decision! It's your decision to go so you should pay for it yourself really.

But their greatest ire was reserved for the welfare state:

ME: Is the welfare state one of Britain's proudest achievements?

STUDENT 6: Definitely not! I hear all the time about people who have got like fifteen kids! And they're scamming the system. You've got the things for massive families – the money is supposed to be for the kids but they just spend it on alcohol and cigarettes and fake nails.

STUDENT 7: There are plenty of jobs but they just don't want to do them. You can get more on the benefits system.

ME: What do you think of the NHS as a principle? Do you support it as a principle?

STUDENT 1: In some ways yes – but, you know, drunk people? That's their own fault so they should pay for that!

ME: Say I'm a heavy drinker – should the NHS pay for a transplant?

STUDENT 2: It's about priorities – heavy drinkers or someone who has looked after their health?

ME: What about overweight people – should they have access to NHS care?

STUDENT 2: They shouldn't pay for a gastric band!

STUDENT 3: They've done it themselves! Why should they get the care?

STUDENT 4: Oh come on, what are you supposed to do, just leave them? We're in danger of stereotyping massively here ...

STUDENT 2: I'm sorry but you should help yourself before you get help – if the government helps you all the time then you will develop a mindset that you don't have to do anything for yourself.

Opinion wasn't monolithic, some had harder views on welfare than others. But several themes were constant, those of choice, agency and a forthright individualism. Indeed, there was no evidence of any political analysis beyond that of the merits of individual agency, and almost no sense of the constraints that society might impose on others. Hence the concept of inheritance tax is anathema: why should the state be able to distort the will of an individual, especially after that individual has used their agency to accumulate their own wealth – after all, everyone has had the chance to make their own money. And let me stress these were not some extreme, unpleasant group. As I sat chatting to them and their teacher in a big common room, they came across as the most civil, charming young students. They just don't believe that the state should be the individual's first port of call. In that they are apparently speaking for their generation.

Interestingly, one of the reasons why they're so reluctant to rely on others is that millennials simply don't trust other people. According to polling, when asked if they would trust the average man or woman on the street to tell them the truth, in every age group seven in ten agree that they would. Save for one group – you guessed it: millennials. Only just over 40 per cent of young people agree with their elders, and a clear majority say they wouldn't trust the average person to tell them the truth.*

It seems that those stories of not talking to strangers were a little bit too effective. If we take the prewar generation, a full 73 per cent have trust in their fellow men and women. Gen X, our parents, when they were the same age as Gen Y are now, also trusted, with 60 per cent agreeing that others were trustworthy. We are, it seems, a uniquely suspicious bunch.

Many explanations have been proffered for this: one is that the solidarity fostered by the Second World War engendered a sense of trust in others. That trust and solidarity have gradually dwindled. More important is probably the widening inequality and a sense of generational injustice. Either way, it helps explain the scepticism Gen Y has towards the welfare state, people on benefits and raising taxes to pay for them, etc. If you generally believe that the average person is lying to you, why would you believe that they require extra benefits – you certainly wouldn't believe that you should pay for them in the form of extra taxation. After all, our common institutions are made up of individuals, and if you don't trust them, how could you possibly trust the institutions themselves? Why would you trust the government to do good on your behalf? And why would you be social democratic, a philosophy centred in the belief in the common good and that we can achieve more together than we can alone? And we should not slam young people as a bunch of misanthropes – as Robert Putnam has argued: 'The social distrust among America's youth should be seen not as a character flaw, but rather as a mirror held up to social mores of recent decades. Our youth are, in effect, telling us that in their experience most people really *aren't* trustworthy.'

---

* Another reason why, in today's politics, authenticity is so valued.

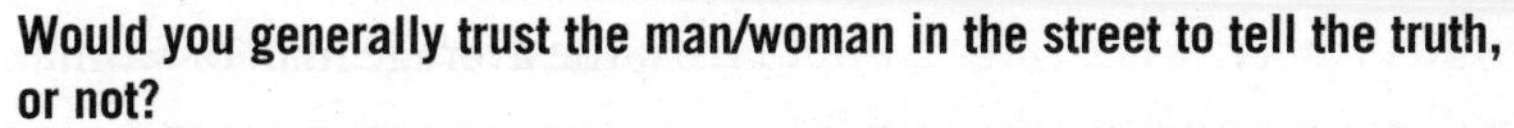
Would you generally trust the man/woman in the street to tell the truth, or not?

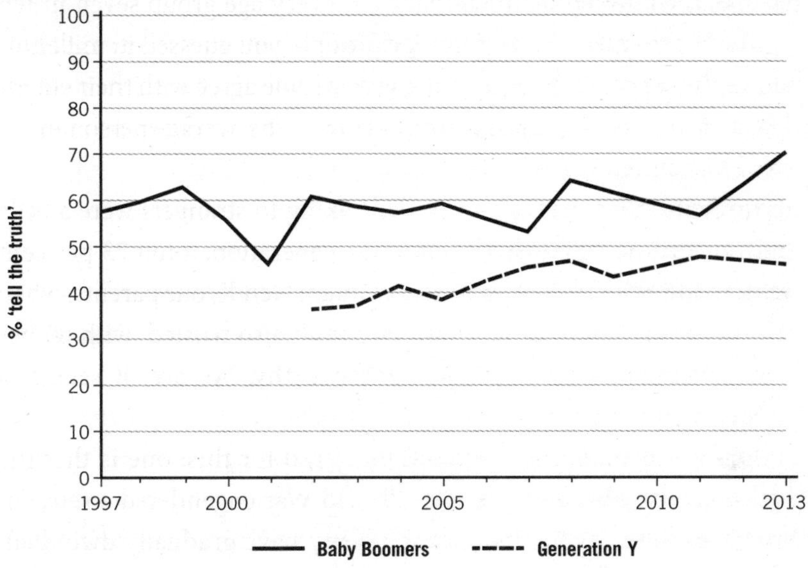

Source: Ipsos MORI Generations Project, 2013

This greater scepticism towards collectivism has doubtless been shaped and perhaps even largely forged by the internet. We are the first generation to grow up with the internet as a ubiquitous presence in our lives.

We've seen in other chapters how important the changes in technology are for the future of the left, so I don't propose to rehash all of that again. It is worth noting though that millennials are at the very forefront of the political changes that technology is driving and there are things peculiar to them.

It has been argued that social media and technology have precisely the opposite effect on millennials. That, far from being driven into ever smaller pockets of ourselves, we are better connected than any generation before, that by definition we are more social than individual – after all, the clue is in the title, right? It's 'social' media. But this is to fundamentally misunderstand the nature of the internet and technology. We may indeed be better 'connected' or 'networked' than our forebears but that does not equate to not being highly individualistic. Bernie Hogan is a psychologist who has studied the effect of the internet on the mind:

'These revolutions in technology make it very easy to connect but connect in a peer-to-peer or diatic way, it's not that I'm connecting to this group or this community organisation, it's I'm connecting to you and I'm connecting to you – these factors lead to us being very networked rather than very grouped, and networked as individuals, and the technology fosters that, this isn't everyone coming to a website and then collectively coming together to do something as a community. Group – rather, person *A* replies to person *B* and those specific very particular relationships are all laid out there.'

This is mirrored in social media. As with technology generally, millennials are the first generation to grow up on social media, documenting our lives on sites like Facebook, or (remember it) Myspace (note, it's not 'Ourspace'). Martha Gill, fellow millennial journalist, says she feels the competition they engender, daily: 'We all grew up in the age of the internet, which has given us a thirst for individualism and has made us quite competitive, documenting our lives competitively on social media.' And that competitive social media use is connected with our poor levels of social trust. We are used to seeing a constant stream of highly curated information about others, tailored, 'spun', to project the very best possible impression and even, at times, with the express intention of making others envious. We've all been there, a Facebook post from a friend apparently introducing irrigation to Costa Rica or curing bubonic plague in Rwanda. Or, more prosaically, clear attempts to project success and perfection. How many of us haven't logged on to a Facebook account or Instagram and felt deflated at the thought that the lives of our friends seem so much more joyous than our own? Sites like Instagram take active steps to make tinkering and enhancement easier and part of the process. People take pictures of their own food, filtered and enhanced, accompanied by a hashtag like '#winning'. What is this if not an attempt at psychological competitiveness and even aggression? It is nauseating but it's more than that – there are wider political effects too.

A recent episode of Charlie Brooker's *Black Mirror* explored the idea. In 'Nosedive', every character's eyes are equipped with technology that allows them to see the social media profiles of everyone around them, including an Uber style 'rating' out of five, which is reached by the assessments of everyone with whom the person has a social interaction. It has led to a saccharine, pastel-coloured world, where everyone must maintain eerie artificial smiles with the facade of happiness and of leading a perfect life. Eventually the main character, Lacie, in an attempt to improve her social standing to a chimerical '4.8', suffers a series of missteps, breaking down in anger at a wedding party after being thrown out. Her anger liberates her, as she realises what an artificial pursuit the whole thing has been, and when she is detained by police starts swearing joyously at her cellmate. She's been freed from the need to maintain her social standing.

All of this channels millennials into an instinctively conservative, free-market direction. Yet, today, 50 per cent of millennials say they would not contemplate voting Conservative. In theory, the Conservatives had a golden opportunity with Britain's young, a generation that was temperamentally attuned to its instincts on economic and political matters. This was borne out by the results of the 2015 election, in which Labour only beat the Conservatives by three points (36–33). Yet, mainly as a result of Brexit,* a Tory retreat from social and political liberalism, and a comprehensive failure on

* Even here, we might ask ourselves why that is and why millennials (and millennial graduates in particular) are so in favour of Europe. I'm not entirely convinced it's because of shared social bonds with Europe, but rather because we love the idea of a liberal Europe: the liberty to travel anywhere, the liberty to work anywhere, the liberty to move anywhere, the liberty to live our lives on a broader continental stage rather than a national one. It maximises our liberalism, our freedom, our ability to project ourselves as individuals. That we could leave work at 5 p.m. on Friday and be sipping cocktails with friends in Barcelona by 9 p.m. the same evening; all documented on our respective social media feeds. It also speaks to a sense that the nation state is less important, that the bonds we feel with those of our national state are also weaker; that what matters is our individual rights rather than nationalism or national solidarity.

housebuilding, the party stupidly finds itself at loggerheads with this generation of its own making.

The irony is that my generation, the great liberal generation, is unwittingly becoming a central part of the most collectivist enterprise British politics has seen in some time. It may be that Corbyn's cultural cachet is able to ride that out and paper over the cracks and that the Conservatives don't realise what a stupid mistake they have made. Or it might not. Generational cleavages are an unknown quantity in British politics. For virtually all of the twentieth century, the entirety of the Labour Party's history, its electoral coalition has been based on class. What is sometimes proposed, or if not proposed assumed to be virtuous, in Labour circles now is that the returns on class politics are diminishing and that the new Labour coalition will be a generational one. This new politics, it is supposed, will be a politics of identity and social virtue, intensified by and played out on social media, for which the Corbyn project is uniquely positioned.

This might work fantastically well. It might be better than class – after all, class has hardly guaranteed Labour's success in the past. If all of the working class had voted Labour all of the time it would have scarcely ever left office. It could be that the forces of the culture war, Brexit and the dysfunction of capitalism are creating a phalanx of young Labour voters who, once aligned with the party, will never desert it. If so, Labour can look forward to decades of dominance. Alternatively, it could be much more contingent. But, whichever way you slice it, it is an unknown. We just don't really have much precedent for it. If the young really aren't all that left wing and their party attachment is much weaker than that of the generations before them (as polling suggests it is), then the young may be more capricious than we think and open to a pitch from a younger, more socially liberal Conservative leader.

A NEW PARTY PROBLEM

Pretty much ever since the beginning of Jeremy Corbyn's leadership there has been lots of speculation that a new, breakaway party might emerge. These dark whispers have become more numerous since the Brexit referendum, in which the lack of a convincing social democratic, unequivocally pro-European voice seemed to damage the Remainer prospectus, then and since.

I have always been sceptical about it. I've never really believed that the Labour moderates would take the plunge for three main reasons: (i) our first-past-the-post system makes the barriers to entry for such a party impossibly high; (ii) it's been done before and failed, and worse still it was done recently – the folk memory of the SDP breakaway hasn't receded; and (iii) the sheer bloody-mindedness and tribalism of many moderate Labour MPs and members are profound.

That changed with the Brexit referendum. Just as the common passion of the EU brought strange bedfellows together, so the zeal for the European project is forming odd alliances across the usually impermeable political spectrum. There is now talk of a cross-party alliance, bringing figures together like George Osborne, Chuka Umunna and Nick Clegg. This is not ideologically implausible – such liberal and globalist figures have more in the way of common thinking than they do with the outriders in their respective parties (think Osborne and Jacob Rees-Mogg or Umunna and John McDonnell), but still strikes me as politically unlikely. Nonetheless, the common enemy of Brexit makes it more likely than it would otherwise be, though given it hasn't happened after so much time in the Brexit process has already elapsed it still seems relatively remote.

Nonetheless, sustained Corbynist success might yet give the project wings. In the aftermath of the Corbyn leadership victory, moderates consoled themselves that his success would be fleeting. The party would see what a failure the man and his mission would be and it would not be long before the activists and country would turn to them to pick up the pieces. The 2017 general election put paid to such a notion. Moderate MPs who had come to look at their period in the wilderness as a sabbatical, a brief sojourn on the backbenches to recharge body and mind, suddenly found themselves staring at a career abyss.

Faced with that prospect and the feeling that their party is irrecoverable, moderate MPs may well decide to bite the bullet. I suspect, however, that won't come without the stupidity of the more hardline Corbynist elements pushing them to the exit. Instead of 'taking the fight to the Tories', plenty of key voices on the left are keen to press home the left-wing advantage by purging the party, especially through reforms to make deselection of sitting MPs easier. Such a move would be politically combustible and force MPs into a corner: after all, in a situation where they were facing deselection from their local party, what would they have to lose? The last thread of self-interest that bound them to the Labour Party would be gone – why not throw the dice on the gamble of a new party?

When I have made that argument (both publicly and privately) to key Corbyn allies, they are unmoved. As Matt Zarb-Cousin, usually one of the moderate Corbyn voices, told me: '[It's] thirty-five to forty wreckers who are obstructing a Labour government anyway. They'd do less damage standing for a party no one has heard of. Good luck to them if it comes to it. It would harm the Tories more than Labour. In the same way we wrongly thought UKIP had the potential to harm the Tories more than Labour, people are getting this one the wrong way round again. Electoral contours are totally different.' Aaron Bastani, another key Corbyn outrider, agreed: 'I've presumed split always inevitable. Happened in response to each of last two crises: Ramsay MacDonald capitulation mid-thirties and SDP to crisis of 1970s. I've priced in to be honest. It will be failure.'

With the greatest of respect to both men, such insouciance seems extraordinary. We could be on the verge of a Corbyn government, the first government of that kind in British history, and some of its key architects seem blinded to the possibility of allowing such a magnificent prize to slip through their fingers in the name of cleansing a party of a few Blairite MPs who don't matter at all anyway.

When I put this point to Zarb-Cousin, he replied: 'Ah but they would. Unless he gets a majority of fifty-plus they could have it hamstrung. You're quite right [to be wary of prediction], and I am far from certain on anything, but think it's actually more of a risk to have so many members of the PLP actively opposed to the leadership.'

This speaks to two things: (i) the fact that many Corbynistas still, in my view, think of the Corbyn project as primarily one about party rather than country; despite the general election success, its first reflex is to spend that capital on purifying Labour, rather than getting rid of all possible barnacles on the boat in order to achieve true political power; and (ii) that they don't really take the threat of a new party seriously anyway, that it would (like the SDP before it) have no chance of genuine political success.

But they ought to be warier, because the definition of success is subjective and it is shifting. Most moderates who have entertained the idea of a breakaway had resiled from the idea because they were aware it had little chance of winning many MPs, much less supplanting Labour as the opposition, much less form a government. But now, as they become increasingly desperate and their brand of pro-European centrism seems, along with their party, more lost, their minds have become open to other possibilities. Many more too are disgusted with the party's seemingly never-ending row over anti-Semitism and the leadership's refusal to defuse it. As a former Labour activist, Nora Mulready, told me:

'Yeah. It's happening. I'm fairly certain that party is going to happen. How many people have you read on a daily basis saying we need a new party? There's a hole in the centre! This is actually meeting a massive groundswell of support. It's needed, there's no doubt, it's needed. We can't just sit around waiting for Labour to be different in twenty years. It might fail. I think that's a complete possibility. Although I think that depends how you define the parameters of success. If you're objective, at minimum is to stop Corbyn from getting to Number 10, to stop Milne, Stop the War, the SWP, from being the residents of Number 10, this could achieve it. One of the things this new party might achieve is, if it does end up with Labour losing the next election, and this party has something to do with that, it might be the case it gets us closer to Corbyn's end and the hard left's dominance of the Labour Party more quickly.

'So instead of that taking ten years, it might take five years. So I think the new party could help in that regard. Actually it may go well beyond that. We just don't know. There's a pessimism and a caution that is quite an English trait, and that's fine, that's good. First past the post makes it very hard. But I think nothing ventured nothing gained. I really do. We've got nothing to lose.'

THE POLLS PROBLEM

As you're reading this the Conservatives may be languishing at 30 points below Labour in the polls, the public may be crying out for a change and Corbyn measuring up the curtains for Number 10. But the remarkable thing since the general election is how remarkably static the polls have been; there has been almost no movement at all. Labour and the Conservatives have each hovered at the 40 per cent mark, sometimes a bit more, sometimes a bit less, occasionally swapping places as being marginally in the lead.

What is remarkable about that is that Conservative support has held up so well, despite a pretty catastrophic year: the botched general election, whispers of coups, cabinet dissent, Grenfell, the disaster of May's party conference speech when even the set conspired against her; huge problems over Brexit; Windrush; continued austerity and yet – still around 40 per cent in the polls.* Labour hasn't really gained much either, apparently unable to eat into the Tories' vote and unable to press down any further on the other parties. Result? Two polarised blocs.

* By the summer of 2018 there had been a modest shift of votes from the Tories to UKIP as the implications of Theresa May's Chequers deal became clearer. It is entirely possible, however, that a UKIP revival could damage Labour as much as the Conservatives.

This would confirm my culture war thesis: in this new age, bifurcated by the Brexit division but also by wider cultural and political change, there is less crossover between the two parties than there might have been in the past. When politics was about what was in your pocket, about economic division, perhaps the pool of voters in the middle who might cross from one side to the other was greater, depending on what each party might be offering. When the primary points of political antagonism were class-based and economic, then the resolution was relatively straightforward – there could be resolution based on bargaining, of an alteration in the division of the national pie. In a politics where the main division is cultural, however, there is less crossover. When politics is based on your identity, your fundamental cultural outlook, then you are less likely to be able to make a change and nor would you wish to. That is certainly the case in the United States, where politics has become much more polarised for longer. Likewise, we have some experience of this in the UK with Northern Ireland, and perhaps that (startlingly) is the best way to think about the direction of our political life. In Northern Ireland there is obviously much less transference between parties than in the rest of the UK; politicians and parties represent distinct communities of which you are inalienably a part. Though the religious sectarian conflicts do not (thankfully) exist in the mainland UK, nonetheless we are seeing a more subdued secular political equivalent emerge.

In such a circumstance, both main parties will struggle to reach into the other's tent, and that would partly explain why the polls have been so sticky. It also explains why smaller parties like the Lib Dems are struggling to make much headway. In this polarised political culture, voters are much warier of the other side getting into office. They are less prepared to take a risk on a smaller party, lest they waste their vote and let the opposing bloc in; the stakes are just too high. It is perhaps no coincidence that the smaller parties and a more pluralist politics seemed to flourish most when the differences between the two main parties were at their smallest, especially in the mid-1990s to late 2000s.

For all the reasons outlined above, it's going to be much heavier weather for Labour at the next election than many believe. And that itself will be a walk in the park compared to actually governing.

A GOVERNING PROBLEM

There are moments when the public decides that a government has run out of time, that it is not fit to govern. Such moments are rare but, once they come, things are irrecoverable. The Winter of Discontent in 1978 for Jim Callaghan, Black Wednesday in 1992 for John Major, the election that never was in 2007 for Gordon Brown. After those moments, it seems not to matter what a prime minister or their ministers do or say, the die is cast. It doesn't feel to me that we are quite at that moment yet for this government or the Conservatives. That moment might come (by the time you're reading this it might have come already), but as things stand a party that has averaged 40 points in the polls in a year of hell is not to be underestimated. Taking that and given what we know about the uphill struggle Labour has in terms of the sorts of seats it needs to win and the coalition it must build, it seems sensible to conclude that Labour will not be looking at landslide territory. Indeed, more likely it may only have a very small majority, or even more likely be the largest party in a hung Parliament, where it must look to others for support.

This prompts a number of problems – what will the price be for the Scottish Nationalists (whose support would be crucial)? Could it be a second independence referendum? Although we've reason to believe that Corbyn might be personally sympathetic to the prospect of so-called 'IndyRef2', the bulk of the Labour Party would be bitterly opposed. It would also endanger the Scottish Labour Party's nascent revival.

The other problem a hung Parliament or small majority would pose is one of expectations. Jeremy Corbyn is promising – in rhetoric if not in policy yet – nothing short of a transformation of the political and economic order of Britain. As he put it at the end of 2017: the

Tories stand 'for a failed and broken system which Labour must and will replace'. Labour, he claimed, has a 'new model of economic management', and it would 'replace the failed dogmas of neoliberalism'. Labour's mission was not simply reversing austerity, 'but to transform our economy with a new and dynamic role for the public sector'. Owen Jones, an ally of the Labour leader, wrote in his *Guardian* column on the eve of that year's party conference that 'Like Attlee and Thatcher, Corbyn will completely transform Britain.'

Those expectations will be entirely of the left's own making but they are essential to the project. Without those expectations, what is Corbynism? It is not a project of half-measures. But the parliamentary arithmetic will be difficult. The contrast again with New Labour is telling; there too expectations were high. Blair and Brown had the parliamentary numbers on their side, yet they had done virtually everything they could do to lower expectations; they had promised to match Tory spending plans and they consistently said that they would not promise anything they couldn't be assured they would deliver. Their infamous pledge card contained five pledges that, looking back, are almost hilariously banal.

Therefore, Blair was elected on almost no promises at all but still public faith eroded, partly (though not exclusively) because it was perceived that he had promised the world and not delivered. Jeremy Corbyn is promising a total transformation. The capacity for disap-

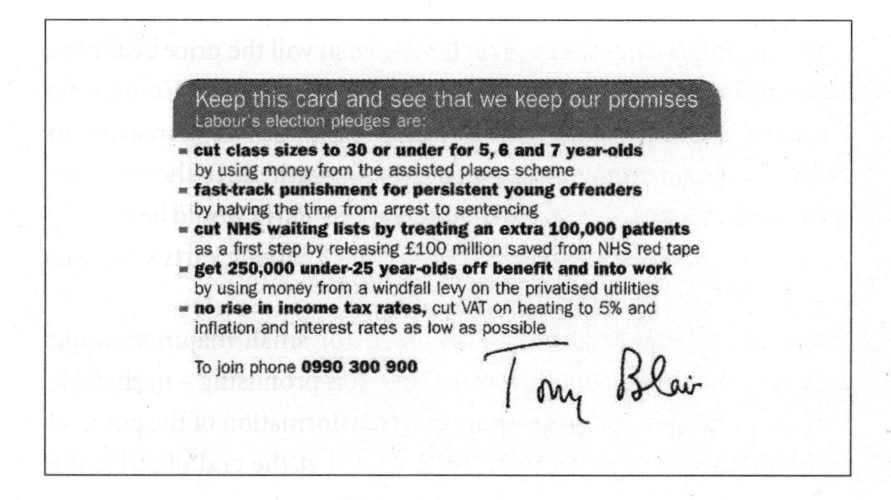
Keep this card and see that we keep our promises
Labour's election pledges are:

- **cut class sizes to 30 or under for 5, 6 and 7 year-olds**
  by using money from the assisted places scheme
- **fast-track punishment for persistent young offenders**
  by halving the time from arrest to sentencing
- **cut NHS waiting lists by treating an extra 100,000 patients**
  as a first step by releasing £100 million saved from NHS red tape
- **get 250,000 under-25 year-olds off benefit and into work**
  by using money from a windfall levy on the privatised utilities
- **no rise in income tax rates,** cut VAT on heating to 5% and inflation and interest rates as low as possible

To join phone **0990 300 900**

Tony Blair

pointment and disillusion is probably greater than for any incoming government since 1945. And its ability to implement its programme won't just be restricted by Parliament. It'll be restricted by vast economic forces outside the control of any government.

Throughout this book, I've made the argument that Corbynism (in attitude if not always in practice) is new, that there is no British parallel against which to compare it. So much then of trying to predict its future, as a political project and in government, is reduced to guesswork. There is, however, one example, one control, one lesson from history, from which all Corbynistas ought to learn. It is a salutary example of overreach, retreat and leftist destruction. Across the Channel, they've seen this story before.

MITTERRAND: LE PREMIER CORBYNISTA?

Brighton isn't so far from Paris, and indeed there's something in the city's raffish, bohemian approach to life that feels a little French. But I doubt even in this Remainer citadel, awash with Bordeaux and bloated on brie (with thousands of actual French residents to boot), that many of its citizens are ever much preoccupied with thoughts of François Mitterrand. Many will never have heard of the famous *grand mec* of French politics, who departed his own national stage long ago. But it seemed to me, as I sat not ten metres away from him, that one man certainly had Mitterrand on his mind: John McDonnell. Indeed, as he addressed his audience, at a Momentum fringe event at the Labour Party conference in the city in 2017, it was obvious it was Mitterrand's government to which he was referring when he made the comments that were to dominate the next day's headlines:

'What if there is a run on the pound? What happens if there is this concept of capital flight? I don't think there will be, but you never know, so we've got to scenario plan for that. People want to know we are ready and they want to know we have got a response to everything that could happen. Because if we can demonstrate that, that will calm things down.'

At the time, though my eyebrows raised slightly at his candour, it didn't strike me as being noteworthy enough to report the comments in to my newsdesk. It was a classic example of (a) my being a bad journalist, and (b) being a bad journalist as a result of being too close to something. I thought it self-evident that what McDonnell was saying was true and that he believed that in no small part because of the spectre of the Mitterrand experience, something which happened when many of those who currently comprise the Labour leadership were cutting their teeth in elected politics: McDonnell was trailblazing at the radical Greater London Council (GLC) as Ken Livingstone's treasurer and Corbyn was on the threshold of entering Parliament. At yet another false dawn for the left in the early 1980s, it was a searing experience.

And it's hardly surprising the man the French now affectionately call '*tonton*' (uncle) should attract the Labour leadership's thinking. The parallels between Mitterrand and Corbyn are striking: in May 1981 a socialist president and government were elected in France, promising a 'complete rupture with capitalism', and with a slogan no less grandiose: 'Change Life' was the mantra plastered on every billboard and empty wall from Biarritz to Besançon. 'Class struggle is not dead,' Mitterrand told his campaigners, 'it is going to have a second youth!' Mitterrand was elected as a radical, to transform France's economic model, and the panic across the French right and the wider establishment was absolute. As Mitterrand's lover Anne Pingeot was to say years later: 'There was real terror. People thought it would be the French Revolution all over again and they'd bring out the guillotine. You can't imagine how frightened they were.'

Newspapers like *Minute* warned that the country would soon effectively become a branch of the Soviet Union. Inauguration day was full of the socialist great and the good from around France and the world: the widow of the assassinated Chilean president Salvador Allende, the socialist prime minister of Spain, Felipe González, the writer Gabriel García Márquez, the playwright Arthur Miller, the Greek actress Melina Mercouri. A new start for the leftist family.

And boy, did they need it. For the left the world over, battered by the revanchist forces of neoliberalism and a renewed lust for free markets, this was the brightest beam of light; finally, a new beginning. As he addressed the crowd, the assembled masses on the hill of the Panthéon in Paris chanted Mitterrand's name: 'Amid injustice and intolerance there can be no security – we must end a situation where two-thirds of the planet provide men and goods and return hunger and contempt.' Amid the chants and the rhetoric and sense of moment, it is not hard to imagine Corbyn in Mitterrand's place, using Mitterrand's words in our own age.

Mitterrand's manifesto for government was called '*110 propositions pour France*', a series of eye-catching Keynesian proposals to inflate the French economy and get people back into work. They included an expansion of social housebuilding and a massive programme of public works, the nationalisation of certain key industries and utilities, and new investment in science, development and research. For the first year or so things went according to plan. The retirement age was lowered, a wave of nationalisations was carried out, the minimum wage was raised. Government ministers, including Mitterrand, spoke of a desire to show that voters and the world did have a choice, that there was a difference between the parties and that political consequences mattered, and in this case France was going in an anti-capitalist direction. And, indeed, at the beginning it looked like it was working. Jacques Attali, a close adviser of the president, recorded in his diary that American officials told him they didn't see much difference between French and Soviet economic policy.[1]

Within two years, however, Mitterrand's government found itself in turmoil, facing a third devaluation of the franc after his attempts to stimulate the French economy through extra spending had failed. By 1982 concern was growing that money, people, valuables and investment were fleeing the country. Wealthy families were caught driving to Switzerland with the boots of their cars stuffed with fine jewellery and gold bars. One estimate put the value of capital leaving the country at a rate of some 2 billion francs a day. Inflation reached 12.6 per cent and the country's trade deficit ballooned. In order to maintain the value of the franc and continue inflating France's economy through the leftist economic policies he was pursuing, Mitterrand would have probably had to pursue a siege economy, much like that Tony Benn had proposed for Britain during the IMF crisis of 1977. The French government would have needed to impose stringent exchange and capital controls, plus a whole series of extra measures and regulations that would have effectively removed France from much of the network of international capital that, while comparatively juvenile by comparison to our own hyper-globalised age, had already put down firm roots by the early 1980s.

In the late 1970s this might not have been such a dramatic shift as it would be today. But Mitterrand chose not to do so and instead proceeded to do precisely the opposite, embarking on a programme not of Keynesianism but deflation, the so-called '*tournant de la rigueur*' ('turn to austerity'). He did this not because he had any great truck with the bankers, but for two reasons: (i) he perceived the risks of pursuing a sort of equidistant economic course between the capitalist West and communist East as being considerable and a near unknown quantity, and that the cost to the economy would be enormous; but also (ii) because to do so would have almost certainly meant France leaving the European Economic Community (the precursor of today's EU). The strict set of regimes on tariffs, markets and currency alignments, as well as membership of the European Monetary System (a sort of forerunner system of the Euro) would make an alternative set of economic policies of that kind impossible. Mitterrand opined: 'I am divided between two ambitions: constructing Europe and social justice.' In fact, Mitterrand didn't struggle that much in making his choice. Retaining in his childhood the folk memory of the first French defeat against the Germans in 1870, the horrors of the trenches running through northern France like stitches, and then experiencing the humiliating surrender in 1940, Mitterrand would never choose to endanger European integration (and by extension Franco-German co-operation), irrespective of the socialist prize. In this context it is easy to see why Jean-Luc Mélenchon* wants to

* Long-standing socialist candidate of the far-left La France Insoumise front in 2017.

leave the EU, and likewise why other politicians of his vintage, such as Jeremy Corbyn and John McDonnell, believed the same thing throughout much of their careers.

Mitterrand had chosen and he had chosen to abandon socialism. Within a couple of years, he had dispatched the communist ministers from his cabinet and had even called for (the unthinkable) modernisation of the French economy 'à l'américaine'. The Mitterrand of the end of the 1980s cut a very different figure from the one who entered the Élysee at their start. He had reformed social security, engaged in monetarism and initiated a series of privatisations.* The most ambitious socialist experiment since the social-democratic high noon of the late 1940s was over, almost before it had even started. He was re-elected, and became a very popular figure, but the transformation of French society never came.

If I were a member of the Labour Party and a Corbynista I'd read as much as I could about François Mitterrand and what happened to him. If Mitterrand struggled in the early 1980s to overcome the problems of capital flight and international investment drying up, then, goodness knows, a far-left Labour government in the late 2010s/early 2020s would have far greater difficulties. It wouldn't have to worry about EU membership, but that advantage would be dwarfed by the major structural changes to the global economy that have taken effect in the interim. The world has become hyper-globalised by comparison to the early 1980s, when the internet had not yet been invented and Bucks Fizz had just won the Eurovision Song Contest. Worse still, Britain is at the very nexus of that world – one of the most open, exposed economies to international economic headwinds on the planet. The UK's current account deficit of 5.9 per cent of GDP is the biggest of any major economy. In plain English, that means we buy about 6 per cent more of our economy from abroad than we sell. If that gap weren't plugged our currency would plummet in value because there wouldn't be enough demand for sterling to buy things

* Some of these included many of the very same firms he had nationalised himself at the start of his first administration.

from us. The reason the pound isn't worth only half a peso is because we rely – as the Bank of England's Governor, Mark Carney, says – 'on the kindness of strangers'. Essentially foreign investors (either individuals, companies or governments) investing in Britain and buying British government bonds, all denominated in sterling. Fortunately, Britain has been a top destination of international investment for decades, buttressing our economy and plugging that gap.

But it is possible to imagine a perfect storm: a Corbyn government elected, possibly off the back of a Tory government falling over the Brexit process after being unable to pass a deal in the House of Commons. This would spook the markets enough – the uncertainty over Britain's European future would be profound – and a Corbyn government, elected on a more radical prospectus than the manifesto outlined in 2017, would frighten the horses further. The Bank of England would have little choice but to raise interest rates – possibly substantially – to try and maintain sterling's value and see off a run on the pound. But those very rate increases – while encouraging investors to leave their assets denominated in sterling and discouraging them from taking money out of the country – would depress the economy. Government debt, at record levels, would also become considerably more expensive to service, prompting the demand for further public-sector spending cuts from the markets. Tens of thousands of people, accustomed for so long to rock bottom interest rates, would find themselves in a position of default on their loans – and, even worse, their mortgages. Asset prices, especially homes, have been inflated tremendously by the Bank of England's enormous programme of 'quantitative easing' (printing money) since the financial crisis. One of the only ways people have been able to cope with this is a combination of artificial government intervention in the mortgage markets (Help to Buy) and uber-low rates of monetary policy in the form of interest rates. Should, through a crisis, those rates be raised to anything approaching normal levels, then hundreds of thousands of people might not be in a position to pay their mortgages and would risk default and repossession. This isn't an apocalyptically outlandish scenario: British householders and lenders have become so used to such abnormally low levels of interest that even a modest increase, of a few percentage points, would push thousands of homeowners into default.

Moreover, a return to more normalised monetary policy (in whatever form it takes) is intrinsically difficult for Corbynism. As a policy prospectus, it is an embodiment of the age of cheap money. Corbynism's spending pledges and promise to reinvigorate and transform the state would have no credibility at all in the world of the 1970s or even the 1990s, where interest rates were considerably higher than they are today. In September 2007, on the eve of the crash, the base rate stood at 5.75 per cent and was forecast to rise further as increasing inflation spooked the Bank of England. For much of the period since they have hovered at around 0.5 per cent, the lowest figure since the bank was founded in 1694. This situation has been mirrored all over the West.

We do not know how long this will last. The economic effects of the era of easy money are well documented: the economies of Europe and North America have become addicted to cheap credit and finance, thousands of zombie companies exist that probably ought to have gone bust but have survived thanks to the availability of money, probably increasing inefficiency and decreasing productivity in the process, and that's without taking account of the huge generational fissures that have come about too.

What is less obvious and less well documented are the political effects of such policies. One such effect has been the rise of a space through which Corbynism and far-left politics can thrive.* Consider for a moment if interest rates in the UK were at 10 per cent; what would, what could, Corbynism be? What promises could it make? How could it promise to nationalise, to reverse austerity, to abolish

---

* Although we think of the last decade as being volatile, in one respect it was not. The monetary environment, so unstable over the decades previously, has been sanguine. Such low interest rates have given credibility and succour to populists and to political insurgents. After all, if interest rates are so low, governments can do almost anything. The only organisations that the markets have wanted to lend to, they can borrow with abandon.

tuition fees, to reinvigorate the public realm, when it would be so prohibitively expensive to borrow the money? Corbynism is rooted in the low-interest-rate environment of the 2010s. It is a political response to the exigencies of the post-crash world. In a situation where those taps were turned off, it is not clear to me how it could reform. Moreover, I'm not sure many at the top have much idea either. By 2022, that world will be closer and at the end of a Labour government's first term in 2027, if monetary policy hasn't stabilised and returned to more normal levels, it will be a sign of tremendous global macroeconomic weakness.* Labour needs to be considering a return to the end of post-crash economics.

So whether it comes from a run on the pound or a return to macroeconomic normality, McDonnell was certainly right to be thinking about the future on that night in Brighton, albeit perhaps not right to be so candid about it. It's worth remembering that the day after Mitterrand was elected – before he had even done anything – the franc went into freefall. In the ten days between his election and investiture the Banque de France spent $5bn, a third of the country's capital reserves. It's not beyond the realms of possibility that the same could happen here. Paul Mason, the journalist and new darling of the Corbyn movement, also on the panel that night, said chillingly: 'They – the neoliberals – are coming for us. We have to be ready.'

There is another respect in which the French socialist experience ought to loom large in the minds of all of those contemplating the fate of the British Labour Party and others around the world.

THE CLASS CONUNDRUM

No one does solemn introspection quite like the British Labour Party. Psychologically it always feels like the younger sibling of British politics, consistently measuring itself against its overachieving (and much

* Indeed, if it wasn't for Brexit, the Bank of England, like the Federal Reserve, would have already long-started this readjustment.

despised) older Tory sister. Its inadequacies are oft-repeated, some of them in the preceding pages: that for much of the last century it consistently lost elections, that it failed on most occasions to move the dial of British politics in its direction. Occasionally its members look enviously across to the continent with its nationalised industries, its high public spending, a political culture with egalitarianism woven into its warp and weft, and they sigh wistfully, if only we could have a bit of that.

But they ought not to have such political FOMO, because, whisper it: the French socialists aren't all that. France can kid itself with as many monuments to radicals of the past as it likes. The truth is, socialism has never been especially strong in France or Germany or Italy or Spain. By comparison with their continental counterparts, the history of the British Labour Party is one of solid success.

Let's take recent history. Of the eight presidents elected during the Fifth Republic, only two, the two François, Mitterrand and Hollande, have been from the left. In presidential election after presidential election the party underperformed; indeed, it has been in crisis for decades. As far back as 2002 – long before the day of the populists – their presidential candidate, Lionel Jospin, came third behind the Front National in a presidential election. If we compare European socialists to the British Labour Party since 1945,* we find that Labour has been in office for 33 of the 72 years since then. Not stellar but solid enough. The German SPD have been in power for 20. The Italian left barely got into government until the late 1990s.

In France this malaise was a source of deep introspection for decades. Some commentators concluded that without their communist allies the left-wing base in France simply wasn't large enough to win an election. In an article entitled 'La résistible ascension de Nicolas Sarkozy', one noted columnist wrote in *Libération*: 'there is no more PCF [the Communists] and the PS is weaker'.[2]

---

* Before I get letters I know that the Socialist Party in its modern guise was created only in 1969. Instead, there was the French Section of the Workers International (SFIO), plus other smaller groups.

The reason that, say, the French socialists have performed so poorly vis-à-vis the British Labour Party is centred on the very different electoral bases on which the two parties rely. The French Socialist Party has more or less always been a party anchored in bourgeois France, the largely urban middle class. The party, unlike the British Labour Party, never enjoyed much support from the industrial working class. Instead that was left for their comrades in the Communist Party (PCF), on whom the socialists depended to reel in the working men and women, much like the Italian Social Democrats and several other important European democracies. In the English-speaking world we've almost totally forgotten just how important the communists were in sustaining the European centre left; to our minds they've virtually slid into the same league as the Whigs in a big historical wastepaper basket of political anachronism.* Nonetheless, they were the largest left-wing political party in France from 1945 to 1960 and took part in three governments in the Assemblée Nationale since its formation in the 1920s. Even today they retain a significant, if much reduced, membership. France wasn't alone. The Italian Communist Party (PCI) was a major player in much of the country's postwar history. At its peak in the 1970s it boasted over 3 million members and 34.4 per cent of the vote. Nowhere in postwar Europe did the Communists come as close to power as they did on the Italian peninsula.[3]

This allure was sustained for two or three decades and in France and Italy communists proved natural allies for the centre left.† As communism imploded, not only did the ideological repercussions send shockwaves throughout Western social democracy, but they also had a more practical effect on the bread and butter of social democracy

---

* Our ignorance of this is understandable given the communists' desultory performance in the UK or USA. For example, in Britain the Communist Party reached its peak at 95,000 in the 1945 general election (or 0.4 per cent of the national vote) and won only two seats in the House of Commons.

† Of course, it is also the case that in some respects the presence of the communists held socialist parties back, spooking more moderate voters who were suspicious of communism and the Soviet Union.

too. A French communist intellectual said in 1987: 'There have been ups and downs of Communism ... But this is not that – it is an irreversible regression. There can be remission, but this is a fatal cancer.' What was not obvious at that time was that the cancer would soon spread and slowly metastasise, not just attacking and consuming the communist vote but social democracy itself too. With the communists in long-term decline from the late 1970s onwards, both of the main centre-left parties in France and Italy and elsewhere in Europe struggled to appeal to working-class voters who the communists reliably delivered in election after election. The socialists failed to win their support and have limped along electorally ever since. In French political thought, they are called 'social-démocratie des élus', narrow parties based on a small, often wealthy slice of the electorate.

It is therefore no coincidence that the two European socialist parties in weakest shape are those that once shared this symbiotic relationship with the communists. By contrast, those that made appeals and inroads to the working class in their own terms – like the British Labour Party or the Scandinavian socialists – have managed to better weather the storm.

The warning from France, Italy and the rest of southern Europe for Labour has to be this: the French Socialist Party is a living example of the limits of a left-wing party when its coalition is drawn from too narrow a social base – especially a bourgeois, urban one. Without their communist allies, with their entrenched roots among the industrialised working class, the electorate of the socialist party hovered at around one quarter of the vote and remained there, losing election after election, its bastions of support limited to the culturally rarefied, the educated, the urban, wealthy and the bourgeois. Or to put it only somewhat crudely: the Corbyn coalition. Sociologically speaking, if you plotted the Venn diagram between the sorts of people who voted Remain, the traditional base of the French socialists and the Corbyn coalition you'd have to get your coloured pencils out because you'd spend a lot of time shading it in. Problem is, as electoral forces go, just as in France, just as in the European referendum, just as in the general election of 2017, it is for the moment at least a losing one.

And that matters. Because in all the talk of the culture war in the US and UK, there is sometimes a proclivity, a tendency, to suggest that the left has evolved, that to survive it must realign and develop a new coalition and leave its uncivilised, socially illiberal base behind, so that a new purer, more politically coherent coalition might emerge. This way lies ruin. The test case is France, continental European democracy and the United States too, not just in 2017 but over the past five decades. We've seen what happens there. It wilts and it dies. You can't just leave the 'gammon' behind.

I set out to write a book that examined the causes of the decline of the Labour Party, inspired by the great 1935 work of George Dangerfield, *The Strange Death of Liberal England*. The legacy of that idea survives in the subtitle of this book.

In *Strange Death*, Dangerfield shatters the conventional historiography on the decline and collapse of the Liberal Party, which during the nineteenth century had been the main opposition to the Conservatives. Up till Dangerfield's analysis, it had been received wisdom that the Liberals had been in rude health and would have survived but for the ravages of the First World War, which introduced lasting and lethal splits into the Liberal ranks. That division allowed the nascent Labour Party, which had been but a neophyte before the war, to fill the vacuum. The Liberals never recovered as a result.

Dangerfield argued that the real explanation was more complex. He said that even before the war, the decline of liberalism was chronic, not acute. That the writing was on the wall not because of the First World War but because of deep structural problems within liberalism itself. That as a governing philosophy it was out of date, ready to be supplanted by socialism and social democracy. That it was psychologically, temperamentally and philosophically ill-equipped and ill-suited to dealing with the problems that the modern world was throwing up: of mass labour participation in democracy and the workforce, of trade unionism, of the politics of heavy industry and the universal franchise. He argued that liberalism as a governing credo belonged to the nineteenth century and that socialism was a natural twentieth-century replacement. The fundamental political fissure had become that of capital vs organised labour, and liberalism was squished in between that divide. The questions it sought to answer, about the established church, Ireland, land reform and free trade, were out of date. It was a set of answers to a set of questions that no one was asking any more. That, Dangerfield said, was the real reason why liberalism and the Liberal Party failed to survive – not just in Britain but in its equivalents across Europe and the West.

When I began to think of the ideas behind this book, I imagined that it would be an update and transposition of Dangerfield's thesis. It seemed obvious to me that social democracy and socialism were struggling, not only in Britain but across the Western world, because the questions that it sought to answer were outmoded, just like liberalism before it. It was clear that its fundamental assumptions had been shattered by the collapse of the Soviet Union and the subsequent triumph of liberalism – a world where the ground had given way beneath its feet. Even the language of social democracy, with its emphasis on solidarity, collectivism, the pooling of risk, seemed, to my generation, antiquated and obsolete in the age where the individual was king. Moreover, socialism, especially British socialism, with all of its innate (small 'c') conservatism and eccentricities, had been forged in the fire and heat of the furnaces and the factory floor. It had been made in Longbridge and thousands of places like it. Without that spine of organised labour, it was limp and listless. It had tried to respond, in the form of the Third Way and taming as much of international capital and the new order as it could, but when the crash came, even that half-formed thing was spat out by the system. In what should have been a prime moment for the left, it seemed that the primary opponents of the market had nothing to say. This was not just a British phenomenon: from the French Socialist Party, to the US Democratic Party, to the German SPD, to the Italian Democrats, to the Spanish PSOE, to Greece's Pasok, to the Dutch socialists, everywhere you looked, conservatism in whatever form was dominant and the left was nowhere. In that context, Corbynism, it seemed to me, was the last gasp of a waning philosophy. It was a party, a movement, raging against the dying of the light. It was in grief, looking back in anger, lashing out with the truest version of itself.

Yet out of that darkness Corbynism has shone light. The British Labour Party alone is the only major Western European socialist or social democratic party to be doing *well.* Against all expectations it gained seats in an election designed to destroy it. It has polled at around 40 per cent ever since.

How has it done so? Corbynism has succeeded because it has been led by a man who has appeared decent and fair. Who has had clear, principled answers in an age of social democratic muddle. Corbyn, unlike so many of his fellow Labour politicians, has never forgotten that politics is about hope and possibility. After 20 years of being too constrained by ideological forces and constraints not of the left's making, no politician has done more to shatter consensus and break the mould. He remembered that the best leftist politicians do not seek only to assume government but to move the boundaries of what is and isn't politically possible too, to not be of the system but to stand outside it.

Corbyn and British social democracy have also been lucky in the way that Asquith and liberalism were not. Dangerfield was right: liberalism's decline was in the making but its fate was sealed by the political landmine of the First World War, accelerating trends that might have taken longer to come to fruition. Brexit, by contrast, has been a lifeline for Corbyn and British social democracy. It ignited a growing but largely sleepy British culture war. It has accelerated political trends that had been developing and disrupted long-standing political norms. It has helped reform British electoral sociology: the rise of the graduate class, the cleavages between the educated and less educated, town and country, liberal and illiberal, the citizens of nowhere and the citizens of somewhere – Brexit helped transform British politics and lifted its lid, exposing the shifting molten interior, for all to see.

It is impossible to argue that Jeremy Corbyn and Labour have not been enormous beneficiaries. It has allowed him to bring together a new, liberal, progressive coalition. Strange bedfellows flocked to his banner. He brought together the anti-system vote, the disaffected, the none of the above and the broader liberal left and promoted it to its maximum. He has united Kensington and Canterbury, Warwick and Warrington, with enough residual Old Labour voters behind him to match. Nor would it be fair to say that Corbyn was a mere passive recipient of the rise of this new culture war. His team were alive to it and rode the wave, through their messaging, branding, policies and positioning. Corbyn himself, though ambivalent towards some of these developments and to Europe itself, was the politician of the moment. In an age when virtue is values, where approbation is in authenticity, who could be better than a very English sexagenarian old socialist who 'meant what he said and said what he means'?

But what of the politics of tomorrow? There is not nearly enough appreciation of the contingency of the Corbyn surge. Too many believe that his ascension is destined. It is not. The realignment of British politics is a process, not an event, and it is a process that is ongoing. Theresa May and Nick Timothy, when they called the general election of 2017, thought that tearing asunder Labour's historic working-class base could be done in one go. It could not – the pieces of the kaleidoscope had yet to settle properly. But it is happening, slowly but surely. The local elections of 2018 showed that far from the great onward march of Corbynism, his advance halted. Labour continued to shed working-class support and the Tories picked some up. The Tories, who after eight years in government should have experienced major losses, suffered almost none at all. This new culture war insulated them. The old patterns of party politics, of a big pool of voters, swinging from Labour to the Tories and back again, is over, at least for a while. The parties are settling down to a new reality.

We can say that, yes, the British (Brexit) Culture War saved the Labour Party. I didn't see it coming. In 2015 liberalism was hegemonic, not only in the Conservative Party but across the British political state and the West generally. Within 18 months that had collapsed. The Corbyn Labour Party, against all the odds, became the vehicle to save it. But beware, Jeremy Corbyn, the hand that feeds you. Because the Culture War is doing odd things to British politics. It is creating two zombie parties. Far from being able to create a big political tent, both sides are trapped in their own, unable to explore the pastures outside. That was fine in 2017, when the objective was survival, when maximising your own support was all that mattered. That won't be the case next time. It is possible that the next election, with our two culture war blocs, will yield a very similar result to last time around. The forces that saved Corbyn, which made Corbyn the man of the moment, may be the same ones that place a ceiling on his ambition. Nuneaton was the place where in 2015 Ed Miliband's hopes of being prime minister died. At the next election, the Warwickshire town could yet do the same to Jeremy Corbyn. There just aren't enough Islingtons and Cambridges and Warwicks to make him prime minister. There are plenty of Birmingham Northfields and Birmingham Erdingtons though. And whenever I go home, I look around and I listen to what people are saying, how they think about politics, how they see Britain and the world, how they think about London, how they think about their country and how it's changing around them, and I wonder how long, in its current form, they'll keep voting Labour.

Postscript

GRANDAD

He has conducted himself well.

Mr V. Reynolds, engineering tutor, North Birmingham Technical College, writing on my grandad's final apprenticeship assessment, June 1960

Not long ago, I was running in Brockwell Park, just near where I live in south London. When I run, I don't usually listen to heavy, pulsating music to propel me forward; instead, tragically, in this case it was a programme about Black Wednesday, the 1992 run on the pound, which resulted in the UK crashing out of the European Exchange Rate Mechanism (or ERM). The byzantine details of its operation are irrelevant but suffice to say it was an important forerunner to the development of the Euro, pegging the value of European currencies together, specifically by tying them to the value of the German deutschmark. It became a running political sore for the Conservative governments of the early 1990s. In the end, sterling fell out of it in dramatic circumstances – the government simply couldn't maintain the British currency at such a high level. However, that was not before Norman Lamont as chancellor sold billions of Britain's foreign-currency reserves and raised interest rates to eye-watering levels, some 15 per cent (rising 5 per cent in a single day). Lamont emerged late at night in front of the Treasury, puffy, sweaty, to announce that this had been 'a very long and very difficult day'. It was the official baptism of Euroscepticism as a legitimate and mainstream political creed. Look closely at the news footage from the time and you'll see a tall, rosy-faced young man walk behind him, just in shot. It's a 25-year-old David Cameron, then Lamont's special adviser.

This programme brought together many of the players of that era, including Ken Clarke, Lamont's successor, and the man himself. As they were reminiscing, Clarke remarked that the economic effects of Black Wednesday were 'pretty benign'. Lamont and the others around the table agreed.

I stopped running. I listened to it again and I took a moment and I realised I had a tear in my eye.

I think I might have been the only person to have listened to that broadcast to cry at it. International currency stabilisation mechanisms don't usually bring out the weepers among us. But as I picked up the pace again, their words, their self-satisfaction and bonhomie, kept ricocheting around my head, until the offending sentence itself started to match the rhythm of my feet on the tarmac: 'pretty benign'.

The truth is Lamont had got it right, not on the radio broadcast but a quarter of a century before, when he'd said Black Wednesday had been 'an extremely difficult and turbulent day'. But it had been more difficult for some than for others, and the shadow it cast much longer than any of those septuagenarian politicians today realise. Some of us are still living in its darkness. Including my nan and grandad.

Well, just my nan really. Because in December 2017, just before I went running and just before Christmas, my grandad, Alan John Page, died suddenly at the age of 72.

It was the worst night of my life. Every hour exists vividly, as if on continuous replay, in the recesses of my mind, escaping often to its fore. He was my hero, everything that I ever wanted to be. All throughout my life, he called me 'son'. He'd had three daughters and I, as the eldest grandchild, born in unexpected circumstances, was the closest thing he had to one. He, in turn, was like a father to me.

I'm so glad, living all together in Erdington as we did, my first days were with him. Later in my childhood, I would relay to my mum, in a way that children often do, memories and events that their parents themselves possess much more sharply; I would inform her that it was a huge house, wasn't it? There was, I would insist, room for everyone. In my small head, the ceilings were so high, the garden so vast, the rooms cavernous. In reality it was a Victorian terraced house, packed to the rafters. But how lucky I was. I had not just one set of parents, but two. Not one father but two – and one who was as besotted with me as I was with him, who had so much to teach and to give; and at 44 and 45 apiece, both my grandparents were easily young enough to live up to the task.

When we moved to Longbridge, Mum, who couldn't bear being apart from her parents, used to take me up on the train nearly every day. Even then I still thought of Wesley Road as home. I can remember every room, its layout, conversations, hushed whispers, dinners, breakfasts, books and bonfires, Christmases too; my first set of everythings, all of the little landmarks of my then little life, in those four walls.

It was also my first heartbreak. One day, when I was about five or six, my mum told me that Nan and Grandad were having to look for somewhere new to live. When I enquired as to why, I remember, so clearly, her telling me that they'd lost the house. She had tears in her eyes. In retrospect, it was an odd thing to tell a little boy – but I suspect she was just very upset, she was only a child herself. But I didn't understand what she meant: how can you lose a house?

Later, I came to understand only too well. They had lost their house because they couldn't afford the mortgage repayments after the enormous increases in the Bank of England base rate, as a result of the Black Wednesday crash. Like hundreds of thousands of others, they lost their home, for reasons few could understand. This particular 'economic effect' didn't feel especially 'benign' to them. They tried to cling on for as long as they could, but after their savings were exhausted, their house was repossessed by the bank.

After they lost the house, Grandad remained assetless for the rest of his days. He, along with my nan, had to move from house to house, from rented accommodation to rented accommodation, aged itinerants. Moved on, turfed out, shoved along, always at the whim of another. Not for them the bounty of the baby boomers; instead, the sadness of seeing their friends, relatives and acquaintances enjoy their golden years, while they looked on, knowing in their heart of hearts that for them those years would not come. They never again enjoyed a day of security, another day of the reassurance anyone has of looking around their own home and their own possessions and feeling that this is mine and no one can tell me otherwise. I know that insecurity haunted Grandad until his last day.

To make ends meet, he became a shopkeeper in north Wales, in the small seaside town of Towyn. He sold ornaments, knick-knacks, CDs, DVDs, shoes, clothes, porcelain dolls, slightly dodgy perfumes with very odd names,* bonsai trees – you name it, he sold it.

He was never one to complain, never one to project on to others his despair. But I know he ended his days miserable. He had to spend his last years working in the cold, long after he should have been enjoying the fruits of his many long years of labour. Yet he couldn't. I spent every summer with him, at his side, talking, learning, laughing, taking on his traits. Every school holiday, from ten past three on the Friday till the last possible moment before term resumed, there was only one place I would be: by his side. There was nowhere else, no other place, I wanted to spend my time. It wasn't until I got into my late teens that I stopped going so religiously; until then I would be there, every Easter, half-term and summer: helping him in the van, on the way to warehouses in Manchester for ornaments and toys, to Rossendale for shoes, and Blackpool for tapes and CDs, Radio 2 on in the background, helping him with the boxes, learning my 12 and 18 times tables to impossibly high numbers as we ordered pallets of every useless knick-knack Britain had to offer. We'd buy crossword

* 'Bondage', like Jean-Paul Gaultier, was a personal favourite. 'Old Jazz', like Old Spice, was another.

puzzle books, ceramic cats and oversized blouses, keyrings, yo-yos, aliens in an egg – no object was too eclectic or kitsch. Then every tape and CD known to man – Spotify had nothing on Grandad's selection; most were utterly obscure and ancient: 'Death row,' he called them. When work was finally done, we'd get home and spend the late night watching the TV, mainly *Question Time* and *Newsnight* and other political shows and when they were finished we'd plot and scheme as to how we could finally make our (his) millions, me the Rodney to his Del Boy. We never quite managed it, and so he went back to the shop. In his fifties he enjoyed it, in his sixties it was harder, in his seventies, impossible. I wouldn't swap those memories for anything. Save, perhaps, for his having to be there at all.

Don't misunderstand, his life wasn't joyless: he had his wife, his family, his fishing, his endless online poker (not for money, inexplicably, just 'for fun'), his football, his painting and his liquorice; but he never had his retirement, for which he'd worked so hard. Worse, not only did he never enjoy the leisure he deserved but his life was buffeted in other ways beyond his control. His company pension was much less than it ought to have been following plummeting annuitisation rates as a result of the financial crisis; he was made redundant a number of times; whatever modest savings he had accumulated were reduced in value by QE and low interest rates. He died with barely £1,000 in his bank account and credit card debt to boot, to help pay for rocketing private rent. His widow, my beloved nan, had no means to pay for his funeral. In the days after, we had to navigate the vast bureaucracy of the state. It proved almost impossible to claim the new benefits she needed. The state was, as it so often is, chillingly impersonal and disempowering. It seemed a sad end to a wonderful, brilliant life that now she was widowed, Grandad's wife of fifty years should have to beg the government to which they had paid so much for financial absolution.

Grandad's life, to me, is a reminder of how this book began: that politics is important and that what happens in Westminster and the City can wreak havoc on people's lives. My grandparents were some of the hardest-working people you could ever meet. Grandad had left school at 15, completed his City and Guilds apprenticeship and become a draughtsman. Eventually, after many years in industry, he worked himself up the ladder to become the works manager at the Birmingham mint. My nan, too, worked, often in two jobs. They had obeyed the law, worked as hard as they could, brought up a family: they had done everything right.

So much of our politics, our sense of justice and morality, rests on the idea that if we work hard enough everything will come good in the end – but it just isn't true. For so many of us, like Grandad, find our lives disrupted and destroyed by vast impersonal forces beyond our control. Neither the free-market right nor the big-government left can be absolved from blame, they are both implicated; forces of both the state and the market buffeted him and blew him off course, decisions taken by men and women of power in both the boardroom and the cabinet. He was failed by both, in life and death. He and millions like him were and have been let down by a political society and elite that know little of how many ordinary people live their lives. From Grenfell to Brexit, those who govern us are surprised by the views and material circumstances of our fellow citizens. When I was at *Newsnight*, I had to walk away when a senior colleague expressed disbelief and scorn at those who played the lottery: 'Anyone who plays the lottery are just fucking morons,' they drawled. They (rightly) remarked at how absurdly unlikely any player was to win and how they'd be better off 'throwing their pound coins down the drain.' I thought of my grandad, walking to the newsagent's twice a week, spending his pension and earnings on lucky dips and birthday numbers. He knew how unlikely it was – he was not a fucking moron. But for him – and millions like him – it was the only hope of a better life and a way out. Far from being fanciful, it was the most realistic option in an economic and political order that had failed him.

When I was a little boy, I wanted to be prime minister, because of my grandad. Not only because he gave me everything – knowledge, love and the introduction to a political world on which to feast – but because he gave me passion. I was – I am – appalled by the injustice of his life.

I used to want to be in politics to help right it and others just the same. I wanted to look after 'my people'. I no longer want to be prime minister, I no longer have a party, and I don't even know who my people are, any more. I'm not the same person I was. In an era of identity politics, I've never been less sure of my own. I feel neither middle nor working class, part of a media and political elite but not of it. When I was a boy, much of that identity came from a sense that I was a Labour person, that my family was too and that Labour was for us. For me, that sense, for both personal and political reasons, has gone.

It was brought home to me at the Labour conference in 2017 when I was sitting at 'The World Transformed', the Momentum fringe event, with, among others, John McDonnell.

I'd sat down and chosen a seat early. A woman in her fifties sat next to me. We initially bonded over the fact we both had a strong distaste for the man sitting next to us who was eating a box of what I cannot stay, but it stank.

She was a civil servant, she was clearly well-heeled. She informed me she had recently rejoined the party.

She then asked what I did – things quickly took a turn for the worse. Naturally, as soon as I told her I worked for Sky: 'Ah, so you work for Murdoch.'

I explained that I didn't: his company owned a third of Sky plc shares, but, in any case, Sky News, like the rest of broadcast news, is regulated by Ofcom so even if he wanted to interfere in our editorial line he couldn't.

She considered this.

'Yes, but it doesn't matter – you get it through osmosis.'

We talked a bit more. She said: 'Well, it doesn't matter about Murdoch anyway, you speak like that, you act the way you do. What hope is there?'

I asked her to explain what she meant.

'Well, the way you speak, the way you are. You'd never cover any working-class people.'

I pointed out to her that my family is working class, I was brought up in a council house, I was the first in my family to go to university.

She looked uneasy. 'Well perhaps – but, look, you went to university, why? Why not just do something for your class?'

I know what would have happened if this had taken place a few years before. I'd have snapped back: 'How dare you! You know nothing about me. I've worked hard all my life; I was bloody proud to go to Oxford. And I finally make it and I have bloody privileged people like you daring to tell me I'm a class traitor! And this from someone who has a degree and was almost certainly middle class to begin with!'

But I didn't, I couldn't. I just smiled and said, clearly we don't agree. She decided to leave the room, roundly denouncing me as a capitalist stooge.

That civil servant didn't speak for the Labour Party, nor Jeremy Corbyn. But something clicked in me. I realised I wasn't even angry, or annoyed. I was just bemused. The Labour Party was no longer part of my identity. I no longer cared as I once did.

In so many ways, my identity has changed. In a weird sort of way, the Labour Party has followed me. As I graduated, became better educated, moved to London, took my place in Britain's new rentier generation, so Labour's base too began to shift in my direction, this new thing I'd become. Yet, that process hasn't moved me closer to this new Labour Party. As it has followed me, so I feel, for whatever reason, pushed away. I'm now neither one class nor the other: like thousands of working-class kids before me who 'make it', there's always a little bit of us sticking out, whether back home or in our new lives, at home everywhere, yet not entirely at ease anywhere. But if I'm not sure of my identity, then I am sure of my values, the values my grandad gave me.

Those values leave me restless. I know there are millions of people, young and old, like my grandad. I think they're forgotten by politics – he certainly was by the politicians around that Radio 4 studio table, reminiscing fondly of days and crises gone by. I used to think that that is why the Labour Party existed – to remember him and people like him. I'm not sure that's the case now: I think it's moved on, socially, demographically or politically. Whether I'm right or wrong,

I fear that with a Labour Party dominated by visceral questions of identity, internal strife and factional purification, and a Conservative Party by abstract questions of sovereignty and its own endless Brexit psychopathy, people like him are left in an even deeper darkness.

There's not a party for me now. I don't need one. But I'm not sure if, as I deeply wish, he were still alive, there would be a party for him.

NOTES

Chapter 1 – What Went Before: New Labour and the Left

1. https://www.theguardian.com/commentisfree/2015/jan/01/dear-tony-blair-electorate-shifted-left-ed-miliband
2. Chris Mullin, *A Walk On Part* (2011), p. XXX
3. David Marquand, *Britain Since 1918: The Strange Career of British Democracy* (2008), p. 363
4. From Tony Benn's *Diaries* (2005)
5. Tony Blair, 'The Economic Framework for New Labour', Mais Lecture, City University, May 1995
6. Harriet Harman, *A Woman's Work* (2017), p. 230
7. *The Wilderness Years*, BBC Two, December 1995
8. *The Wilderness Years*, BBC Two, December 1995
9. Harriet Harman, *A Woman's Work* (2017)
10. Roy Hattersley, quoted in *The Wilderness Years*, BBC Two, December 1995
11. Herbert Morrison, *Manchester Guardian*, 2 July 1934

Chapter 5 – Corbyn the Culture Warrior

1. Tony Judt, *Ill Fares the Land* (2010), p. 88
2. Thomas Piketty, *Brahmin Left vs Merchant Right: Rising Inequality and the Changing Structure of Political Conflict* (Evidence from France, Britain and the US, 1948–2017), March 2018

Chapter 7 – The Takeover

1. Denis Healey, *Time of My Life* (1989), p. 159
2. Ben Pimlott, *Harold Wilson* (1992)
3. Tony Benn, *The New Roman Empire* (2004)

Chapter 9 – The Night Everything Changed: The 2017 General Election

1. Chris Hanretty, 'Areal Interpolation and the UK's Referendum on EU Membership', *Journal of Elections and Public Opinion* (2017), 12
2. Oliver Heath and Matthew Goodwin, *The 2017 General Election, Brexit and the Return to Two-Party Politics: An Aggregate-Level Analysis of the Result* (2017)
3. *The Wilderness Years*, BBC Two, December 1995

Chapter 10 – What Comes After: The Next Election and the Future of the Left

1. Tony Judt, *Postwar* (2008), p. 553
2. Joffrin, L., 'La résistible ascension de Nicolas Sarkozy', *Libération*, 4 May 2009
3. Jan Werner-Muller, *The Paradoxes of Postwar Italian Political Thought* (2008)